D1432553

THE MIDDLE OUT

ALSO BY MICHAEL TOMASKY

Left for Dead

Hillary's Turn

Bill Clinton

If We Can Keep It

THE MIDDLE OUT

THE RISE OF PROGRESSIVE ECONOMICS AND
A RETURN TO SHARED PROSPERITY

Michael Tomasky

DOUBLEDAY   NEW YORK

www.doubleday.com

Doubleday and the portrayal of an anchor with a dolphin are registered
trademarks of Penguin Random House LLC.

Jacket design by Matt Chase

Library of Congress Cataloging-in-Publication Data
Names: Tomasky, Michael, [date] author.
Title: The middle out: the rise of progressive economics and a return to shared
prosperity / Michael Tomasky.
Description: First edition. | New York: Doubleday, [2022] |
Includes bibliographical references and index.
Identifiers: LCCN 2021058667 | ISBN 9780385547161 (hardcover) |
ISBN 9780385547192 (ebook)
Subjects: LCSH: United States—Economic policy—2009— |
Middle-class—United States—Economic conditions—21st century. |
Economics—United States. | Capitalism—United States.
Classification: LCC HC106.84 .T66 2022 |
DDC 330.973—dc23/eng/20211227
LC record available at https://lccn.loc.gov/2021058667

Manufactured in the United States of America
1 3 5 7 9 10 8 6 4 2
First Edition

Neoliberalism forthrightly aimed to dismantle the social state. . . . it is not only social regulation and redistribution that are rejected as inappropriate interferences in markets or as assaults on freedom. Also jettisoned is democracy's dependence on political equality.

—WENDY BROWN

CONTENTS

Part Two
DIGGING OUT OF THE MESS

PREFACE: IT'S ALL ONE ARGUMENT

Conservatives have convinced most Americans that the free market means personal freedom. And it does, for those with the means to eat at high-end locavore restaurants or purchase the right to skip the lines at Disney World. But that isn't most people. Most people live with a constant, low-level anxiety about potential job loss or unexpected bills. An ongoing Economic Anxiety survey sponsored by National Public Radio's Marketplace found in October 2020 that more than half of all Americans were fearful of losing their jobs and nearly half couldn't cover an unexpected $250 expense. Yes, this was during the pandemic, when economic anxiety was certainly nudged higher, but this anxiety has been a fixture for many Americans since the survey began in 2015. Millions of Americans live in towns where the free market has produced for them the career options of working at the Dollar Store or selling a little Oxy.

What sort of freedom is that?

This book is about changing that; changing, as Joe Biden was fond of saying when he unveiled his ambitious economic plans in the spring of 2021, the "economic paradigm." Through a combination of historical exposition and present-day reporting, I hope to show readers two things: first, how we got into this predicament where so many people put faith in an economic arrangement that immiserates them; and second, that there are people, from the president and his aides down to activists and economists and folks in the foundation and nonprofit worlds, working hard to move the country to a better place. The Biden administration has made some commendable progress in changing the economic circumstances of Americans, even if inflation understandably dulled the luster of the biggest GDP increase in almost forty years and record employment gains (6.6 million jobs created in 2021). But the immense difficulty the administration faced, even within the Democratic Party, in passing the legislation it did, and the failure as of this writing to pass the Build Back Better bill thanks to one senator's opposition, showed that the battle of ideas will be a long one. And so this book will conclude with my views on how liberals can win this fight.

Here is a truism of our political discourse that is not widely enough recognized: the right thinks in terms of morals, while the left tends to see matters through an economic lens. That is, ask someone on the right what ails America, and he or she will almost certainly begin with a discussion of moral decay: we've lost our way, left God, abandoned the old values of thrift and hard work that made America great. Ask someone on the left the same question, and she or he will much more likely start by citing statistics on wage stagnation and the transfer of wealth from the middle class to the rich over the last fifty years.

It's not hard to see why, to your average person, the right-wing argument is more compelling. It's emotional. It resonates. Everyone in the world thinks things were better when they were young. Nearly everyone is patriotic in a basic, uncomplicated way. Most people are religious to one degree or other. So the right's rhetoric along these lines hits home. And the hypocrisy argument doesn't work. No matter how many evangelical preachers are caught in love nests, no matter how much un-Jesus-like hatred some of them spew from their pulpits—this perception will never be dislodged.

So the broad left, by which I mean everyone from the House members who make up the Squad to more centrist senators, can't win a morals argument. True, Joe Biden's deeply held Catholicism has helped bulletproof him against charges of radicalism. Nonetheless, religious morality is not the terrain on which the left will win political arguments. We can win, though, on economics.

Here's why. People have two lives: material and spiritual. Modern liberalism is ill-equipped to make people's lives spiritually better. But it can make people's lives materially better—with better wages and health care, less fear of financial crisis, better roads, a faster internet, and more. If liberalism can deliver those things, I believe it can cobble together an electoral coalition that can win most of the time. But we can't do it solely by citing statistics. We—more precisely, elected Democrats, because they're the ones who have the megaphone—can win by tying economic policies to the larger ideas that Americans care most deeply about: democracy and freedom.

We happen to be deep in a historical moment when our democracy is under assault from the right as never before and when "freedom" has been grotesquely redefined to include the right to get other people sick. Democrats have to fight these fights. But they also have to recognize that these aren't separate fights from the battle to reimagine economics in a way that delivers fewer benefits to the rich and more to the middle class. It's all one argument: economic inequality and concentration of wealth and political power in the hands of the few weaken democracy and limit freedom. Liberalism tends to treat these as separate issues. Conservatism, as I will show, has tended to fuse them into one argument, and it has done so to considerable success. It's time for Democrats to seize that high ground. This book is my attempt to help them make the case.

How Do You Change an Economy?

•

Heather Boushey remembers when it struck her that the work she was doing had taken a more serious turn. An economist who grew up in Washington State, she earned her PhD in economics from the New School for Social Research, a center of progressive thought since its founding in 1919. Boushey (boo-SHAY) had joined Joe Biden's presidential campaign staff in March 2020, just as the coronavirus pandemic was upending the nation's daily life and its politics. She was one of a relatively small number of younger economists who had, since the Great Meltdown of 2008–2009 (she was thirty-eight when the global economy nearly collapsed), produced work that challenged her profession and asked probing questions about how most of that profession had failed to see the collapse coming.

She had been a staffer on Hillary Clinton's 2016 campaign, and in the wake of Clinton's devastating loss to Donald Trump she worked on a range of fronts—through her think tank, the Washington Center for Equitable Growth; through her writing; through dinners and seminars she helped arrange—to get more Democratic elected officials to

pay closer attention to new economic ideas that were bub-
bling up from this younger cohort of economists, ideas built
around what Boushey calls "the care economy." These were
ideas related to government support for initiatives like child
care and elder care and family leave and higher wages for care-
givers and a generally modernized social safety net, the kinds
of ideas that the U.S. government, and the Democratic Party,
hadn't pursued aggressively in the decades since the mid-
1970s when the dominant thinking in economic policy was
that the government should get out of the free market's way.

Over the months of the 2020 campaign, she watched,
encouraged, as candidate Biden's rhetoric changed from
talking about restoring the Barack Obama era, which was
his main pre-pandemic theme, to something much more far-
reaching, summed up in his phrase "Build Back Better." She
was co-chair of the campaign's economic policy committee,
helping to coordinate input from some seven hundred different experts. After Biden won, in late November 2020,
she was named one of three members of Biden's Council of
Economic Advisers (CEA), the policy team that presents any
president with a menu of economic policy options to confront whatever crises he faces. Another body, the National
Economic Council (NEC), generally guides policy after the
CEA narrows the options. The NEC is usually considered
the more powerful of the two, but the CEA wields enormous
influence, too. At any rate, her team helped assemble what
came to be known as the American Rescue Plan, the ARP,
the $1.9 trillion COVID relief bill that passed Congress in
March 2021.

I first met Boushey sometime in the early 2010s, and her
writing has included several pieces on the need for a new
economics published in the quarterly journal I edit, *Democracy: A Journal of Ideas*. When I asked her in an interview in

mid-2021 to re-create for me how Biden's team of economic advisers put together the ARP, she described a process that started during the campaign and involved dozens if not hundreds of experts; finally, it produced a bill that fulfilled candidate Biden's pledges to voters, if not in every single detail, then at least in the way it began to change how Washington thought about economic policy. Boushey: "We were sitting here trying to figure out, how big does this need to be? What is the scale and scope? How many bites at the apple will we have? And how are we going to [address] this pandemic?" She paused for a moment and continued: "And God help us. This is my third recession in this town. And I know I for one, and the people I was working with, all thought, we need to make sure that this meets the scale and scope of the problem [in a way] that cannot leave Americans behind."

Jared Bernstein had been named by Vice President Joe Biden as his chief staff economist. That appointment surprised me and a number of other observers at the time, and in a good way. Bernstein was then working at the Economic Policy Institute (EPI), a labor-funded think tank whose work product has been consistently excellent—and consistently out of fashion in the free-market era. If you are aware, for example, that CEOs in America make some three hundred times the salary that their average worker makes, you know that because of work done by EPI, which tracks such matters closely and has always occupied the left edge of the mainstream.

That is something that can't be said of Joe Biden. Disparagements from the left notwithstanding, he was never a centrist; he never, for example, joined the Democratic Leadership Council, the avowedly moderate, pro-business group formed in the 1980s. But neither was he a crusading liberal. Biden always found the center lane of where his party was as a whole. If Ted Kennedy was over here to his left, and Sam Nunn was over there to his right, Biden would usually land in a place equidistant between them. So his choice of Bernstein in 2009 seemed out of character—until one thought about Biden's devotion to labor unions, a passion that's well known now that he's president but was less evident in the Obama years. As a senator, Biden had spent much of his career chairing the Foreign Relations and Judiciary Committees, so he became more associated with foreign policy and high-profile Supreme Court nomination fights (on neither of which was he particularly progressive).

Back in 2009, as the Obama-Biden economic team surveyed the wreckage of the meltdown and tried to figure out what to do, Bernstein usually found himself in two positions: first, representing the leftmost opinion in the room; and second, being badly outnumbered by those urging smaller or more cautious or more political approaches. But by 2021, two things had changed. First of all, Bernstein was now not the guy representing the vice president, to whom people didn't *really* have to listen; he was now a member of the Council of Economic Advisers, with Boushey and Cecilia Rouse, a Princeton economist whose scholarship focused on labor and education economics and who became the first African American to head the CEA. Bernstein was much more central to the policy-making deliberations than he had been in 2009.

The second thing that changed was Biden himself. His instinct for finding the center of his party remained intact, but now the party as a whole had moved left, and so that center lane was to the left of where it had been in 2009. And there was the matter of the pandemic, which Biden believed opened up political possibilities for government intervention in the economy that hadn't existed before. So there was no doubt the new administration was going to be as aggressive as it could be, and this was a tone, Bernstein says, set by Biden himself. "He was and is acutely aware that the virus pulled the curtain back on a set of inequities that he is talking about when he says 'Build Back Better,'" Bernstein told me. "He recognized the idea that hundred-year storms happen every two years and that people of color and people in the bottom half of the income scale were much more subjected to both the economic and the health crises."

The tone of deliberations in 2021, Bernstein told me, was "hugely different" from that of 2009. There was a commitment to being bold. "If we're going to get in here, let's get in big; that was the president's very clear guidance," Bernstein says. And he was no longer the lonely voice in the room. Biden had appointed a team very different from the more establishment one Obama had assembled. "Some of the policies that we're putting out are happening in part because of the people who are here, and in part because of the people who are not here," Bernstein told me. He didn't name names, but it seems clear that by "not here" he meant figures like Larry Summers and Tim Geithner. The new direction, he told me, was very much a function of personnel: "Sometimes I'm on these calls where it's an economics call and there are seven people on the call, and I'm the only man. In fact, every morning when the CEA has our morning briefing, there are typically five to seven people, and I'm the only male. In *economics*. Wow."

Boushey, too, had her "wow" moments. She recalled working on a document, she couldn't remember whether it was about child care or climate or what exactly, but she remembered that there were repeated mentions in quick succession of labor rights. "And I just remember thinking to myself, 'Oh my God, we have mentioned the right to join a union something like eight times in this paragraph,'" she told me. "And I remember stopping myself and thinking, 'What a problem to have.'"

And so the American Rescue Plan grew, to $1.9 trillion. Such numbers take on a surreal and incomprehensible quality, so it's understandable if people react to them with a bit of an unknowing shrug. But this was a staggering amount of money. A good guesstimate for federal spending on welfare in fiscal year 2020 is about $31.5 billion. That's a lot. But $1.9 trillion is sixty times that amount. It's hard to compare spending today to New Deal–era spending because today's economy is so much larger than that of the 1930s, but *The Washington Post* estimates that New Deal spending from 1934 to 1940 amounted to 2.8 percent of all produced goods and services; the Great Society figure was 0.9 percent, while Biden's number is a little under 2 percent. Republicans dismissed it as just more taxing and spending from Democrats. In fact, there were no taxes to speak of; the most notable item on the tax front was the dramatic increase in the child tax credit for families, which Democrats like the Connecticut representative Rosa DeLauro had been pushing for years and which families started seeing in their bank accounts in July 2021 (it was temporary and ended when Congress failed to pass Build Back Better). As for spending, yes, there was a lot of that. But what the Republicans called spending, one might also label investing: investments in public goods that had been underfunded for years or even decades during which conservatives argued that public investment was bad economic policy. The ARP sent $350 billion to states, counties, cities, and tribal governments for schools, public safety, pandemic response, water and sewage systems, broadband infrastructure, mental health services, and other initiatives. On the pragmatic level, it was a vast reversal of policy direction. But the more important and heartening reversal occurred on a different plane, the plane where these ideological battles are really and truly won and lost: on the level of economic theory or philosophy, it was a frontal assault on the country's reigning economic policy assumptions.

This was jarring and frightening, even for a number of Democrats. It wasn't just West Virginia's senator Joe Manchin, who at least has the excuse of representing a state where Donald Trump carried nearly 70 percent of the vote. Many congressional Democrats had come to believe over the years that "spending" equaled deficits equaled political suicide. Republicans ran up the deficit, largely through giving tax cuts to the rich, whenever they had power, obviously as part of a broader plan (though they would never admit this) to starve the government so that when the time came that Democrats took power, increasing investments would be politically harder, and Republicans could accuse Democrats of running up the deficit. However hypocritical that charge was, coming from the people who actually *had* run up the deficit, it terrified many Democrats.

But the mood was changing now. Even though Democrats clung to narrow majorities in both houses of Congress (indeed, by one tie-breaking vote in the Senate, Kamala Harris's), and even though a lot of them were still spooked by deficits, they were resolved to do something with their power. They knew, given the historical likelihood that they'd lose the House in the 2022 midterms, that their time to act was limited. Their president wanted to do big things. Beyond Biden himself lay, as this book will explain, groups of activists and policy intellectuals and economists and others who'd spent years tilling this Keynesian soil, trying to shift economic policy making away from the "neoliberal" free-market policies that Ronald Reagan and others had ushered in. They wanted big things, too.

There was new spending that was clearly COVID related, notably the benefits paid out to people who'd lost their jobs. But there were also a number of items that had been on liberal wish lists for years that had never made it through. The most prominent of these was the child tax credit, delivered to families partly through a credit at income tax time and partly through a check directly from the government. Representative DeLauro first came up with the idea in 2003. The Republicans controlled the House at the time, "and it lost on a party-line vote," DeLauro told me. "But I introduced it year after year from that point on." Finally, the time was right.

The bill passed in early March. Manchin provided some heart-stopping last-minute drama (and not for the last time) by holding up the bill in the Senate and insisting that monthly relief checks expire sooner than had been agreed upon. Such is the power of the fiftieth vote in the Senate. But it all got sorted out. It passed with no Republican support in either house. It was just one bill, but symbolically it was much more. It was the beginning of a new economic era.

"I want to change the paradigm," Biden said in late March at his first press conference. "We start to reward work, not just wealth." He reiterated the point the following week in a speech unveiling his infrastructure plans in Pittsburgh—the old steel city, a perfect symbolic location to talk about work and investment and unions and the middle class. Liberals could hardly believe their ears. Joe Biden, talking like peak–New Deal Franklin Roosevelt. And he didn't just talk. After the American Rescue Plan there was the bipartisan "hard" infrastructure bill, supported even by Minority Leader Mitch McConnell. This was the biggest such bill Congress had passed since the original Interstate highway act during Dwight Eisenhower's presidency.

That the third bill, Build Back Better, got stalled shows that the work of changing the country's economic paradigm is the work of many years, and if Republicans retake power, of course, all progress will cease and some will be reversed. Some version of Build Back Better may have passed by the time this book appears. But even if not, its constituent elements—childcare, healthcare, universal pre-K, green investments—are firmly part of the conversation. Despite all the media caterwauling about "#demsindisarray," the fact remains that in late 2021, there were 271 elected Democratic legislators in Washington, and 268 of them either voted for the $3.5 trillion version of Build Back Better or were prepared to do so. It's hard to picture the party retreating from these commitments.

Most of us think of the economy on two levels. The first level, for most people, is personal. The economy is about their job, their income, their prospects for advancement, their 401(k)s, their expenses. The second involves the sets of numbers that the media report to us on a regular basis: the Dow Jones Industrial Average, the S&P 500, the previous month's job numbers, the unemployment rate, the rate of inflation. These statistics press their way into our brains insistently, daily, even hourly for news junkies, and they collectively constitute what we think of as the economy.

But the economy is something else, too. It's a set of ideas. Ideas about human nature, about how generous or selfish we are; ideas about how and why people conduct commerce and about what motivates their economic decisions; ideas about what people want and need out of work; ideas about what constitutes the good life and how we as a society can best get there. These ideas reflect a society's reigning values at any given historical moment. What do we value more—the individual pursuit of wealth or the communal pursuit of basic comfort for all? What is government's role in shaping the market? The economic ideas that we choose to promote reflect the principles we've chosen to elevate.

The promulgation of these ideas, at least in ways that remain meaningful to us today, dates to the eighteenth century and begins with the work of the famed Scottish economist Adam Smith. He is known today for having developed ideas that conservatives celebrate, like the notion of the "invisible hand"—the unseen forces that keep a free market moving, and the idea that if people act in their rational self-interest, and if production and consumption are unfettered, the best interests of society are met. It's part of the broader theory—another phrase most people have heard—of laissez-faire economics, which is essentially the notion that through such free exchange the market will find its equilibrium (in other words, no government interference needed). Smith was more complicated than that—he took a dim view of monopolies, and today's Republicans would despise him because he believed in inheritance taxes high enough that today's conservatives would call them extortionate, a fact I've long thought Democrats and liberals should do much more to push into public consciousness than they do—but Smith is known, by those who know him, as the father of free markets.

Others appeared with other ideas. In the nineteenth century, Karl Marx insisted that what Smith's disciples called freedom was in fact slavery for the workers in the then-burgeoning factories of Manchester and the other centers of the Industrial Revolution. A working man had no more business smelting iron for a factory owner who would soak up the profits, Marx held, than he had giving that owner the chickens he raised and the cabbages he grew. The labor was *his*; thus, the workers should own the factory (and, eventually, the state should own it, to remove the profit motive entirely). Still later, in the twentieth century, John Maynard Keynes split the difference: he accepted a market-based, capitalist economy, but he posited that state intervention was required to satisfy demand, especially during downturns. Their ideas were very different, these three men, but they had in common that they were all extraordinarily influential. For good and ill, their ideas changed the world.

Keynes's ideas held sway in most of the developed world from the 1930s through the 1970s, when economic woes opened the door for critics of Keynes. They argued that "stagflation," a term coined in the 1970s to refer to raging inflation and high unemployment producing stagnant output, and other failures like deindustrialization and spiking oil prices, were the fault not of the market but of the government—the makers of both economic and monetary policy. Liberate the market, they said—reduce taxes, especially on the wealthy, decrease regulation, and expand the supply of money—and all will correct itself. To make a very long story very short—and I'll cover some of this ground in more detail in chapter 2—even though reality has rarely supported their theory, they won the argument. We've been living under, and the bulk of our government's economic actions have been predicated upon, these anti-Keynes ideas ever since, and as a result inequality has exploded, and prosperity and opportunity have retreated in vast swaths of the country.

The chief characteristics of the American economy

became these: concentration of wealth, inequality, crushing costs of health care and a college education, disappearance into vapor of that core characteristic that made American capitalism the envy of the world for many years—the broadly shared prosperity that lifted so many millions of families into the middle class. And while it was Republicans who led this charge, economic elites of both parties largely bought into this worldview.

Liberals, and occasionally a few conservatives too, have been fulminating about these matters for years. But what liberals have not done is present the American people with an alternative to supply-side economics.* That is to say, forty or forty-five years ago, Milton Friedman and others centered mostly at the University of Chicago seized upon the 1970s downturn and gave Americans a whole different story about how an economy was supposed to work: We don't need government intervention. Free markets work best. Those whom the market rewards deserve reward, and those whom the market punishes deserve punishment. Growth is what matters, and it's bound to be unequal, but if you get the government out of the way and let the market work, the "rising tide lifts all boats," as Ronald Reagan liked to put it.

And they did something else, too, these free marketeers, something very smart and strategic and important. They tied these rather drab economic principles to a couple of stirring ideas, ideas that every American is taught to love from kindergarten on: liberty and freedom. Because who cares about

---

* Supply-side economics and neoliberal economics are not the same thing (supply-side economics is an aspect of neoliberalism, which is a broader philosophy), but I dislike the word "neoliberal" in this context, for reasons I'll explain in chapter 2; besides, no normal person has the slightest idea of what "neoliberal" means, whereas everyone knows roughly what supply-side means, so for now permit me my usage.

theories of growth? Nobody! But who cares about freedom? Everybody! And so Friedman's famous 1962 book, which had sold half a million copies by the time the fortieth anniversary edition was published in 2002, was called *Capitalism and Freedom*. That is, Friedman didn't merely extol a set of economic principles. He tied them to an idea Americans cherish. Not just *Capitalism*. Or *Capitalism and Growth*. Or *Capitalism and Sound Monetary Policy. Capitalism and Freedom*. The title announced, in other words, that the book wasn't really about economics at all. It was about politics. It was about life. And the title of the book's first chapter, which cuts right to the heart of things, is "The Relation Between Economic Freedom and Political Freedom." That chapter's very first paragraph gets right to the point; it's a punch in Keynesian liberalism's nose and bears reprinting in full here:

> It is widely believed that politics and economics are separate and largely unconnected; that individual freedom is a political problem and material welfare an economic problem; and that any kind of political arrangements can be combined with any kind of economic arrangements. The chief contemporary manifestation of this idea is the advocacy of "democratic socialism" by many who condemn out of hand the restrictions on individual freedom imposed by "totalitarian socialism" in Russia and who are persuaded that it is possible for a country to adopt the essential features of Russian economic arrangements and yet to ensure individual freedom through political arrangements. The thesis of this chapter is that such a view is a delusion, that there is an intimate connection between economics and politics, that only certain combinations of political and economic

arrangements are possible, and that in particular, a society which is socialist cannot be democratic, in the sense of guaranteeing individual freedom.

I disagree with every single word of that paragraph, including the "ands" and "thes," and believe it to be—know it to be—demonstrably wrong. To take but one of many available examples from recent human history, look at the U.K. in the mid-1960s: arguably at its dour socialistic nadir under the Labour prime minister Harold Wilson (he "nationalised" 90 percent of the British steel industry), but undergoing one of the most gobsmacking explosions of personal freedom in human history (rock 'n' roll, loud amps, long hair, fashion, drug laws relaxed, homosexuality decriminalized, and so on). It's balderdash. Or, to use a concept to which this book will return, it's an assertion based on theory rather than data. The data in this case show that while Wilson was crushing market freedom under the state's remorseless jackboot, the young people of Swinging London were shagging their brains out. There are so many other examples. If Friedman were correct, the Scandinavian countries—liberal social democracies, and as such economic nightmares by Friedman's lights—would all be gulags. But personal freedom is doing just fine in those nations. In fact, in the World Population Review's Personal Freedom Index for 2021, Denmark, Finland, Norway, and Sweden all have higher personal freedom rankings than the United States. Friedman was either a liar or a fool, or both (yes, brilliant people can be fools).

But I admit that he came up with a great way to open a book. Friedman is no cagey welterweight feeling the opponent out in round one. He's a heavyweight who comes out swinging right at the opening bell. This is not about economics, he wrote. It's about freedom. *Your* freedom, citizen.

And by the way, how contemporary it still feels, with that reference to democratic socialism, made back when Bernie Sanders was still in college, probably just starting to dig into his Marcuse. Plus, Friedman had a skill most economists, in my experience, do not: he could write, and speak, plain English. No wonder he won so many converts—along with the fact that his message was exactly what rich people wanted to hear!

So free-market economics took over. And liberals have never really had an answer. Many liberals supported aspects of this agenda—a number of Democratic politicians, and quite a lot of economists, including famous ones who might surprise you. The *New York Times* columnist Paul Krugman, for example, was a strong free-trade advocate in the 1990s; his tenure at the *Times* has roughly coincided with the Republican Party's war against facts and science, and he became more political and more partisan in reaction, and these days is one of the country's most important advocates for the new economic paradigm. Others were not swayed. But even the ones who didn't go along and offered plenty of critiques never succeeded in putting forward an *alternative*: not just an alternative set of economic ideas, but an alternative explanation of how society ought to work that ties economic ideas to some greater good, like freedom.

This book is my attempt to do just that. I am writing this book because I believe Americans need to know this story, and because I believe elected Democrats need to develop some language that they can take to voters to help this new paradigm take hold. Because the status quo won't change until that happens. The new language begins with a phrase that you might have heard Biden invoke, a phrase I borrowed for this book's title: "middle-out economics." It was coined in 2011 by my friends Nick Hanauer, the swashbuckling Seattle venture capitalist whom you'll meet in this book, and Eric Liu, who these days devotes his time and bottomless energy to citizenship and civic health. It means, as Biden has said, that the economy grows not from the top down but "from the middle out" (he often adds "from the bottom up and the middle out, not the top down," which is even starker in class terms). What it means is, invest in creating a large, stable, and comfortable middle class, and the economy will not only be fairer but grow faster. It holds that we are all better off when prosperity is broadly shared, and that the public sector—government—must play a vital part in shaping that prosperity. It insists that this prosperity be inclusive in terms of race and gender, to correct for past (and present) discrimination, but also because greater inclusiveness means greater growth. More theoretically, middle-out economics maintains that the assumptions of classical and neoclassical economics about what motivates our economic decision making are wrong. We are not purely self-interested maximizers; we (most of us, anyway) are also generous, reciprocal, and concerned about this thing called the common good that today's right wing dismisses. So middle-out economics is more than just a theory of growth. It's a vision of a better society, one that takes seriously John Adams's conviction, borrowed from Jeremy Bentham, that "the greatest happiness of the greatest number" is the point of government.

I'm not an economist. This book will dip into academic economics here and there, but the focus is much more on economic policy making—that crucial junction point where economic ideas enter the sausage factory I've been writing about for three decades, namely, the political process. And, especially in the last chapter, the focus is on the kind of political rhetoric I believe Democrats need to employ to sell their economic ideas, because right now, they do a pretty poor job of tying those ideas to a larger vision of the kind of society they want. I know this much: the economic paradigm that has reigned for the last four decades is destroying the country. The central political-economic fact of the last forty years in the United States is the massive transfer of wealth from the middle to the top. A Rand Corporation study in 2020 concluded that from 1975 to 2018, nearly $50 *trillion* in income had been moved from the middle class to the top 1 percent. Put another way, to use numbers people can grasp: If all this money had not been shifted away from the middle class, the median individual income in 2018 would have been not the $36,000 it was, but about $57,000. That's what neoliberal economics has done to the middle class.

Donald Trump used to like to brag before the virus hit that he was presiding over the greatest economy in the history of the solar system, or whatever self-aggrandizing term he chose to apply on any given day. And it's true that by the standard measures—the Dow, the unemployment rate—the economy was doing well. Median household income did increase significantly, and across the board, in one year, from 2018 to 2019. But it was doing best for people at or near the top. If you were in the 90th percentile—that was $184,200 in 2019—then you were fine; you could afford most anything you wanted, within reason, especially if you didn't live in an expensive city or suburb. If you were in the 95th ($248,304), you were living a very good life—nice vacations, some college savings, and you could absorb the hit of an unexpected $600 car repair. If you were in the 99th percentile ($475,116), you were on easy street. But if you were in the 50th percentile, you made, or rather your household took in, $63,030. That's not much. Especially for a family. No nice vacations, no college savings; not even much in the way of taking the kids to a ball game. And remember—even at that level, your household brought in *more than half of all American house-holds*. And the really rich were getting tax cuts bigger than your annual income.

So no, Trump's economy was not great for most people. For that matter neither was Barack Obama's. I admire him infinitely more than I do Trump, but his economic policies could certainly have been bolder. The last time wages rose in a meaningful way was during Bill Clinton's second term. But even then inequality raged and got worse; the middle class did well, but the rich did light-years better.

No one would have guessed a few years ago that Joe Biden would be the person who would start to lead the Democratic Party and contemporary liberalism down a new path. But he and his team have at least begun to create a new conventional wisdom. The inflation problem that hit us in 2021 ignited a debate about whether government spending was to blame—that is, most observers acknowledged that inflation was driven chiefly by the lingering pandemic and the supply-chain issues it created, but conservatives also argued that government checks sent to people to get them through the downturn drove consumer demand to levels that supply couldn't accommodate (later, after Russia invaded Ukraine, inflation became partly Vladimir Putin's fault as well). The inflation scare has been a sobering reminder that making change on this scale is never easy. Meanwhile, though, polls have continued to show that people want universal pre-K and subsidized childcare and so on. This will be a long battle. This book is about how we can win it.

Part One

GETTING INTO THE MESS

CHAPTER ONE

The Golden Age

•

EMERGING FROM THE WAR

This book will end by looking forward, but it will open by looking back. Specifically, we will look back to the era after World War II and examine how economic policy making changed over that time so that we have a fuller understanding of how we got to this point, when (most of) the Democratic Party has embraced a much more economically populist agenda. What made that happen? This book offers four different answers to this question, all to be discussed in coming chapters, and each answer zooming the historical lens out a bit more broadly than before. In the short term, the main answer is the pandemic—a crisis that created the conditions that made a greater level of government intervention in the economy possible. In the slightly longer short term, say the last fifteen or so years, it's changes in economic thinking and in political activism and in the often-overlooked but important foundation world that opened up the space for ideas that challenged the reigning conventional wisdom. In the longer term still, I examine the free-market economic ideas and principles that were incubated in the 1940s and that came to dominate policy making in the 1970s, because all that new thinking and activism of the last fifteen years represented a reaction to them. And finally, my fourth answer to the above question lies in the fact that those ideas, the ones that came to prominence in the 1970s, were themselves a reaction to the reigning ideas of the earlier era, which takes us back to the end of World War II. We could do this forever, I suppose, and there's a good argument for going back to the New Deal, but I choose the late 1940s because that was the time when our modern world and economy were, in many important senses, born. Before 1945, as the labor historian Joshua B. Freeman has written, the United States "was much more a conglomeration of regions with distinctive forms of economic activity, politics, and culture" than it would become.

So this returns us to what is often called the golden age of capitalism—that postwar period when the middle class exploded, wages grew steadily, American homes added comforts that would have been inconceivable in the Depression era, and everything just seemed to work. As we'll see, everything didn't work for everyone. Black people, other people of color (who didn't exist in the United States in large numbers yet), and women were largely cut out of the action, a historical error that any new golden age must take pains to correct. And even beyond that, there were problems aplenty, as there always are: intense labor strife, deep ideological divides over communism and anticommunism fueled by demagogues like Joe McCarthy, violent battles for civil rights, bitter division over the war in Vietnam.

But economically speaking, it was a comparative golden age. And this is the first important point that needs to be made today about this period. It was an age of shared prosperity compared with today, and it was such because *our economic values were better.* Coming out of depression and war—two experiences shared by the whole population that demanded sacrifice and made people think about not just their own well-being but that of their neighbors—the United States of the 1940s through the 1960s had morally superior economic values to the United States of, say, the 1980s.

But let's put morality to the side for now and establish that the period was materially better. Robert Skidelsky, the economic historian and biographer of John Maynard Keynes, wrote in his short post–Great Meltdown volume, *Keynes: The Return of the Master*, of the two broad postwar periods that he refers to as the Bretton Woods era and the period of the so-called Washington Consensus. Bretton Woods refers to the Bretton Woods Conference of July 1944, when representatives of the Western democracies met at a resort in New Hampshire to set up a system of global economic cooperation to take hold once the war was won. Bretton Woods established the International Monetary Fund and provided for a system of fixed exchange rates; in addition, the Bretton Woods system encouraged government intervention in the economy to promote full employment as a chief goal. Thus, the Bretton Woods system was, Skidelsky writes, broadly Keynesian. The "Washington Consensus" was a phrase coined by the British economist John Williamson in 1989, referring originally to a set of policy ideas that Washington sought to impose on developing economies. These ideas included lower tax rates, deregulation, privatization, and kindred notions; given that, the term came to refer to neoliberal market fundamentalism more generally. The Bretton Woods system lasted, according to Skidelsky, from 1951 to 1973, when the first OPEC oil crisis caused a number of economic shocks. After a transition period, the Washington Consensus era ran from 1980 to the time of Skidelsky's writing (the book was published in 2009).

Skidelsky compared global and Western economic performance during the two periods using a variety of metrics. He begins with real global GDP growth, which ran at 4.8 percent during the Bretton Woods period, and 3.2 percent during the Washington Consensus period (and remember, the neoliberals say that it's all about growth!). He also notes the existence of five global recessions since 1980, and none during the Bretton Woods era (and one large one in that mid-1970s interregnum). Likewise, global unemployment grew in the Washington Consensus period; Skidelsky tracks the unemployment rate in the five major industrial democracies, and all rose during the latter period (most dramatically in the U.K. and Germany; in the United States, the increase was from 4.8 percent to 6.1 percent, which isn't as sharp as the U.K.'s 1.6 percent to 7.4 percent but still means a few million more people out of work). Inequality was, not surprisingly, "stable in the Bretton Woods age, but it rose sharply in the Washington Consensus years from 1982 and all the way into the new millennium." World growth volatility—changes in the growth rate of real GDP over time—was characterized by large spikes in the mid-1970s and early 1980s, but overall was about the same in the two periods. Only on inflation did the Washington Consensus period produce better results, but the numbers weren't as different as many might expect—3.9 percent in the Bretton Woods period to 3.2 percent in the Washington Consensus period. Likewise, four economists taking a longer historical view found that the average annual growth rate for the advanced democracies in the 1950 to 1973 period was 4.9 percent, compared with 2.2 percent for 1820 to 1870, 2.5 for 1870 to 1913, 1.9 percent for 1913 to 1950, and 2.5 percent for 1973 to 1979 (when their study ended). They note also that the growth was broadly shared—that wages grew steadily on pace with productivity, a key measure indicating that gains weren't just concentrated at the top as they have been in more recent decades. So the economy really *was* better for middle-class families than before or since.

It should be said that none of this growth and prosperity was inevitable. Early during World War II, as it became clear, in the United States and the U.K. in particular, that the Allies were likely to win the war eventually, economic and political minds turned toward the postwar economy. They did so with considerable trepidation. To appreciate this, we have to imagine the wartime economy, barely comprehensible to us today in our age of unquenchable consumerism. This was a time when millions of people were doing without. Meat, sugar, rubber, gasoline, and many other goods were rationed. Governments issued pamphlets to housewives instructing them on how to squeeze everything they could out of the groceries they were allowed to buy. There was a Home Front Pledge that even Eleanor Roosevelt took: "I will pay no more than top legal prices. I will accept no rationed goods without giving up ration points." As the end of the war approached, some critics observed that the upper classes were growing a bit weary of all this. The historian Isser Woloch wrote that in the summer of 1944, in his regular newspaper column, George Orwell noted that certain cars on the British rail system were once again being designated first-class, a distinction that had disappeared after the war's onset, and that some gated private parks in London, "which had been opened to the public when the government requisitioned their iron railings for scrap metal in 1940," were once again being closed off.

There was deep fear among policy makers in both the United States and the U.K. that the economy would tank when the war ended. The wartime economy put everyone to work, including women, who had previously mostly stayed at home; the transition to a peacetime economy would surely reduce employment and lead to some serious dislocations and a period of labor strife. Inflation fears were rampant, too, because wartime laws on price stabilization across a host of sectors were due to be lifted.

Wartime planners like the New Dealer Chester Bowles, who as the war drew to a close headed the Office of Price Administration (where a young Richard Nixon worked for a time), saw all this coming and wanted to avoid these shocks. But they were also driven by larger, historic motivations in both the United States and Britain: that these nations, the world's two most durable democracies, must not simply revert to the way things were before; that they were going to emerge from the war, first, in a new position of economic and political supremacy vis-à-vis the rest of the world and, second, with something of a duty to deliver on the mighty ideals they had invoked in fighting Hitler and would continue to invoke against Stalin during the Cold War.

This meant, in short, that new degrees of social provision would be necessary and that government would have to drive this activity because the private sector on its own would not. In the U.K., this thinking was most famously made manifest in the Beveridge Report. On June 10, 1941, the War Cabinet commissioned Sir William Beveridge, an economist who had served in a range of government posts, to conduct "a survey of the existing national schemes of social insurance and allied services, including workmen's compensation and to make recommendations." In November 1942, he issued his report, which he packaged as an assault on the "five giants" that plagued the lives of the greater proportion of the British population: want, disease, ignorance, squalor, and idleness. The two that you couldn't get away with today, ignorance and idleness, were seen in the report as reflecting not moral failings of the people but rather the failure of society to properly educate people and provide them with sufficient motivational opportunities. The report's recommendations were sweeping, especially so in a country that had not embraced government expansion in the 1930s in quite the way Roosevelt's America had. By 1945, the Labour Party released its manifesto for that year's campaign, called *Let Us Face the Future*. While a bit vague on the particulars on matters like housing and health care, the manifesto nevertheless committed the party to expansive measures ("the best health services should be available free for all").

Something similar was happening in the United States. It was happening without quite the same level of commitment, because the American Democratic Party was more ambivalent about such matters than the British Labour Party, and because the American president was ideologically elusive; yes, despite all that Franklin Roosevelt accomplished and all the change he oversaw, he was in some ways a cautious politician, unwilling to confront his party's segregationists, backpedaling toward deficit reduction after his 1936 reelection. But he was being pushed on this matter of the postwar economy by his advisers, and none more so than Chester Bowles. Around Thanksgiving 1943, as Roosevelt was preparing to leave for the Tehran Conference with Churchill and Stalin, at which the Western powers committed to opening up a second front against Nazi Germany, Bowles sent Roosevelt a memo. He urged the president to return from Tehran with the message that the soldiers were asking him about what kind of country they would be returning home to—one still stunted by unemployment and poverty, or one committed to a new dynamism. It had to be the latter. And so Bowles advised FDR to return from Iran and give a speech that might go as follows:

Therefore, I propose a second Bill of Rights in the field of economics: the right to a home of your own, the right of a farmer to a piece of land, the right of the businessman to be free from monopoly competition, the right to a doctor when you're sick, the right to a peaceful old age with adequate social security, a right to a decent education.

Roosevelt did not exactly respond with enthusiasm. He shared the memo with another aide and asked, "What the hell do I do about this?" But he did come around. The next January, in his State of the Union address, Roosevelt unveiled his proposal for an "Economic Bill of Rights": the rights to work, food, clothing, and leisure; freedom from monopolies and unfair competition; additional rights to housing, education, medical care, and Social Security. Bowles and other New Dealers were hopeful that Roosevelt would make this the theme of his reelection campaign. He didn't; he ran largely as a wartime president, and he mentioned the Economic Bill of Rights only one other time, in a speech in Chicago in late October that was broadcast nationally on radio. But it was enough. The Democratic Party was committed now to postwar Keynesianism in a way it had not been before Bowles's intervention and Roosevelt's speech.

WHAT MADE THE GOLDEN AGE GOLDEN?

The golden age, it must be said, got off to a rather leaden start. It didn't help the national morale that as Hitler was locked in his bunker, two and a half weeks shy of putting a bullet in his mouth, Roosevelt died, handing leadership of the nation to a vice president the people (outside Missouri) barely knew. Harry Truman, who today regularly ranks as one of our great presidents, inspired little confidence in April 1945. And as far as the economy was concerned, many of the postwar fears of the New Deal men were quickly realized. Inflation surged. The price of steel rose almost immediately after the war. Likewise, the price of meat—so strictly rationed during the war—spiked in 1946 as price controls expired over President Truman's veto. The controls were reimposed, but the supply of meat disappeared "as the big meatpacking companies held back supplies and cattlemen kept their steers in feed lots awaiting higher prices before they would send them to slaughter."

The immediate postwar period also saw an enormous amount of labor strife. Organized labor, then very powerful and quite left wing, reined in its militancy during the war, with unions in many sectors accepting wage freezes (that's how health insurance became attached to employment in the United States; it was a nonwage benefit management could offer workers) and agreeing not to strike (although there were literally thousands of wildcat strikes, sometimes pitting workers against not only bosses but their own leaders). Then, after the war, labor unrest exploded, and 1946 saw more strikes than any year in American history. A mere three days after V-J Day, the United Auto Workers (UAW) requested a 30 percent pay increase; this was at a time when wages in most sectors were going down, in part because of the oversupply of labor, what with several million men returning home from the war. Electrical workers followed, then oil workers and coal miners and lumber workers and longshoremen and more. All told, in 1946, about 4.6 million workers were involved in strikes. This was in a workforce of around 60 million people.

Over the next couple of years, inflation abated and labor unrest quieted (not entirely voluntarily—the Republicans took over Congress in January 1947 and passed just one big bill, the anti-union Taft-Hartley Act, which made it much harder for unions to organize and to strike; Truman vetoed it, but Congress, with more than half of all Democrats joining the Republicans, overrode his veto comfortably). A recession hit in November 1948—well-timed from the perspective of Truman, who'd just pulled off his upset victory over Thomas Dewey. Pent-up wartime consumer demand had been over-satisfied, as department store sales crashed by 22 percent. Unemployment began to rise because, with all those returning veterans, there were far more people than jobs. The downturn wasn't severe, but it lasted nearly a full year. Everything was sorted out by 1950, though, and it was off to the races. From 1950 to 1973, the gross domestic product *averaged* 4.06 percent. For a little perspective on that, we've had just two years above 4 percent in the entire twenty-first century—its first year, 2000, when GDP was 4.1 percent, and 2021's rate of 5.7 percent.

What made the golden age golden? Economists point to such factors as "an unprecedented growth rate of labor productivity along with a similarly high rate of capital accumulation." Conservatives would put it all down to a newly dynamic private sector—innovators like Abraham Levitt and his sons William and Alfred, who built the American suburbs, and the engineers at GE who started bringing more good things to life in postwar America than ever before, and more than dazzled consumers could believe. The explosion in international trade was important; the World Trade Center that ceased to exist on September 11, 2001, opened in the early 1970s but was being planned by the Port of New York Authority (as it was then known) as far back as 1946. Increased military spending to fight the Cold War and the Korean War—and to sustain this new national-security state on a permanent basis—was a huge factor. Indeed, "military Keynesianism," a concept that first came into vogue in the United States during World War II, was firmly established as national policy by the time of Truman's National Security Council directive NSC-68, which advocated a massive expansion of the U.S. military budget. By 1953, writes the historian Jonathan Levy, "total federal government expenditures accounted for nearly a quarter of GDP—nearly two-thirds of which was military spending."

Levy posits that the golden age was harmonized by a "fiscal triangle" that consisted of the federal government, the private for-profit sector, and the nonprofit sector. The private sector, of course, drove the economy and was still dominated at that point by the production of actual goods (as opposed to services; the United States transitioned to being a service economy from the late 1960s through the 1980s). The nonprofit sector at the time was growing by leaps and bounds. Nonprofit philanthropy had received favorable tax treatment for decades, but the big moment came when Congress passed the law establishing tax-exempt so-called 501(c)(3) organizations in 1954. The government was also growing and becoming more professionalized. Truman signed a law creating the Council of Economic Advisers to give presidents objective and professional economic advice (although they often lose arguments to the political people). The second CEA chair was Leon Keyserling, a liberal Keynesian who had studied at Columbia under FDR's adviser Rexford Tugwell. No one called the government the enemy in those days. The government, the private sector, and the nonprofit sector worked together, wrote Levy, to become "the dominant political-economic coordinating mechanism of Cold War liberalism. Its task was the production, distribution, and redistribution of industrial income."

That last noun is crucial. Redistribution on a vast scale was accepted more or less across the political spectrum, except by a few cranks—some Texas oilmen, a dean at Notre Dame named Clarence Manion, assorted capitalists like Walter Knott of Knott's Berry Farm fame—who had no political power at the time. The top marginal tax rate was 94 percent during the war; it was lowered to 91 percent in 1946. "Marginal rate" means that rich people paid these rates only on dollars earned above $200,000, an amount of money that almost no one not named Rockefeller made. (A small sign of how our values have changed: in 2021, that $200,000 would equate to about $2.8 million, which is made by roughly 300 Major League Baseball players, as well as something approaching 5.5 million other people.) However, taxation at lower levels of income was still quite high. For example, on dollars earned above $90,000 ($1.2 million today), filers paid 87 percent. On dollars earned above $50,000 ($697,000), they paid 75 percent. On dollars earned above a relatively modest $16,000 ($223,000), 50 percent of each of those dollars went to Uncle Sam. Even the lowest rate then, 20 percent, was twice today's 10 percent. And compared with today's seven tax brackets, there were a staggering twenty-four in 1950. At all levels, if you made more, you paid more.

Of course, then as now, the tax code was festooned with deductions and ways to avoid paying the posted rate. Still, those are rates that would be impossible to replicate today; antitax forces would literally start a war. Rates that high would also be bad policy today, in a world where capital is so mobile. (If they made me emperor, I'd probably impose a top marginal rate of about 55 or 60 percent on some quite-high dollar figure, like $5 million.) But those tax rates did one salutary thing: they brought in a ton of revenue. Despite what the supply-siders say—and we'll dig into this in more detail in a later chapter—the history on this point is as straight-forward as it can be: higher tax rates produce more revenue. There was money for the government to spend, and it spent it. Yes, on building up the military, but also on things like rebuilding Europe and Japan: the Marshall Plan cost around $15 billion, or $180 billion in today's dollars. The Federal-Aid Highway Act of 1956, which built the Interstate High-way System (on the basis of a military-emergency rationale), cost more than $100 billion over ten years. That would equate to about $1 trillion in today's dollars.

Corporate tax rates were higher, too. The statutory cor-porate tax rate in the 1950s was 50 percent. The effective rate jumped around but was typically in the 30 to 40 percent range. The maximization of profit that became holy writ in corporate America later in the century wasn't part of the equation then. Shareholders in publicly held companies had a right to expect a reasonable return on their investment, but only that—a reasonable return. Such was the ethos of the time. There was a business group, the Committee for Economic Development (CED), that was started during the war by executives from the Studebaker auto company and Eastman Kodak to plan reconversion to a peacetime econ-omy. The CED got corporate America behind the Marshall Plan, and it enlisted private-sector CEOs and university presidents to describe the social role of business. An econo-mist named Howard Bowen published a book in 1953 called *Social Responsibilities of the Businessman.* Interestingly, it was one of a series of books on Christian ethics produced by the Federal Council of the Churches of Christ in America. This paragraph sums up the book's, and to some extent the era's, ethos:

The unrivaled freedom of economic decision-making for millions of private businessmen, which characterizes our free enterprise system, can be justified not if it is good merely for the owners and managers of enterprises, but only if it is good for our entire society. We can support freedom and private control of enterprise only if it is conducive to the general welfare by advancing progress, promoting a high standard of living, contributing to economic justice, etc. We judge its success or failure in terms of the public interest. When we consider proposals for its modification, we do so with the public interest in mind. Business, like government, is basically "of the people, by the people, and for the people."

And so General Motors consummated, with the UAW's leader, Walter Reuther, the Treaty of Detroit in 1950, in which management for the first time accepted the idea that the union was its legitimate bargaining partner. Health care and pensions became a permanent part of labor contracts. In that same year, Truman signed into law amendments to Social Security that dramatically expanded that program. Yes, the amendments raised the level of taxation, to 6.1 percent of payroll (it's 6.2 percent today, for both employer and employee), but they increased average benefits from $26 a month to $46 a month, added ten million new workers to the rolls, and greatly increased benefits for widows and orphans. And of course Medicare and Medicaid were created in 1965 (these were technically also amendments to Social Security).

This little section barely scratches the surface of a remarkable time. There was still a lot wrong with that America, as the next section will discuss. And even as the country committed to these liberal public investments, a new conservative movement was taking shape that would change the country entirely by 1980. But in sum, the golden age of American capitalism was golden because that America had better economic values. We invested in ourselves. We cared about inequality. We did not venerate extreme wealth. We taxed the well off to pay to improve the lives of working people. In other words, I'd argue, the America of that era practiced middle-out economics. And working people saw their lives improve in dramatic ways.

IT WASN'T GOLDEN FOR EVERYONE

It is important to note, though, that this golden age had deep defects, defects we've only just started to reckon with. Our political culture—and yes, this was true of mid-century liberalism, not just conservatism—was built around the understood presumption that the chief beneficiaries of all this public generosity would be white men.

In fact, if the postwar era was a time of rare consensus on behalf of public expenditure, that was probably *because* of this presumption. This is the argument of some recent and important works of history, notably Jefferson Cowie's *Great Exception*. Cowie's main thesis was that those of us who came of age during the Bretton Woods era thought of it as "normal" and the Reagan counterrevolution as aberrational. Cowie argues that that has it backward—that the New Deal and the postwar period of vast public investment were the actual outliers in American history. But another point he makes is about race: that the broad social cohesion that characterized the United States during the Bretton Woods period happened because most people were white. The United States in 1950 was roughly 88 percent white, 10 percent Black, and 2 percent other. To Cowie, "a sort of 'Caucasian' unity took place among a historically divided working class." As we know well, many, many white voters resent government doing things perceived as benefiting people of color. It's hard to avoid the grim conclusion that America was okay with redistribution provided the goods were going to white folks.

That Blacks were legally excluded from most of the postwar bounty is well known. The GI Bill, officially the Servicemen's Readjustment Act of 1944, may be the most often cited example. But what many people don't understand is that the bill's discriminatory effects were smuggled in through a side door, very slyly constructed. The bill provided numerous benefits to returning soldiers—the cost of college or vocational tuition, money to start a small business, unemployment benefits as they looked for work, and, most of all, home loans at very favorable rates, financed and administered by the Federal Housing Administration (FHA) and the newly created Veterans Administration. Racial exclusion was not written into the law, so officially the bill's benefits were available to Black veterans. Instead, according to Richard Rothstein, author of the searing book *The Color of Law*, which documents the ways in which federal policy underwrote segregation, FHA regulations promulgated after the legislation was passed stated that "incompatible racial groups should not be permitted to live in the same communities." In effect, Blacks couldn't get home loans under the bill. They couldn't get home loans generally to move to the new suburbs, which were virtually all built with racial covenants. This, it has to be said, was chiefly the work of liberalism, not conservatism. The FHA subsidized the explosion of the American suburbs after the war—literally millions of homes that African Americans were simply not allowed to buy.

Blacks were excluded from many jobs as well. The story here is sometimes a little more complicated than just a simple tale of intransigent racism. But only a little. Here, we see leading American corporate CEOs who in some cases held fairly progressive personal beliefs on race but did next to nothing to integrate their workforces. Robert Woodruff, the head of Coca-Cola in the postwar period, donated money toward educational opportunities for Blacks and raised millions for the United Negro College Fund. Coke advertised to Black consumers in Black newspapers, using figures like Jackie Robinson, Jesse Owens, and the Harlem Globetrotters. But it hired few African Americans, either at the Atlanta headquarters or within its far-flung network of bottlers and distributors. General Electric had promulgated an antidiscrimination policy as early as 1935, but by the 1960s "less than 1 percent of salaried employees, and less than 2.5 percent of GE's overall workforce, were people of color." Roughly the same was true of General Motors—where, by the way, UAW members were nearly as racist as management. The most infamous postwar story of all involved Eastman Kodak in Rochester, New York. For decades, Eastman Kodak *was* Rochester, and it had a national reputation as a benevolent employer that paid good wages, promoted from within, and took care of its people—as long as they were white. When Black ministers and others pushed the corporation to hire people of color after the passage of the Civil Rights Act (which, officially anyway, barred discrimination in the workplace), Kodak dug in its heels. The famous radical organizer Saul Alinsky eventually showed up in Rochester, quipping that "the only contribution the Eastman Kodak Company has ever made to race relations was the invention of color film." The future senator Daniel Patrick Moynihan eventually mediated a settlement between the company and the community that did result in more Black hires.

Most of us tend to think about racism before sexism, because racial discrimination was this country's original sin, and it often (not always, but often) assumed uglier public forms than sexism, like lynchings and murders. But however sexism was expressed, women were denied untold economic opportunity during the golden age as well. Women, especially white, middle-class mothers, were supposed to stay home and raise the kids. Most women accepted this state of affairs. A *Fortune* magazine survey from 1946 found that just 22 percent of men—and 29 percent of women—thought women deserved "an equal chance with men" for jobs.

But not all women went along. At the Detroit-area auto plants during the war, women constituted a quarter of the workforce or more. When the war ended, the percentages went back down to nearly prewar levels. Again, as with race, this wasn't just on management. The UAW went along with this for the most part, too. For example, one hundred women worked at Ford's Highland Park plant before the war; during the war, that number spiked to fifty-eight hundred; by November 1945, when the plant had reconverted to the manufacture of tractors, the number of women workers was back down to three hundred. Women workers organized and fought back. At the UAW's March 1946 convention, they forced a floor vote on a resolution calling on the union not to collude with management in upholding sexual discrimination. It actually passed, but it didn't change anything in practice.

On the issue of wages in particular, "equal pay for equal work" had been a rallying cry of Susan B. Anthony and Elizabeth Cady Stanton in the 1860s. Very little progress was made, though, for decades. In 1944, while all those women were working in factories, the upstate New York congresswoman Winifred Stanley introduced an act calling for equal pay. It never even made it out of committee. It took until June 1963—four months after the publication of Betty Friedan's *Feminine Mystique*—for Congress to pass an equal pay act, as part of President Kennedy's New Frontier program. By that time, it passed the House overwhelmingly, by 362–9. The nine were southern Democrats, five from Texas and four from Mississippi (seven of the eight Alabamans voted for it!); there were in addition 62 members who voted "Present." This was landmark legislation, although of course the problem persisted and continues to persist: in 2019, women made 82 cents to men's $1.

New research in recent years has emphasized that with respect to both race and gender, the economic costs of institutional discrimination were borne not just by people of color and women but by the whole society. Just a couple of quick examples: Heather McGhee's 2021 book, *The Sum of Us*, provides a brilliant analysis of the economic costs to society of institutional racism, expressed in a small but telling way in her metaphor of swimming pools, revenue-generating public goods, being filled in with cement and shuttered rather than integrated. Similarly, an OECD study from 2016 emphasized the link between gender discrimination and economic growth. If the G20 fulfilled its target of reducing the gender gap in labor force participation by 25 percent by 2025, 100 million women would be brought into labor markets in those countries.

If the United States is to embark on a new golden age, these issues must be squarely addressed. We need to be able to look back at the golden age to see what about it was good, and there *was* a lot that was good: in terms of opposing economic inequality, accepting labor unions, enforcing progressive taxation, and making broad public investments, our economic values were far better than the values that took hold in the mid-1970s. But a second golden age would have to proceed by undoing the discriminatory legacies of the old age. This is something that a lot of powerful people in this country are against.

CHAPTER TWO

Who Were the Neoliberals?

•

A DIFFERENT PERSPECTIVE ON THE GOLDEN AGE

Not everyone was thrilled about the golden age, and they weren't upset because of all the racism and sexism. Their concern was the ism that consumed such people throughout the twentieth century and still does today: socialism.

From a certain mid-twentieth-century perspective, Western societies, all Western societies, were just a dangerous blunder or two away from falling under socialism's trance. This was never truer, probably, than in the late 1940s, when the Cold War started and the countries of Eastern Europe became part of the Soviet bloc. That change everyone knows about; less well remembered is the fact that there were robust communist parties in several nations of Western Europe, notably France and Italy. The Italian Communist Party, formed in the 1920s by Antonio Gramsci and others, did well enough in the elections of 1947 to be offered some cabinet seats under the Christian Democratic prime minister, Alcide De Gasperi. But 1947 was also the year of the Truman Doctrine, which laid down the policy of containment of communism in Europe. After it, the U.S. secretary of state, George Marshall, told De Gasperi that if he wanted continued U.S. aid, he'd need to give the communists the boot, so he did. In France, the party (called the PCF) had a wide following after the occupation ended and was a part of the governing Tripartite Alliance for two years. But, again in 1947, the communists were ejected from the government.

That year, 1947, comes up a lot in such discussions. In addition to all the above, it was the year that Poland began to align itself with the Soviet Union after an election the communists rigged—a crushing blow to the West inasmuch as Poland, having been ravaged from both sides in 1939 by the Nazis and the Soviets, occupied a special place in Western hearts (and more to the point, strategic calculations). It was a pivotal year for world communism and for political anticommunists—those whose concerns about the spread of communism were formulated first and foremost around the concepts of political freedom. But there was another group of people whose chief concerns had to do with economic freedom. They were the most alarmed anticommunists of all. Taking a somewhat darker view of human nature, they feared that the countries of the West and their "soft" anticommunist leaders didn't grasp the severity or immediacy of the Red Threat.

These men (plus a small number of women) were conservatives. But don't call them that! They thought of themselves as the true liberals, and they came to call themselves, in 1947, neoliberals. Here, I think it's worth taking a little detour down an important rhetorical side road to examine the history of the word "liberal." It's fascinating to me, given how detested the word is in today's America by the right, and given that even many people in politics who obviously *are* liberal are terrified of having the word applied to them, that it is also one of the most contested words in the history of the English language.

THE MANY MEANINGS OF "LIBERAL"

We all know what "liberal" means today. Whether used as a compliment on MSNBC or a term of abuse on Fox News, a liberal is someone who holds a handful of core beliefs: government intervention in the economy; government-driven action on issues like environmental protection; promotion of civil rights and racial and other forms of justice; defense of abortion rights; support for a reasonably generous social safety net; higher taxation on the wealthy to finance initiatives like health care; and more. But let's step back for now from specific policies and think of the word more historically and philosophically.

First and foremost, a liberal believes in progress; change. A conservative believes in the preservation of old things—that is to say, in conserving. I've always felt we liberals got the short end of the etymological stick in this sense: The very word "conservative" communicates a value, a goal—to conserve. The word "liberal," in and of itself, connotes nothing. So liberals are at a disadvantage right out of the gate: Any person with no knowledge of politics but a modest ability to reason logically could figure out what kinds of things a conservative believes in just by hearing the word. The same can't be said of the word "liberal."

Tracing its roots, though, the word "liberal" doesn't have anything to do with progress or change. It comes from the Latin *liberalis*, which meant "of or relating to free men" (as opposed to slaves, who were at different times anywhere between 25 and 40 percent of the Roman population), or "worthy of a free man," or even "decent." It could also mean "generous," which remains its nonpolitical meaning today: a liberal dollop of ketchup on those fries.

The English word "liberal" was in general use by the fourteenth century, according to the Online Etymology Dictionary. It mostly meant "generous," although it could also be used to mean "free" and "nobly born." But there were negative meanings as well. Back in Elizabethan England, "liberal" could be a pejorative term, meaning extravagant, unrestrained, licentious. In William Shakespeare's *Much Ado About Nothing*, the nobleman Don Pedro rats out his friend's female love interest by describing her midnight assignation with another man—right before her wedding, no less. The Leonato to whom Don Pedro delivers this grim news is the woman's father:

> *Leonato, I am sorry you must hear: upon my honour,*
> *Myself, my brother, and this grieved count,*
> *Did see her, hear her, at that hour last night,*
> *Talk with a ruffian at her chamber-window;*
> *Who hath indeed, most like a liberal villain,*
> *Confess'd the vile encounters they have had*
> *A thousand times in secret.*

Turned out he was lying. There *was* no liberal villain!

We skip ahead now to the late seventeenth century, when the word began to acquire a political meaning, in the writings of John Locke. We think of these old philosophers, when we think of them at all, as remote figures, holed up in their garrets, not quite real and full human beings in some ways. But Locke was far from remote. He lived a life immersed in politics and argument. He was a commanding figure who, with his dramatic cheekbones and wild hair, bore more than a faint resemblance to Pink Floyd's bassist,

Roger Waters. He was, like all of us, a man of certain contradictions: for the most part he was a passionate foe of slavery, but he did spend a couple of years facilitating the slave trade as the secretary of the man King Charles II had put in charge of something called the Council on Foreign Plantations. But we remember him for his great accomplishments. He was the first person to argue that "men" had rights—not bestowed on them as gifts from a king, not earned by some action or deed, just natural and inalienable, to use our founders' word (they adored Locke), and simply by virtue of having been born. These rights were life, liberty, and property, that last of which our founders converted into the broader "pursuit of happiness" (which to the founders, incidentally, meant something akin to the ability to enjoy the fruits of one's labors but did *not* mean unlimited wealth). Either way, it was a revolution. And it was aimed at a target: he grew to despise Charles II and his brother and successor, James II, and in turn he became such a figure of suspicion in their England that he fled for a little cooling-off period to what was then called the Dutch Republic.

When we think of freedom these days, we mostly think of the freedom to do stuff we want. That is certainly how our present-day right wing frames the word. Don't tread on me. This freedom covers the most prominent rights enumerated in our Bill of Rights, freedom of speech and worship and so on. In Trumpy America, it has included the freedom not to wear a mask and go to a grocery store and sneeze on someone in the produce aisle and get them sick, which is a grotesque perversion of freedom, which historically has been generally defined as the right to do as you please until you get into another's space: the right to do what you want with your fist ends where my jaw begins.

The most cherished freedoms in the Bill of Rights

are of course legitimate in part because they respect this boundary: freedom of speech, for example, does not extend to incitement to riot. These freedoms constitute one form of freedom, or liberty. This is called "negative liberty": the freedom to do X or Y without interference from the state or from others. But there's a second kind of liberty that is also important. It's called "positive liberty": the freedom to do X or Y because some other actor (usually the state) makes it possible for a person to have the capacity to do it; the right to vote and, more recently, the right to health care, for example, are positive liberties. Locke's concern was with negative liberty—the freedom of regular people from unjust harassment at the hands of the state. For decades, centuries even, "freedom" meant mainly this: freedom from interference in your life by the king, which is to say, by the *state*. Locke put it this way in the *Second Treatise:* "This freedom from absolute, arbitrary power, is so necessary to, and closely joined with a man's preservation, that he cannot part with it." And since this is what freedom meant, this is what liberalism meant, too. Freedom for the individual from the state's intrusion.

This meaning of the word "liberal" was a political meaning. In the century after Locke, the word took on another meaning—an economic one. And it was closely related. This happened mainly through the work of Adam Smith, the famous Scottish economist who published his most celebrated work, *The Wealth of Nations,* just a few months before Thomas Jefferson wrote the Declaration of Independence. Smith, as I noted in the introduction, argued that if everyone merely acted in "his" self-interest, the common interest would be met. He became with *Wealth* the father of free-market capitalism. The extent of his faith in the unfettered free market is exaggerated by conservatives today. First of all, he wrote extensively about empathy (not exactly a core concern of contemporary conservatism) in his earlier *Theory of Moral Sentiments*, and he held that the invisible hand could work only among people of decency and honor, which would certainly have struck out our forty-fifth president. Further, he did believe that government had several legitimate functions. It should provide for defense, administration of justice, education, and public works. He also got some things wrong; his recent biographer, Nicholas Phillipson, wrote that Smith believed in higher education funded by student fees but predicted that such costs would not be excessive. He failed to foresee all those governors like Louisiana's Bobby Jindal slashing the state income taxes that once upon a time provided the revenue to universities that enabled them to keep tuition reasonable.

Locke argued that individuals deserved to be free from state interference in their political decisions and actions, and Smith posited that people could prosper only with similar freedoms in the economic sphere. Thus, Smith was, by the definition of the word at the time, a liberal. In *Wealth*, he even used the word, a lot—often just in the sense of "generous" but also referring to "the liberal system of free exportation and free importation" that he advocated. And so the system of laissez-faire, free-market economics he outlined became known as liberalism. Today, we call the set of beliefs that Smith set forward "classical liberalism," a phrase you might hear a conservative use on TV from time to time. Here is a definition, for example, of classical liberalism from the website of the Mises Institute, a conservative-libertarian think tank:

> "Classical liberalism" is the term used to designate the ideology advocating private property, an unhampered market economy, the rule of law, constitu-

tional guarantees of freedom of religion and of the press, and international peace based on free trade. Up until around 1900, this ideology was generally known simply as liberalism. The qualifying "classical" is now usually necessary, in English-speaking countries at least (but not, for instance, in France), because liberalism has come to be associated with wide-ranging interferences with private property and the market on behalf of egalitarian goals. This version of liberalism—if such it can still be called—is sometimes designated as "social," or (erroneously) "modern" or the "new," liberalism.

So that's what liberalism meant, for centuries (and evidently still means in France and, the writer might have added, much of the rest of continental Europe). In an economics context, liberal means belief in the free market.

THE MEANING STARTS TO CHANGE

In political contexts, however, the word had started to acquire shades of its current meaning by the late nineteenth century. This was a result chiefly of the Industrial Revolution, because it gave rise to the large and powerful manufacturing concerns, and later the monopolies and trusts, that exerted tremendous power over people's lives. Now, for the first time in history, most men's labor was not their own; it belonged to the steel magnate, the coal operator, the railroad tycoon. The worker's hours (grueling) and wages (pitiful) were set for him. And so liberalism, concerned as it was with personal liberty, began to look not at the king or the state as the chief threat to your average person but at the private sector. And there was only one force capable of checking the private sector and making it play by certain rules: the state. Thus liberalism began, however tentatively, to take up the cause of the state. The Republican Party became the party of Wall Street in the 1870s, but the next generation of GOP leaders saw things differently. Teddy Roosevelt and his Progressive Republicans broke up the big trusts ("malefactors of great wealth," he famously called them) and embraced a range of progressive reforms. And this, according to the historian Heather Cox Richardson, is when "liberal" started to mean what it means today: "After Progressive Republicans came to power, the word 'liberal' would still refer to the inherent worth of individuals, but now those embracing liberalism believed enabling individuals to succeed required a strong, not a weak, government."

TR helped usher in what came to be called the Progressive Era. There were several different kinds of Progressives: agrarian populists like William Jennings Bryan; urban advocates for this new class of industrial poor, most famously the leader of Hull House, Jane Addams, in Chicago; many preachers and other religious figures preaching what was called the social gospel, which fought urban poverty, child labor, and the like; and the new class of social scientists and urban planners emerging from these brand-new academic disciplines established in the universities. They were all liberals (except for the ones who were socialists). But they didn't use the word. They used "progressive." The Progressive Era ended in the early to mid-1920s, and the word "became a somewhat tainted term for some of those who favored a degree of government action," according to A. James Reichley in his history of U.S. political parties.

So it wasn't really until the New Deal that "liberal" began to mean what it means today. Franklin Roosevelt himself used the word on numerous occasions, referring not to free markets but to social justice and distinguishing liberalism from both conservatism to its right and radicalism to its left. This is from a radio address he gave in 1938:

> I am reminded of four definitions: A radical is a man with both feet firmly planted—in the air. A conservative is a man with two perfectly good legs who, however, has never learned to walk forward. A reactionary is a somnambulist walking backwards. A liberal is a man who uses his legs and his hands at the behest—at the command—of his head.

But even then, the word remained contested. Senator Robert Taft, "Mr. Republican" and an archetypal conservative, sometimes called himself a liberal. And a man named Ogden Mills, a Republican and a conservative who served in the Coolidge and Hoover administrations, wrote three books in the 1930s critical of the New Deal, one of which he titled *Liberalism Fights On*. The book was reviewed in *The New York Times*, which clearly assumed that its readers would have no trouble understanding that the word still meant what Mills, Taft, and Adam Smith intended it to mean: the review was headlined "Ogden Mills Defends Liberal Standards."

In the main, though, "liberal" was becoming the word of choice for those who wished to signal a set of beliefs that were broadly leftish but not radical. In 1944, a minor political party was formed in New York by two important labor unions, the garment workers' and the hatters' unions (yes, the hatters were important in 1944!), and the famed theologian Reinhold Niebuhr. It was founded as an anticommunist alternative to another small party that had been infiltrated by communists. The leaders named it the Liberal Party. It was in accepting the endorsement of this same party in 1960 that

John F. Kennedy called himself a liberal, making him the last American president to embrace the label:

> What do our opponents mean when they apply to us the label, "liberal"? If by "liberal" they mean, as they want people to believe, someone who is soft in his policies abroad, who is against local government, and who is unconcerned with the taxpayer's dollar, then the record of this party and its members demonstrate that we are not that kind of "liberal." But, if by a "liberal," they mean someone who looks ahead and not behind, someone who welcomes new ideas without rigid reactions, someone who cares about the welfare of the people—their health, their housing, their schools, their jobs, their civil rights, and their civil liberties—someone who believes that we can break through the stalemate and suspicions that grip us in our policies abroad, if that is what they mean by a "liberal," then I'm proud to say that I'm a "liberal."

By this time, the political meaning of the word was clear and was basically what we mean today. But conservative, Smithian liberals did not take this lying down. Milton Friedman, the free-market economist whom we'll discuss in more detail shortly, published his seminal book, *Capitalism and Freedom*, in 1962. So he was presumably writing in 1961, the first year of Kennedy's presidency, when he wrote this paragraph, in the book's first chapter:

> It is extremely convenient to have a label for the political and economic viewpoint elaborated in this book. The rightful and proper label is liberalism.

Unfortunately, "As a supreme, if unintended compliment, the enemies of the system of private enterprise have thought it wise to appropriate its label," so that liberalism has, in the United States, come to have a very different meaning than it did in the nineteenth century or does today over much of the Continent of Europe.

Within those quotation marks, Friedman is quoting Joseph Schumpeter, the Austrian American economist who, like Marx, thought capitalism was doomed but who, very unlike Marx, thought this was not good (the demise, in Schumpeter's theory, would be the fault of lazy and pampered intellectuals, a class of people with far too much time on their hands thanks to the heroic labors of the capitalist innovators; he'd have been a celebrated Fox News regular today). So Friedman was upset in the early 1960s that these ahistorical statists had stolen his word. And as you can see from the Mises Institute quotation above, they're still pretty cheesed off about it today.

It's interesting history, this tug-of-war over this word—especially so since the word is basically quite unpopular today with Democrats and has been ever since 1980, when a Republican political consultant named Arthur Finkelstein won a batch of Senate races with TV ads that called the Democratic incumbents "too liberal for too long." That attack came from the right. Today, within the resurgent left, "liberal" is also a dirty word, because to leftists it connotes (as it has since at least FDR's time) weak-willed reformism that doesn't adequately challenge the powers that be. Still further confusion is added by the fact that there is a whole different meaning of the word "neoliberal," an American meaning, coined in the early 1980s by Charlie Peters, the longtime editor of the *Washington Monthly*, who used the phrase to mean still basically liberal but nipped and tucked around the edges ("we no longer automatically favor unions and big government or oppose the military and big business"). Peters's definition was enormously influential in the United States for two decades or so. Certainly, the first time I heard the word "neoliberal," it was in the Peters meaning, and I'm sure that's true of millions of people around my age. Today, there's even a third meaning, because "neoliberal" has become a favored term of abuse by young leftists of "corporate liberals" like Hillary Clinton. But let's look now at the original coiners of the word "neoliberalism," because they are the ones we're concerned with here.

HOW THE NEOLIBERALS TOOK OVER: THE CREATION OF THE MONT PELERIN SOCIETY

The neoliberals conjured themselves into being in the 1930s. But before we get to them, let's look at the world, and the set of social and political conditions, that led them to choose to become an entity that would try to influence events.

It's fair to say that throughout the nineteenth century, most prominent economists were conservative (that is, liberal, in their parlance). Indeed, there was hardly any basis on which they would have been anything else, because governments weren't intervening very much in economies in those days. The U.S. government, for example, performed very few functions: it ran the military, the courts, and the postal service; it paid pensions to Civil War veterans after that conflict (Union soldiers only); it collected tariffs on imports, then the chief source of federal revenue, before the income tax was imposed for keeps in 1913 (Lincoln had levied a temporary income tax to finance the Civil War). And that was about it. Government spending as a percentage of GDP, typically around 20 percent today, was around 3 percent before the income tax and then our entry into World War I. Under such circumstances, there was about as much call for a state-interventionist economist as there was for an aerospace engineer or an electric guitarist. Economists studied within their discipline and developed important ideas about the functioning of the market: supply and demand, marginal utility, and, mostly from the Brit Alfred Marshall, the idea of the "rational economic man," who weighs the marginal cost versus the marginal utility of something (which we all do all the time: that bag of already shelled pistachios sure looks convenient, and yummy to boot, but is it worth $7.99 to me?). But in terms of economic *policy* in the public sector, there just wasn't much economic policy being made.

This began to change a bit as the universities started cranking out graduates with degrees in economics and other social sciences and the civil service was created. Woodrow Wilson's was the first American presidential administration to be populated by a significant number of these professionals. A bureaucracy began to grow to accommodate their existence: The Federal Reserve Bank was created in 1913, the Federal Trade Commission the next year. The National Bureau of Economic Research, not an arm of the government but a private nonprofit research agency that was created to disseminate information to policy makers and others, was established in 1920. The executive branch Bureau of the Budget, the precursor to today's Office of Management and Budget, was created, perhaps surprisingly, in 1921; that is, it was signed into law not by the academic-minded (though racist) Wilson, which you'd expect, but by the poker-playing Warren Harding.

The 1920s, the Roaring Twenties, were a rambunctious

decade in America: the automobile, jazz, the radio, bathtub gin, Theda Bara, Valentino, Babe Ruth . . . All fueled by a booming economy. The United States took over from England, and New York from London, as the world's financial capital. Indeed, in England, it was by contrast a decade of chaos and misery. Unemployment was high, as was labor militancy. The Liberal Party that had led the country through World War I was split into two; the Labour Party grew swiftly after the war and took power in 1924, though it held it for less than a year and did little to ameliorate the bleak conditions of working-class life. Once the Tories were back in, Winston Churchill, as Chancellor of the Exchequer in 1925, reintroduced the gold standard, which raised interest rates and reduced exports. Coal miners' pay, meanwhile, actually went down over the course of the decade. A general strike was called in 1926, but it ended in utter defeat for labor.

If he'd been an American, living in a prospering nation, John Maynard Keynes might have taken a very different view of matters than he did. But as he watched this squalor take hold in his native England, he sharpened his critique of the conventional economic wisdom of the day. Debonair, tall, erudite, a central fixture of the famous Bloomsbury Group that included Virginia Woolf and Lytton Strachey, married to a celebrity Russian ballerina (although bisexual, in that Bloomsbury way, at least until she coaxed him toward fidelity), Keynes had been famous at least since the publication of his 1919 book, *The Economic Consequences of the Peace*, warning that the high reparations demanded of Germany at Versailles would lead to the economic collapse of Europe and that someday a demagogue just might use the onerous terms to whip the German people into a frenzy. Adolf Hitler was still a minor figure in the mid-1920s, but the inflation-racked

Weimar Republic economy was a shambles, and Keynes was widely seen as prescient.

He was not a socialist; his chief political affiliation had been with the Liberal Party, which was rather more liberal in the old sense than the emerging one. So it was striking when in 1926, the year of that general strike, he produced a short pamphlet with the arresting title *The End of Laissez-Faire*. The content was no less remarkable: In it, Keynes, in the words of his recent biographer Zachary Carter, "was forging a new set of philosophical foundations for twentieth-century society." The essay argued that laissez-faire was failing to produce broad prosperity; it directly and forcefully rebutted the Smithian notion that acting in one's self-interest by definition benefits the common interest ("it is *not* a correct deduction from the principles of economics that enlightened self-interest always operates in the public interest"); and it laid the intellectual groundwork for government intervention in the economy on a large scale. He expanded on this in later works, notably *A Treatise on Money*, in which he argued that the way out of the Depression was through spending rather than saving, and *The General Theory of Employment, Interest, and Money*, which advocated government spending during downturns to maintain full employment.

It would be an oversimplification to hang the New Deal entirely on Keynes's shoulders. Arthur M. Schlesinger Jr., in his authoritative history of the New Deal, traces the various intellectual sources. There was William T. Foster, an American economist who is little known today and who was a leader of the "underconsumption" school, arguing that the government needed to spur consumption and spending; he referred to the free marketeers, quite politically incorrectly, as "lazy fairies." There was his disciple Marriner Eccles, a Utah banker, of all unlikely things, who believed the U.S.

economy could survive only "under a modified capitalistic system controlled and regulated from the top by government." And there were the famous brain trusters, like Rexford Tugwell of Columbia and Adolf A. Berle, who had co-written a stern broadside against concentrated corporate power in 1932.

The New Deal was broadly popular. Hence FDR's overwhelming reelection victory in 1936, literally the most lopsided in Electoral College history, as he inveighed against the "economic royalists." But not everyone, of course, was pleased, least of all those royalists. Corporate America, led by the National Association of Manufacturers and the DuPont family, launched a strident (though obviously not very effective) counterattack on the New Deal. And, on John D. Rockefeller's beautiful University of Chicago campus, as well as in Vienna and London and Geneva and Manchester, economists of a certain stripe grew increasingly alarmed. These were the neoliberals.

One should be careful with blanket statements about intellectual movements. Within any group of people, there are disagreements and debates, and in this the neoliberals were no different from any other collection of smart and passionate people. But it can fairly be said that they shared this general worldview: they were free-market, "classical" economists who fretted that individual liberty was threatened in the modern world possibly to the point of extinction. Remember, this was a time, the mid-1930s, when Stalin and Hitler had consolidated their holds on power. So the concern about individual freedom, with respect to the Soviet Union and Nazi Germany, had a lot of merit to it. More controversially and dubiously, they extended the critique to New Deal liberalism. Ludwig von Mises, for example, generally the most uncompromising libertarian of the bunch, acknowledged that the New Deal was small-*d* democratic, in the narrowly electoral sense, according to the author Daniel Stedman Jones, but he emphasized that "it is obvious that delegation of power can be used as a quasi-constitutional disguise for dictatorship." Henry Simons of the University of Chicago "firmly believed," writes the historian Angus Burgin, "that the main direction of New Deal policies was toward collective authoritarianism."

So men like von Mises and Friedrich Hayek and Karl Popper and Wilhelm Röpke in continental Europe, Lionel Robbins in London, and Simons and Frank Knight and Jacob Viner in Chicago began to communicate with one another about the need for action (indeed, for collective action, perhaps paradoxically). Their first big step was a meeting they held in Paris in 1938 that came to be called the Colloque Lippmann, after Walter Lippmann, the famous American journalist in whose honor the meeting was called. Lippmann was an interesting figure here. He originally supported the New Deal in the main, even though he was no great admirer of Roosevelt's personally. By 1935, he was more mixed and unpredictable; the journalist Heywood Broun once quipped that Lippmann was "quite apt to score a field goal for Harvard and a touchdown for Yale in one and the same play." And by the late 1930s, he was off the reservation totally. He published a book in 1937, *An Inquiry into the Principles of the Good Society*, that was a fierce broadside against state action. It was at this Paris meeting that the assembled decided to call their movement neoliberalism.

Why did they add the "neo"? To separate themselves from the old *laissez-faireistes*, basically—to update the old liberal principles for the modern world. This by definition meant some degree of accommodation with the state. In most contemporary journalism, the neoliberals are painted as free-market absolutists. But in these early days, except for von Mises, they were not. They accepted that the government had to play a role as a sort of market referee. Beyond that, the attendees of the Lippmann meeting had trouble coming up with any sort of plan of action, in part because, as Burgin writes, they "had difficulties identifying constructive 'revisions' that did not violate the philosophy they were attempting to save."

World war broke out, which put all such efforts on ice for a while. The war and its aftermath produced some grim realities from the neoliberal perspective. They were happy to see Hitler vanquished, but from the strictly economic vantage point the war just reinforced everything Keynes and others had said in the 1930s. The American and British governments spent and spent and spent. They took over whole industries. They directly employed millions of people. And they went deeply into debt. There's something called the debt-to-GDP ratio, a standard measurement of a country's financial health that free-market advocates take seriously (or at least pretend to when it goes up while a Democrat is president). In the United States, the ratio hit 114 percent right after the war; in the U.K., it was 270 percent (incidentally, it was above 100 percent for all four years of Donald Trump's presidency, but somehow we didn't hear Republicans complain about it).

So the neoliberals were alarmed as the war was ending. It was right then, as the Allies were planning D-day in the spring of 1944, that Hayek published *The Road to Serfdom*, his most famous book (the spring release was in Britain, where he was living at the time, teaching at the London School of Economics; it came out in the United States that September). It had originated some years before as a rebuttal to the then-voguish argument that the rise of fascism represented the final decaying stage of capitalism and that socialism's triumph was inevitable. The head of the press that published it in the United States estimated that it would sell nine hundred copies, perhaps a couple thousand if he could persuade Lippmann to write the intro. To date, it has sold hundreds of thousands of copies, enjoying a sales spike whenever economic crisis hits, as after the Great Recession.

In our time, *Serfdom* is described as a relentless attack on planned economics and defense of the pure free market. But that's a distortion. The book is certainly a broadside against collectivism, but Hayek had the Soviet Union much more in mind than the New Deal. He saw, Burgin and Stedman Jones and other historians of the neoliberals agree, a reasonably substantial role for the state in economic affairs. For example, Stedman Jones writes, "So while Hayek wanted to critique the idea of the middle way associated with Roosevelt, Keynes, and the mixed economy, he ended up sounding as though he might support it." Keynes himself wrote to Hayek (the two had been friendly sparring partners for two decades) to say that "morally and philosophically, I find myself in agreement with virtually the whole of it; and not only in agreement with it, but in a deeply moved agreement," offering only the gentle remonstration that while Hayek acknowledges that there is a line to be drawn across which the state should not intrude, "you give us no guidance whatever as to where to draw it."

I don't want to overstate this and turn Hayek into a liberal (in the modern sense). He was not. He lived to see Ronald Reagan elected, a development that delighted him; Reagan even had him to the White House. Hayek was upset by some oversimplifications of his thesis, such as a *Reader's Digest* condensation that emphasized the book's anti–New Deal points (and that made the book famous, vaulting its sales and launching Hayek on a Stateside lecture series). But his overriding concern—that collectivism would destroy individualism and freedom and make of us slaves or serfs—was clear. And so he proceeded from the success of *Serfdom* to a key moment in our narrative: the formation of the Mont Pelerin Society, a group of like-minded economists from Europe and America, which took its name from the Swiss mountain in whose shadow the group held its first meeting in early—note the year—1947. The thirty-nine economists, social scientists, businessmen, and journalists—thirty-eight of them white men, the exception being the British historian Veronica Wedgwood, a descendant of Josiah Wedgwood, maker of the famous blue china, and, interestingly, the maternal grandfather of Charles Darwin—met for ten days to try to hash out something resembling a program. As I noted above, they feuded on a number of points, but they agreed on four core principles: rejection of collectivism; defense of markets; insistence on a link between economic and political freedom; and "an acknowledgment of the importance of moral absolutes."

They felt pretty good about that first meeting, and they continued to meet every year. But they were hamstrung by two realities. First, stern disputes, and ultimately a kind of schism, arose over the question of whether they should have it as a goal to exert direct influence on public and political events. Hayek was of the view that "any turn toward propaganda . . . would challenge [the society's] identity as a venue for serious inquiry." As Angus Burgin put it to me in an interview, "Hayek's concern was that if you start bringing in lots of people who are involved in thinking about the politics, it makes it very hard to legitimately address foundational questions, because you're always navigating between these spheres. He said there's the philosophical sphere and the political rhetorical sphere. And the latter necessarily tends to dominate the former."

The second reality was far harsher. The world wasn't the least bit interested in their ideas. This was the era of Keynes's triumph. Even the Republican president of the 1950s, Dwight Eisenhower, declared himself a New Dealer and a Keynesian and famously wrote to his brother of opponents of Keynesian economic principles that "their number is negligible, and they are stupid."

So the neoliberals would have to wait for the world to accept their ideas. Something would have to happen to make their explanation of how the world should work seem more appealing than Keynes's. That something wouldn't happen for three long decades. In the meantime, one neoliberal—smart and argumentative and decidedly not hesitant about taking positions on the issues of the day—would do much to alter the intellectual landscape of America.

THE TRULY IMPRESSIVE, DEEPLY UNFORTUNATE RISE OF MILTON FRIEDMAN

The second most famous economist of the twentieth century—I suppose some would say the most famous—was born in Brooklyn in 1912 to parents who had emigrated from Hungary. In a Jewish-immigrant milieu in which many people were socialist or on the left in some form or another, Milton Friedman seems never to have been so seduced. He was supersmart, a mathlete long before that coinage (but, at five feet three, not an athlete). He got into Rutgers at sixteen, read some John Stuart Mill (a godhead of classical liberalism), studied under Arthur Burns, a conservative economist who would become Richard Nixon's none-too-successful Fed chair, and never looked back, possessed of that self-assured serenity about the correctness of his views that conservatives seem to come by so much more easily than liberals.

He was studying at Chicago in the 1930s, under Frank Knight and Jacob Viner; after the war, he returned to Chicago as a full professor in 1946. He attended that first meeting of the Mont Pelerin group the next year. Throughout the 1950s, most of his work was academic rather than oriented toward public policy. His big book of that decade, published in 1957, was called *A Theory of the Consumption Function* and was a critique of Keynes on a central point of Keynesian economics about aggregate consumption. Basically, Keynes had made some arguments about why people made their consuming, saving, and spending decisions as they did. Friedman countered those with different arguments of his own. It was all theoretical and academic, but the *policy* implications were clear. If people didn't make their decisions as Keynes argued they do, and if savings were good, not bad, then the whole edifice of Keynesian policy prescriptions crumbled. You didn't have to discourage savings by taxing high-income people, or encourage consumption by giving tax cuts to low-income people (also an important Keynesian principle), and you didn't need government to create demand during times of high unemployment (or ever, for that matter). In issuing these challenges, wrote his biographer Lanny Ebenstein, "Friedman helped to pave the way academically for the intellectual rehabilitation of free private property capitalism from the 1960s to the present."

Over the course of the 1950s, Friedman's views became more rigidly libertarian. Earlier, for example, he had supported the idea of some government regulation of monopolies, the one point on which almost all the Pelerinistes acknowledged that the government must play a role; by the end of the decade, Friedman had decided the government shouldn't do even that (as I will explain in chapter 5, he changed his mind not on principle but because a funder told him to). He also engaged in what seems today some wishful thinking along ideological lines. In the early 1960s, he smelled a libertarian revolution among the young, sensing "a rising tide of support among the young for the party of liberty, for the principles of free, private enterprise, and a strictly limited government." That didn't work out so well. Neither did his support for Barry Goldwater's presidential campaign, which Friedman enthusiastically backed and advised.

His greatest hit came in 1962, when he published the book that brought him fame: *Capitalism and Freedom.* It was aimed at a nonacademic audience. It was forcefully and briskly written. It was brilliantly titled. Its thesis is simple and direct: without economic freedom, there can be no political freedom. This was, as noted above, a core belief of the Pelerin crowd; as I wrote in the introduction, I think it is invidious buncombe that has provided the philosophical basis for our descent into oligarchy. But a lot of people liked the idea. Especially rich people, most of whom had always despised Roosevelt and Keynes and taxes and government but hadn't had anyone of prominence and authority come along to start ripping the clothes off the emperor. Now they did.

Read today, it's an odd book. Friedman lists fourteen activities the government performed that he said could not be justified (although he hastens to note that the list is "far from comprehensive"). A few make a certain amount of sense; for example, he opposed the government's monopoly on carrying mail for a profit; the rise of FedEx and DHL have borne out his point. Others are simply daft: he was against national parks. Still others are dangerously reactionary: he was against Social Security. Elsewhere in the book, he compares the wartime Fair Employment Practices Committee, created by FDR to outlaw racial discrimination in all war-related work, to Hitler's Nuremberg Laws, which barred Jews from attaining German citizenship, on the grounds that laws opposing discrimination and laws promoting discrimination are morally indistinguishable because they are based on the same principle, that it's okay to think about race in the first place. He writes, "Opponents of such laws [as Nuremberg] who are in favor of the FEPC cannot argue that there is anything wrong with them in principle. . . . They can only argue that the particular criteria used are irrelevant." By that logic, laws raising taxes and lowering taxes are indistinguishable in principle, too, because both involve the state mandating a change in the tax rate.

This little jewel is embedded in a chapter titled "Capitalism and Discrimination," which vectors between being merely ridiculous and starkly offensive. The central point of the chapter is that markets can end job discrimination more efficiently than government edicts because when bosses don't hire the best candidate irrespective of race, they pay a penalty because that best person goes elsewhere. This sounds nice, but it isn't remotely how the world works, except *maybe* at the level of professional sports. There have been many studies over the years testing this hypothesis, and they show that hypothetical job applicants with names like Lakisha and Jamal are, as the economist Robert H. Frank wrote in *The New York Times* in 2008, "less likely to be considered for jobs, even when they had qualifications on paper that were similar to those of applicants named Emily or Greg."

Friedman writes in this chapter that he is no racist ("I believe strongly that the color of a man's skin or the religion of his parents is, by itself, no reason to treat him differently"), and there is no evidence that he was personally racist. But he implicitly or explicitly endorses much racist policy in this chapter. Implicit: He writes that in a free society, the best way to end discrimination is "to seek to persuade [people] that their tastes are bad and they should change their views and their behavior, not to use coercive power to enforce my tastes and my attitudes on others." Right—that was working so well in Mississippi as Friedman was writing. Market forces and persuasion left apartheid in place in the South; it took government to topple it, which Friedman aggressively opposed. Explicit: He writes approvingly of a plan adopted by the State of Virginia to address school segregation, admitting that while it was adopted "for the purpose of avoiding compulsory integration," he, Friedman, predicted it would have precisely the opposite effect. He does not name this plan, but writing when he was, he can only have been referring to the diabolically named "freedom of choice" plan, which was the state's 1961 attempt to keep schools segregated while appearing to be comporting with the letter of the law as laid down in *Brown* by giving vouchers to white students to attend private segregated schools. It was the brainchild of Leon Dure, a journalist (he'd been *The Washington Post*'s White House correspondent during FDR's first three years in office) and segregation supporter who argued that "freedom of association carried with it a corollary freedom not to associate." Dure's plan would have permitted integration, but with the winking understanding that most students wouldn't want to do so. In any case, Friedman's prediction couldn't have been more wrong. Virginia's schools did not peaceably integrate. Black people, sensing that the free market was not fixing their problem, went to court. In 1968, by a unanimous 9–0 vote, the Supreme Court ruled that the freedom of choice plan had failed to integrate the schools as promised.

But people didn't bother about such things in 1961 in quite the way we bother about them today. The book made

Friedman a star. He got a column in *Newsweek*. "He became less a social scientist," Ebenstein writes, "and more a public figure, less an economist and more a political philosopher." The very next year, though, he returned to a more scholarly work, producing (with co-author Anna Schwartz) *A Monetary History of the United States, 1867–1960*. This book took aim at the conventional wisdom about what caused, and prolonged, the Great Depression. In Friedman's telling, it was not wild market speculation but government mismanagement of the money supply, especially in the years right after the crash. Friedman argues that the Depression would have been rather brief or might not have happened at all if the Federal Reserve had only expanded the money supply. Was he right? Certainly, the Fed's failure to stem the decline in the supply of money is a commonly cited reason for the duration and intensity of the Depression. Ben Bernanke said as much in his widely admired history of the Great Depression. In 2002, at a dinner honoring Friedman on his ninetieth birthday, Bernanke said of the Depression, "We did it. We're very sorry. We won't do it again." At the same time, though, it doesn't seem obvious that increasing the money supply would have been the panacea Friedman claims it would have been. This is exactly what Bernanke did as Fed chairman in the wake of the Great Recession. His three quantitative easing (QE) programs were just that—efforts to increase the money supply by purchasing government mortgage-backed securities and Treasury securities. QE is judged to have done some good—it stimulated bank lending and mortgage refinancing—but it certainly didn't bring the economy roaring back to life.

At any rate, on Friedman sauntered. In 1965, he wrote an article for *National Review* called "Social Responsibility: A Subversive Doctrine." This is the so-called Friedman Doctrine—that corporations have no responsibility to country or society or community, only to their shareholders. He famously expanded on this in *The New York Times Magazine* in 1970 under the headline "The Social Responsibility of Business Is to Increase Its Profits" (funny how the "liberal media" such as *Newsweek* and the *Times* kept giving this archconservative a forum). In between, in 1967, he gave an address to the American Economic Association (AEA) that has gone down in economic history as among the most celebrated ever delivered to that group. In it, and in his more popular writings, he seemed to predict the stagflation (high inflation combined with high unemployment, creating stagnant economic output) that hit the country the next decade. His ideas, writes Angus Burgin, "seemed irresistibly prescient."

He advised Nixon, though they didn't always agree, since Nixon, like Eisenhower, broadly accepted Keynesianism. Friedman actually said that Nixon's wage and price controls "did far more harm to the country" than his crimes pertaining to Watergate. He and some other "Chicago boys" did a stint as economic advisers in Chile, after the coup that removed the hated socialist Salvador Allende, undeterred by the murderous dictator Augusto Pinochet's idea of political freedom (Friedman justified it by arguing that if he helped bring economic freedom to Chile, political freedom would surely follow; that too, like Virginia desegregation, didn't quite pan out). And in 1976, he was awarded the Nobel Prize in economics.

It was well-timed, in that double-digit inflation and wage stagnation left Keynesians with a lot of explaining to do. The big hit was the OPEC oil embargo of 1973, which dramatically hiked the price not only of gasoline but of, well, almost everything, because the price of oil is reflected in the price of virtually every good that has to be shipped anywhere. Inflation hit 11 percent in 1974. Keynesianism had no ready response. Reality kicked open the economic theory door, and Friedman and his allies barged their way through.

CHAPTER THREE

Neoliberalism of the Right: From Reagan to Trump

•

SUPPLY-SIDE ECONOMICS: THE ANTI-TRUTH OF THE MODERN AGE

How do things—ideas, movies, songs, fads, anything—go viral in our society? There is of course no clear answer to this question. If there were, there would be no one-hit-wonder bands, because they'd all have figured out how to have a second hit. But what fun would life be without one-hit wonders? We have a soft spot, depending on our generational druthers, for "Dancing in the Moonlight" and "Baby Got Back" precisely *because* they were one-hit wonders; it charms us that the artists found that little indefinable something just the one time.

In the economics realm, Arthur Laffer could reasonably be called a kind of one-hit wonder, but, boy, was that hit big. Whether one should have a soft spot for it is another matter entirely. He's the brains behind one of the most pivotal lies in the American political economy in the last half century—a lie that has radicalized our economic discourse, galvanized the ruling class, and helped create raging inequality. In fact, it's more than a lie. It's an anti-truth—a direct assault on the truth, peddled for a specific and often hidden purpose. A lie is: Mom, I didn't break your heirloom vase. An anti-truth is: Mom, not only did I not break your heirloom vase, but Cindy broke it, and she did it on purpose, and it's all part of Cindy's long clandestine campaign to ruin your stuff and make you look upon me with suspicion. Laffer's anti-truth has been central to the triumph of the neoliberal paradigm since the 1970s.

Laffer is the creator of the Laffer Curve, which he developed right around the time that the ideas of Friedman and other conservatives were beginning to influence public policy. (And yes, Democrats were infected, too. Jimmy Carter pushed for airline and trucking deregulation and cut capital gains taxes, substantially benefiting the rich.) The curve posits that lowering tax rates yields more revenue because lower rates will provide incentive for people to work harder and innovate more and produce more and unleash the American economic tiger to such a degree that before long all that economic action will produce more tax revenue. Specifically, the curve is a hump drawn on two axes, labeled tax rate and tax revenue; without getting too technical, we can say it purports to show that for any given amount of tax revenue, there are two rates that produce that amount of revenue, a low one and a high one. The crown of the curve represents the point at which tax revenue is maximized, and everything to the right of the crown (or below it—the hump is sometimes drawn from the left side) represents taxation that is too high and starts to produce decreasing revenue as the curve slopes downward. So for every kind of tax, there is a point at which the rate is too high, which makes people work less and revenues fall. The curve, it should be stated, was not a finding based on a rigorous study of historical data. It was a mathematical economic model, an unproven theory. And it was a linchpin of another new theory called supply-side economics, which holds that increasing the supply of goods—that is, increasing production—leads to higher productivity and lower prices and thus spurs economic growth. Basically it holds that the economy thrives when businesses thrive, through policies like low taxes and little regulation, not when the government gooses demand, the core of Keynesianism. Supply-side economics had other fathers, people more widely respected in the economics world like Robert Mundell, whose championing of tax cuts gave supply-side economics some intellectual credibility. But from the start, liberals and Democrats gave supply-side economics the derogatory name of "trickle-down economics," attempting to emphasize that what flowed down from the top to the middle wasn't much.

With respect to the curve, you may know the famous story: that Jude Wanniski, an editor at *The Wall Street Journal*, was tremendously excited by the curve and sat Laffer down with Dick Cheney and Don Rumsfeld, then working in the Ford administration, and had him draw the curve for them on a napkin at the Two Continents restaurant in Washington, in a hotel near the White House. Wanniski retailed this story in the journal *The Public Interest* in 1978. Laffer later said he didn't remember the details of the evening and even threw a little shade at Wanniski on one crucial matter: "My only question about Wanniski's version of the story is that the restaurant used cloth napkins, and my mother had raised me not to desecrate nice things." The Smithsonian is in possession of the napkin today, a gift of Wanniski's second wife. And either Arthur's memory failed him, or he wasn't as attentive to his mother's admonitions as he advertises. Peter Liebhold, the Smithsonian curator who collected the napkin and directs the exhibition where it is on display, told me via email: "The napkin is definitely cloth."

Laffer's wasn't a new idea. Even Keynesians—indeed even Keynes himself—readily acknowledged that there was a point at which taxes could be too high. Laffer and Wanniski's talent was the usual talent on the right: packaging. By putting the idea into graph form and giving it a name, they made it seem somehow more real to people, as if it had suddenly acquired the status of immutable law. And after that article in *The Public Interest*, it took off like a rocket. The Nobel-winning economist Robert Shiller, for his book *Narrative Economics*, researched the frequency of appearance of the phrase "Laffer Curve" in news stories and books and found a massive spike in the late 1970s; it went, as we now say, viral, in a way that no economic idea probably ever had before in history. Shiller also drolly noted the real reason for its popularity: the curve, he wrote, "owes much of its contagion to the fact that it was used to justify major tax cuts for people with higher incomes."

Supply-side economics was the point of the neoliberal spear. Neoliberalism is a broader project, built around the concept of economic freedom, the promotion of an unregulated market, and the pursuit of growth, but the tax cuts were a crucial element, and the one that opened the political door. It's very much worth recalling that until this point Republicans were not uniformly dedicated to these ideas. There were still two or three dozen moderate and even liberal Republicans in Congress in the 1970s who backed some taxation and government intervention. A handful of them thought about running for president in 1980, but they either didn't bother or dropped out early (Lowell Weicker of Connecticut, Charles Mathias of Maryland, John Heinz of Pennsylvania). They could sense a stiff wind that was not blowing in their direction.

And so at this point in history, with the election of Ronald Reagan in 1980 (and Margaret Thatcher having become prime minister of the U.K. in 1979), neoliberalism beheld its triumph. Those long decades of wandering in the woods, peering slack-jawed through the glass as even Republican presidents declared themselves Keynesians, were over. Laffer was feted; Friedman and his wife, Rose, were invited by PBS (that liberal media again) to host a ten-part series called *Free to Choose*, funded by the Scaife Foundation, the Getty Oil Company, and the Reader's Digest Association. Now these people had power, and their theories would be put to the test. The ideas formed the core of what came to be called Reaganomics: cut taxes, increase military spending dramatically, decrease the domestic budget, and sit back and watch the deficit shrink (Jimmy Carter left office with a $74 billion deficit, thought scandalous by some at the time) and the economy boom. But the main ingredient, the emotional and psychic ground zero of it all, was the tax cuts.

The Laffer Curve is very famous and has been enormously influential. But is it true? No. It never has been. Now, a couple of caveats. Certainly, as noted above, taxes can be too high, so high as to reduce incentives to work and earn; so sure, there is some theoretical point at which a high tax discourages work. In addition to that, tax cuts to the middle class can certainly have positive impacts on growth even if they reduce federal tax revenue. Money given back to taxpayers is often money they'll spend, which helps to stimulate the economy. Also, according to classic economic theory, a lower tax rate for both individuals and businesses gives them incentive to work more and invest in new equipment and the like; that's more labor and more capital, which means growth. This can be a very slow-moving process, but it can pump up the economy. So Democrats and liberals aren't averse to tax cuts under any and all circumstances. LBJ and

Carter cut income taxes, Bill Clinton cut capital gains taxes, Barack Obama temporarily cut the payroll tax. But what Laffer unleashed was a ceaseless parade of large tax cuts for very wealthy people who have received literally trillions of dollars in tax cuts over the years, sold on the lie that the cuts will, as it is often phrased, "pay for themselves."

Actually, Republicans don't always say tax cuts will pay for themselves. They say it while arguing for tax cuts before they're passed. Then, a couple years later, when the Congressional Budget Office finds or the Treasury Department admits that the cuts have in fact decreased revenue, that's when they tend to say, "Ah, we never said they would pay for themselves." Then, a few years later, when people have forgotten all that and it's time for the next tax cut, they start insisting again that cuts will pay for themselves. This dynamic goes back to Ronald Reagan's presidency, when the top marginal rate was cut—in two chunks, in 1981 and then in 1986—from 70 to 28 percent. The cuts were sold, in part, on the promise that they would raise revenue. That, after all, is the very point of the Laffer Curve: lower rates will bring higher revenues.

If you talk to progressive economists about this, they'll tend to say that no one actually believes in the curve and no one ever did. It's just how they sell tax cuts. "All they know is that their donors want it," says Jared Bernstein, a member of President Biden's Council of Economic Advisers.* "People will say they believe this stuff, but that doesn't prove anything. They sell their tax cuts on how it's going to help the average person, but they know that it won't, okay?"

---

* I should note that this quotation is from an interview Bernstein gave me before he joined the Biden administration, so he's speaking here as a private citizen.

Bradford DeLong, who worked in the Clinton administration and now teaches at UC Berkeley, believes that supply-side boosters *knew* that tax cuts would blow open the deficit and that was exactly the outcome they wanted: "There were four groups. First, there were a lot of grifters. Second, there were a few true believers, ideologues who actually thought there would be enough growth that would pay for itself. Third, there would be those who thought that once the Congress had seen the deficits, then they would find it very easy to cut those who had weak claims on the federal budget, their programs, and so restore the balance by getting to a genuinely superior place in which those with weak claims would lose. And fourth, those who thought that the moochers would lose. And each faction was happy with what it thought would be the consequence of the emergence of a large deficit and so was willing to go through it."

And sure enough, it happened that after 1983, when that first round of tax cuts kicked in fully, the bill lowered revenue rather dramatically. There is a Treasury Department study from 2013 of the revenue effects of every change in tax law since 1940. It's a document with a few columns of numbers for forty-five changes to tax law over that time, and it shows—consistently—that Laffer is dead wrong. The Revenue Act of 1942 is probably the biggest tax increase in American history. Designed to finance the war effort, it (and other smaller wartime measures) expanded the number of Americans paying income tax from under eight million in 1939 to thirty-seven million by 1942 and to fifty million by 1945, and it hiked everyone's taxes substantially, especially rich people's. It raised $10 billion. A smaller tax increase in 1943 raised another billion. Then, with the war won, the Revenue Act of 1945 reduced rates. Sure enough, it reduced federal tax revenues by $5.9 billion. Harry Truman raised taxes in 1950 to finance the Korean War, and again, revenues increased by $4.5 billion. Then, in 1964, LBJ passed the broad-based tax cuts originally proposed by John Kennedy—about 20 percent across the board. This was peacetime and amid general prosperity. Did revenues spike, Laffer style? No—they fell by $11.5 billion, according to the Treasury Department paper. As for Reagan's policies, the 1981 cut cost the Treasury $445.6 billion over four years (that's in 1980s dollars). As that reality became apparent, what happened? Many of the tax cuts' champions, who had thundered with certitude on TV that they would pay for themselves, changed course to argue that no one ever said the cuts would pay for themselves! In fairness, the 1986 cut did actually add money to federal coffers—for the first two years, before it started costing money again. In those first four years, according to the Treasury document, the 1986 cuts cost $1.2 billion.

This debate has never ended. It bubbles up every time a new tax cut results in fallen revenue, or a tax increase doesn't bring the cataclysmic economic collapse that the right-wingers invariably predict. Conservatives say whatever is handy to say under current political circumstances and will advance the argument they're trying to make. And Laffer continued to make the case year after year, in book after book and polemic after polemic, arguing, for example, in a 2015 column—still singing that one old hit, like Barry McGuire on PBS—that during the 1980s "income tax revenues from the top 1 percent of income earners rose like mad as a share of GDP." It's the standard conservative rebuttal whenever liberals argue that the rich are undertaxed. And it's true as far as it goes. But what Laffer *didn't* say in that column is that while the share of taxes paid by the top 1 percent went up dramatically, their share of the national income *increased by nearly twice as much as their tax burden.* The only ones getting richer from Reagan's policies were the rich.

The general consensus of economists, including even conservatives like Gregory Mankiw, is that tax cuts partially pay for themselves—15 to maybe 35 percent, something like that—which means that they 85 to 65 percent don't pay for themselves and thus blow a huge hole in the federal budget that leads either to massive domestic spending reductions or to much higher deficits and debt or, typically, all of those. As Brad DeLong suggested above, this is the point of blowing up the deficit: to force cuts.

The topic of deficits is especially galling. When Democratic presidents are running up deficits, Republicans carry on like Victorians who just heard someone say the word "intercourse." But the truth over these last forty years is that it's Republicans who've saddled the nation with deficits. Under Reagan the deficit went from Carter's $74 billion to $155 billion. Under George H. W. Bush, it shot up to $290 billion. Then Bill Clinton went from inheriting that figure to leaving office with a surplus of $236 billion. George W. Bush converted that surplus into a deficit of $459 billion by 2008. Barack Obama went from that figure up to $585 billion, though it's entirely fair to insert an asterisk in Obama's defense, in that he also inherited a global economic meltdown that pushed the deficit to above $1 trillion for his entire first term; he cut it by more than half from its 2011 peak. Donald Trump inherited Obama's $585 billion and ran it back up to $960 billion in 2019, and that was pre-pandemic. He left office with the deficit at $3.2 trillion. That was pandemic related, but even if we exclude that, we are left with the fact that from 2000 to 2020 the United States dug a more than $3 trillion deficit hole, with the Democratic presidents responsible for only $126 billion of that.

So tax cuts don't pay for themselves. They increase the deficit. And most of the time, their economic benefit is pretty scant. Reagan's tax cuts did help the 1980s economy, since at that point taxes probably were so high as to discourage more work. But the 1980s recovery was also driven by spending, especially military spending. The Bush tax cuts likewise did little to stimulate growth, according to numerous studies at the time and since, and the same was true of the Trump tax cuts. What the tax cuts mainly led to was hundreds of billions back in the pockets of corporations—which they spent on stock buybacks to increase shareholder profits. In this, it's the same as it ever was. The Reagan tax cuts went mainly to the rich, and the George W. Bush tax cuts were even more stacked in their favor. According to the Tax Policy Center, 73 percent of the benefits of the Bush tax cuts went to the top 20 percent of taxpayers; within that, a jaw-dropping 30 percent went to the top 1 percent. Thus revealed, the Laffer Curve's big lie has three hidden purposes: first, to shift wealth from the middle class to the top; second, to give congressional Republicans the cudgel of the deficit to scream about when the next Democratic president comes along; third, to use as a convenient and ever-ready excuse to cut domestic programs, especially for poor people (the "moochers").

At this point in history, with rates already low, tax cuts can perform none of the revenue-boosting magic Republican politicians say they will. But they say it and say it and say it, and they've gotten millions of Americans to believe it. It took a while, but Democrats finally got it. In Reagan's time, and to a lesser extent George W. Bush's, a number of Democrats voted for these tax cuts. In 2017, though, not a single Democratic senator or House member voted for Trump's tax cut. They understand, if voters don't, that it's fantasy.

FROM ECONOMICS TO DOGMA

Laffer's influence on our country has been malignant, but I will say this for him: he was an actual economist and was supposed to deal in theories. But it didn't take long for Republicans to take his theory and turn it into dogma; low taxes are now just one of a handful of conservative fixed ideas that people are expected to believe and spout, whether evidence from the real world supports them or not. And as the years have passed, the party has moved far, far to the right of where Ronald Reagan was. Consider this. Reagan increased taxes four times. It can probably be said that Congress pressed them on him, but he signed them, and without making much of a fuss about it. In 1982, for example, the country was going through a "double-dip" recession (recession followed by short recovery followed by a second recession). It was also apparent—oops!—that the 1981 cuts were creating a huge deficit. So Congress—and not just Democrats; Bob Dole shaped the bill—passed a combination of spending cuts and tax increases, including excise taxes on some consumer items, corporate taxes, and the elimination of loopholes. It was, says Bruce Bartlett, the economist who worked for Reagan but is now staunchly anti-Republican, "probably the largest peacetime tax increase in American history." Then, in 1983, Reagan and Tip O'Neill struck their famous Social Security deal, which increased the payroll tax contribution from both employees and employers by 0.8 percent in increments over the next few years and taxed some benefits on high-income recipients. Finally, there were smaller increases in 1984 and 1987. So Reagan raised taxes several times. Maybe it was the tax *increases* that helped the economy boom! In fact, it was mostly the Fed, which lowered interest rates dramatically after the double-dip recession. Then George H. W. Bush raised taxes in a 1990 deal with Democrats, a move that infuriated Republicans after Bush had famously pledged not to raise taxes at the 1988 convention.

And that was the end of sensible Republican tax policy. With some very minor exceptions, Republicans haven't voted for a single tax increase since in thirty years. This degree of recalcitrance is without precedent in this country's history since the imposition of the income tax in 1913. It is enforced by Grover Norquist of the conservative advocacy group Americans for Tax Reform and his hideous antitax pledge, which large majorities of GOP senators and House members have been dutifully signing since the late 1980s. It's led to pernicious policy, policy that has deprived this country of badly needed public investment and produced enormous reductions in spending, as in the so-called sequestration budget deals of the Obama era, which led to large cuts for military operations and research, the Centers for Disease Control, border security, Head Start, FEMA, NASA, the Energy Department's nuclear security programs, and much more. The pledge has also been a major driver of polarization because it makes compromise on spending bills impossible. In the old days, Democrats would push for tax increases on the wealthy, Republicans for spending cuts, and they'd meet somewhere in the middle. In the age of the pledge, meeting in the middle is impossible.

But we've reached a point now where I think this antitax fervor can't even be laid squarely on Norquist's shoulders anymore. He sold the drug at first, but now everyone is hopelessly addicted, and there are many more suppliers than Norquist. At a debate of GOP presidential contenders in 2011, in the early stages of the 2012 race, the conservative journalist Byron York asked the eight candidates—who included Mitt Romney, Rick Santorum, Newt Gingrich,

Michele Bachmann, and Herman Cain—whether, in getting a budget deal with Congress, they would accept *any* tax increases in combination with spending cuts. York asked Santorum, "Democrats will demand that savings come from a combination of spending cuts and tax increases, maybe $3 in cuts for every $1 in higher taxes. Is there any ratio of cuts to taxes that you would accept? Three to one? Four to one? Or even 10 to one?" Santorum: "No. The answer is no." Bret Baier of Fox News then addressed the question to everyone else on the stage: "Say you had a deal, a real spending cuts deal, 10-to-1, as Byron said, spending cuts to tax increases. . . . Who on this stage would walk away from that deal? Can you raise your hand if you feel so strongly about not raising taxes, you'd walk away on the 10-to-1 deal?" All eight raised their hands. It was a staggering moment, one of those rare instances when you see these people stripped of all misleading rhetoric about willingness to compromise and so on, their true ideology revealed.

Overall, however, the solidifying of Republican economic thinking into dogma since Reagan's time has not happened in dramatic lurches; it's happened slowly and almost imperceptibly, the way blight invades a tree until it's near death. Take the issue of the minimum wage. If we go back to 2007, we find that Republicans generally supported raising the minimum wage. Congress passed the increase from $5.15 to the current (yes, still current!) $7.25 in early 2007, with 52 percent of congressional Republicans in support. And it's worth noting that they were willing to take this position in spite of the standard pro-business, U.S. Chamber of Commerce view that increasing the minimum wage kills jobs and—always a rich thing to hear Republicans say—"hurts the very people it's intended to help."

Fast-forward to 2012, when the GOP presidential nominee, Mitt Romney, supported raising the minimum wage and even proposed indexing it to inflation, assuring that it would steadily rise without Congress ever having to vote on it again; GOP primary voters obviously didn't judge it disqualifying, as they made him their nominee.

Now let's jump to 2016. By that time, the candidates had moved well to the right of Romney. Of the fifteen leading candidates, exactly one, Ben Carson, supported a modest minimum wage increase. Most at least grudgingly acknowledged its existence and said that though they wouldn't increase it, they'd live with it ("I'm not going to repeal it," said Wisconsin's governor, Scott Walker, "but I don't think it serves a purpose"). Others were more hostile. Chris Christie at one point said, "I'm tired of hearing about the minimum wage. I really am." The only one of the bunch to go full Milton Friedman, perhaps surprisingly, was nice guy Jeb Bush, who favored eliminating the federal minimum wage entirely. Donald Trump, as ever on policy questions about which he knew nothing, sometimes said this, other times said that, but was mostly against.

This doubling down was happening, moreover, at a time when evidence was mounting that the old Chamber of Commerce conventional wisdom was dead wrong. Exasperated at inaction on the federal level, a number of states and cities, and not just progressive ones, were raising their own minimum wages. Nebraska and Alaska raised their wages in 2014 ballot initiatives. Ditto West Virginia the same year, by legislation. Numerous cities, from New York to Seattle to Birmingham, Alabama, to Louisville, Kentucky, have done the same. Even a number of companies took it upon themselves to raise their in-house minimums, from Target to Amazon to Costco to Disney. And as far as the states and cities were concerned, what happened? Far from depressing wages and hurting small businesses and all the rest, a number of studies have shown that paying higher wages came with no adverse employment effects.

In fact, this finding goes back to at least 1993, when the economists David Card and Alan B. Krueger compared employment in counties along the New Jersey–Pennsylvania border after New Jersey had passed a wage increase. Their famous (in some circles) paper found that low-wage employment in New Jersey (the state that passed the increase) *rose* a bit relative to Pennsylvania. But no one believed Card and Krueger. Some years later, the success of the ballot initiatives led to more studies, all finding the same thing that they had found. In one infamous case in Seattle, a 2017 University of Washington study found adverse effects of raising the wage. Right-wingers immediately pounced on it. Analysts on the left found methodological flaws, and the next year the researchers reversed field and concluded the opposite, or at least softened their conclusions considerably, acknowledging that most workers benefited from the increase. Finally, by 2019, the Federal Reserve Bank of New York, noted cat's-paw of Vermont-style socialism, conducted a study similar to Card and Krueger's, but this time of the counties along the New York–Pennsylvania border, and found that minimum wage hikes in New York vis-à-vis Pennsylvania had "no discernible effect on employment."

I realize I've carried on at some length about this topic, but I've done so for a reason. It's a perfect case study proving that to today's right no amount of evidence matters. Their economic beliefs are not rational. There is no Republican economic thought anymore. Reactionary posturing and reflexive anti-thought have taken over virtually every aspect of right-wing policy making. There are, to be sure, conservative economists in the United States whose work deserves serious engagement, like Gregory Mankiw and Douglas Holtz-Eakin and Tyler Cowen (a libertarian). There are a few Republican politicians in Washington, notably senators Marco Rubio and the insurrectionist cheerleader Josh Hawley, who argue that their party has to do more for the middle and working classes (although as a presidential candidate in 2016 Rubio opposed even having a federal minimum wage: "The minimum wage is a threat to jobs"). There are a few interesting efforts afoot like Oren Cass's American Compass, a conservative think tank formed in early 2020, which at least acknowledges that there's too much economic inequality in America and purports to argue against key elements of neoliberal doctrine: about economic freedom, and about the Friedman Doctrine of shareholder maximization. And there are conservative policy intellectuals who are respected by their liberal counterparts, like Ron Haskins of the Brookings Institution, Nicholas Eberstadt at the American Enterprise Institute, and Stuart Butler at the Heritage Foundation. They're taken seriously at Washington roundtable discussions, and I assume they meet with Republican legislators at times. But they have little influence. For all intents and purposes, the Republican Party's top economic advisers are Fox News and talk radio hosts. And Norquist, and Tom Donohue of the Chamber of Commerce, and the Koch brothers, and a few oilmen and bankers. Republicans do only what these people want, which is why, for example, they never passed an infrastructure bill when they had unified control of government in 2017 and 2018. Donald Trump talked and talked about infrastructure in 2016, and a lot of people actually fell for it. If he'd really wanted such a bill, he could have made Mitch McConnell and Paul Ryan pass something, even something small, just to be able to tout it as an accomplishment. But he didn't. And he didn't because

the men I named in this paragraph didn't want an infrastructure bill.

AND FINALLY, DONALD TRUMP AND NEOLIBERALISM

Trump fooled many people with his populist rhetoric. And
in fact, the conventional wisdom on Trump is that he is not
a neoliberal. I mostly dissent from this view. The one topic
on which Trump notably rejected the neoliberal position was
trade. His opposition to free trade policies put him at odds
with not just the Republican Party but classical free-market
economics going back to Smith and Ricardo. So it is a meaningful departure from orthodoxy. Whether the Trump policy
was a success was another matter. The U.S. trade deficit with
China, over which Trump obsessed before he took office,
changed very little under his presidency. Before it ended, the
Trump administration did manage to complete a "phase one"
trade agreement with China that included higher import tar-
gets, but they were considered unrealistic by many experts,
and China never met them. And many of the tariffs ended up
hurting American farmers and being absorbed by American
consumers. So this departure from neoliberal tradition and
blow for populism didn't pan out as advertised.

There were also certain ways in which Trump could be
called a statist, but only if the state was an extension of him
personally—the misuse of executive branch agencies to help
industries and states he favored or punish ones he disfavored,
for example. Trump's Justice Department did initiate an antitrust suit against Google. But it did so two weeks before the
2020 election, and it was widely speculated that it was partly
out of personal pique on Trump's part, because conservatives
believed Google stacked search results in a liberal direction
and maintained blacklists blocking right-wing content.

But for the most part, for all his loud and ceaseless talk, Trump governed as a pretty conventional neoliberal. He cut taxes, eliminated a large number of regulations (on the environment, most notably), privileged market solutions to social problems on those rare occasions he paid attention to them, and failed to use the public sector properly when it was needed most, when the pandemic first hit in China and there was time to make preparations, speed the manufacture of ventilators, and so on. That last failure wasn't ideological so much as it was just psychological—Trump's childish inability to accept the reality of the depth of the crisis, as documented by Bob Woodward and in so many of Trump's own absurdly self-justifying public comments. But even beyond the pandemic, Trump opposed government intervention across the board—seen in his attempts to dismantle Obamacare, for example. He had opportunities to govern unconventionally if he'd chosen to—to challenge policies that are manifestations of neoliberal ideology. For example, he talked in 2016 about ending the carried-interest loophole, which allows hedge-fund managers and others to pay a reduced tax rate on capital gains. But he didn't do it. He said as late as May 2019 that he still wanted to eliminate it, but he never did. The problem appears to have had more to do with Congress and the power of private-equity lobbyists, but Trump never really pushed the issue.

But Trumpian neoliberalism is not really about particular policy issues. It gets to something much deeper about the conflict between unchained capitalism and democracy. Unchained capitalism operates under no rules of restraint, whereas democracy requires constant acts of self-restraint to work as intended. In this context, the economist Branko Milanovic offered an interesting take on Trump and neoliberalism in May 2020. Under democracy, decisions are made collectively, with everyone's assent, or at least the assent of the majority, which the minority is expected to accept; under capitalism, decisions are made by the minority at the top, and the majority below has no choice but to follow. Remarking on the tension inherent in a system that is both democratic and capitalist, Milanovic wrote,

> The entire history of capitalism can be readily understood as the struggle between these two principles: is the democratic principle "exported" from politics to rule in economics too, or is the hierarchical principle of company organization to invade the political sphere. Social democracy was essentially the former; neoliberalism was the latter.

Trump, Milanovic argued, represents the unrestrained triumph of hierarchical principles invading politics. This encroachment, he writes, means that "politicians no longer see people whom they rule as co-citizens but as employees. Employees can be hired and fired, humiliated and dismissed, ripped off, cheated or ignored." This pattern long predates Trump, of course; the market devoured the civitas in this country a long time ago. But Trump was in crucial ways its apotheosis.

So that is the story of how neoliberal economic ideas took over the GOP. Again, before the 1980s, Republicans were not of a single mind on these questions. But the dissenters were wiped out in the 1980 election (Jacob Javits of New York) or faded away over the course of the 1980s (Charles Percy of Illinois). Younger and more right-wing senators rode into Washington on Reagan's coattails, and a whole new generation of thinkers and cadre of activists came in as well. However grudgingly, I do have to give them credit. They, behind the persuasive power of a charismatic leader, turned many inside-the-Beltway assumptions on their head, establishing the ideas first laid out back in Paris in 1938 at the Colloque Lippmann as default political fact—such that even Democrats felt they had to adapt to them and adopt some of them, as we'll see in the next chapter.

CHAPTER FOUR

Neoliberalism of the Left: Considering Clinton and Obama

•

BILL CLINTON AND THE NEW DEMOCRATS

There is a story, famous in liberal political circles, about when reality hit Bill Clinton over the head. It takes place on January 7, 1993. He is president-elect. He's sitting in the governor's mansion in Little Rock with some key economic advisers he's already announced will serve in his administration: Robert Rubin, Larry Summers, Robert Reich, Alan Blinder, Laura Tyson, Leon Panetta. The day before, Dick Darman, the budget director in the outgoing Bush administration, had announced that the coming years' budget deficits would be much higher than anticipated. The deficit would be $305 billion by 1997—the year by which Clinton happened to have promised he would balance the budget. The president-elect and his team felt, and pretty much were, totally sandbagged. Wrote James Risen, then at the *Los Angeles Times*, "The numbers almost certainly will cast a pall over a scheduled meeting today at which Clinton and his newly appointed economic advisers will begin to make key decisions on the plan he will present to Congress."

Such was the mood as the new team assembled in Little Rock. Gene Sperling, the noted economist who has worked in every Democratic administration of the last thirty years, recalled to me, "I was the one who ended up having to tell Clinton and Gore that the numbers were like 50 billion, 70 billion worse in the fourth year than we thought. And this is kind of devastating for us."*

I'll let Clinton take it from here, as he told the tale in *My Life:*

> As we sat down to work, Bob Rubin, who was running the meeting, called on Leon Panetta first. Leon said the deficit had gotten worse because tax revenues were down in the sluggish economy, while spending was up, as more people qualified for government assistance and health-care costs soared. Laura Tyson said that if current conditions continued, the economy would probably grow at a rate of 2.5 to 3 percent over the next years, not enough to lower unemployment much or to ensure a sustained recovery. Then we got down to the meat of the coconut, as Alan Blinder, another of my economic advisers, was asked to analyze whether a strong deficit-reduction package would spur growth and new jobs by bringing down interest rates, since the government wouldn't provide as much competition with the private sector in borrowing money. Blinder said that would happen, but that the positive effects would be offset for a couple of years by the negative economic impact of less government spending or higher taxes, unless

---

* All of Sperling's quotes in this book were made as a private citizen, before he joined the Biden administration.

the Federal Reserve and the bond market responded to our plan by lowering interest rates substantially. Blinder thought that after so many false promises on deficit reduction over the last few years, a strong positive response by the bond market was unlikely. Larry Summers disagreed, saying that a good plan would convince the market to lower rates because there was no threat of inflation as the economy recovered.

It was right about at this point that the Arkansas governor, not yet wise in the ways of Washington, exploded with the line that first appeared in Bob Woodward's *Agenda* but has been quoted hundreds of times: "You mean to tell me that the success of the program and my reelection hinges on the Federal Reserve and a bunch of fucking bond traders?"

He does not, in *My Life*, admit to the salty language, but he does cop to his anger at the power of "thirty-year-old bond traders" over the economy (because the bond market, along with the Fed, sets interest rates; "if they didn't like what they saw in Washington, or in the housing market, they'd stamp on the brakes, sending interest rates soaring," wrote the finance journalist James Surowiecki).

This was the seminal fight of the Clinton administration—before it even started—between the spenders and the austerians, the Keynesians and the neoliberals. Sperling, Reich, and George Stephanopoulos argued for public investment, but they were badly outnumbered by the deficit hawks: Rubin, Summers, Panetta, Lloyd Bentsen, Roger Altman, and Al Gore. Tyson and Blinder were somewhere in the middle. And the deficit hawks won. More precisely, the bond market won. Clinton pivoted toward deficit reduction. In fairness, his first budget did include some spending, notably a $20 billion stimulus package, and tax increases (a gas tax increase—the last one we've ever had, incidentally—and a hike of the top marginal rate on high earners). Sperling says the divisions among the team were real but not bitter: "I guess in some ways it was somewhat of the battle of things to come. It didn't feel like this huge ideological divide. It felt more like Reich and I were more on the big spending, public investment side, and the other side was like, 'Oh yeah, we need that. But we still had to meet these deficit targets.'"

But to people on the economic left, it was a betrayal. After twelve long years of supply-side hoodoo, left-populists and left-tilting labor economists like the people at the Economic Policy Institute, a vital think tank on these issues, longed for an emphasis on public investment. The country was in the middle of an economic downturn, or at best a slow and sluggish recovery; this was exactly when Keynes counseled that the iron was hot, just waiting to be struck.

Clinton's reputation today is pretty bruised for reasons that are beyond the ambit of this book. But he's taken a beating on the economy, too. In Clinton's own time, he was criticized, to be sure, from his left—by EPI, by noted journalists on the political economy like Robert Kuttner, by a number of labor leaders. Their audiences, then, were sizable enough but lacking much influence over Clinton or the Democrats more broadly. Now that the political left is resurgent and has more leverage within the Democratic Party, Clinton's economic record has been subjected to a fairly harsh revisionism. The list of grievances begins with the quick pivot to deficit hawkery described above, which came to be referred to as Rubinomics, after Bob Rubin, who was Clinton's director of the National Economic Council during his first term and secretary of the Treasury during his second. The chief principle of Rubinomics was that a balanced budget would keep inflation and long-term interest rates under control. Rubin was no supply-sider; he was not a fan of Reagan and George W. Bush–style tax cuts. But an emphasis on deficit reduction left little room for Keynesian public investments of the sort that Reich and other advisers like Sperling and later Joseph Stiglitz wanted to see. Beyond this core issue, the left critique of Clinton's economic policies extends to his supporting NAFTA and welfare reform, letting China into the World Trade Organization, repealing the Glass-Steagall banking regulations, and endorsing the general financialization of the economy that marked the Washington Consensus period.

This faith in markets and hesitance about public-sector solutions, which leads to policy priorities like free trade and deficit reduction, forms the core of what is called these days by some critics progressive neoliberalism. Progressive neoliberalism is not the same thing as conservative neoliberalism. Progressive neoliberals are not enemies of government. They oppose supply-side tax cuts and back some public investment—once the markets have been reassured. Philosophically, progressive neoliberals are not so attached to the link between economic and political freedom, since progressive neoliberalism does support an interventionist state to some extent. But to critics of Clinton and Rubin and Larry Summers and others, they are still neoliberal in the sense advanced by the Mont Pelerin group because they assume that market solutions will work better than public-sector ones.

How fair are these criticisms? I'd argue that the wholesale dismissal of the Clinton era as hopelessly neoliberal is *too* revisionist. The first thing that should be said in Clinton's defense is the obvious: The economy, in broad terms, performed very well under Clinton. He was, in fact, the most economically successful president of the last sixty years. Job creation was highest under Clinton (yes, higher than Reagan, by about six million). Median household income increased the most during his tenure. The stock market performed best during his eight years in office. And the deficit, of course, disappeared entirely; he left office handing George W. Bush a $236 billion surplus, which Bush instantly squandered on tax cuts that did not pay for themselves and a war the United States did not need to fight. In addition to all that, it must be said that Rubin wasn't wrong about interest rates: They weren't exactly at an all-time low under Clinton, but they were stable in a low-to-middle range, looked at in a historical context. Inflation, too, was generally on the low side during Clinton's term, between 2 and 3 percent most years. More liberal critics have argued, at the time and in retrospect, that Clinton could have been less zealous about deficit reduction and still produced a booming economy. But at a point in history when there hadn't been a Democratic president in twelve years, and the last Democratic president was widely remembered as presiding over economic disaster, progressive neoliberalism seemed to a lot of people to be the only answer a Democratic president could offer.

Yet his critics would argue, and not without merit, that he accepted principles of neoliberal economics much more than he challenged them; he didn't change the country's basic economic paradigm. He (and Hillary sometimes, when she was involved in making policy) sought market solutions where Roosevelt and Keynes would likely have tried or urged public-sector solutions, most notably on the failed health-care reform effort, which was a private-sector-driven plan of so-called managed care competition. He said, famously, that "the era of big government is over," a phrase that will hang over his legacy forever. He signed a Republican welfare reform bill that vastly increased "extreme poverty" (house-holds then getting by on less than $2 per person a day; it should be noted in fairness that overall poverty declined markedly during Clinton's presidency as a result of the general boom and his dramatic expansion of the Earned Income Tax Credit). And for all the economic good he did, inequality continued to rise during his presidency, and pretty dramatically. This happened for a host of complex reasons that Clinton might or might not have been able to address, but he never made fighting inequality an issue. Thomas Piketty, Emmanuel Saez, and Gabriel Zucman found that from 1993 to 2000 the percent of the national income held by those in the top 10 percent of earners rose from 40.5 percent to 47.6 percent. (Quick aside: Their research covers a full century, from 1917 to 2018, and it tells a fascinating, if familiarly grim, tale. Until World War II, the percent of income held by the top 10 percent was usually in the 40–50 percent range. The war—and its high taxes on the wealthy—brought the figure down to the low to mid-30s, where it stayed until Ronald Reagan, under whom it spiked from 34.5 to 40.6. Under George W. Bush, it rose from 44.8 to 48.2 percent. Finally, under Barack Obama, it went from 46.5 to 49.5 percent. In Trump's first two years, it nosed above 50 percent. In other words, we had more economic equality when taxes and public spending and rates of unionization were high.)

Clinton comes in for his most deserved criticisms on the topic of financial deregulation. The most important event here is his signing of the Gramm-Leach-Bliley Act in 1999, also called the Financial Services Modernization Act. This is the law that removed the Glass-Steagall regulations that had kept banks, insurance companies, and securities companies separate since the New Deal and that helped produce the kinds of activities the big banks were engaging in that led to the Great Meltdown of 2008. Congress was controlled by Republicans then, and the three named sponsors were all Republicans. But that didn't matter. In the House, Democrats voted for the bill 138–69, and in the Senate only 8 Democrats were opposed.

Gene Sperling, by this time director of the National Economic Council, the body that recommends policy decisions to the president, recalls that Clinton wasn't personally as invested in this issue as he was, say, in the Telecommunications Act of 1996, another act that decreased regulation and, to critics, has led to excessive market concentration. "This was an area where, for better or worse, the reality was it was seen as largely a technical, Treasury issue," Sperling told me. "I think for Clinton, it was kind of, okay, it's very hard to get any legislation done. If this is something my team, Rubin et cetera, feels is taking out irrationalities in the economy and creating greater certainty for investment, then it's fine."

Clinton certainly celebrated the act's passage. There exists today on YouTube, courtesy of the Clinton Presidential Library, a half-hour video of the signing ceremony. Larry Summers, Treasury secretary at the time, kicks it off: "With this bill, the American financial system takes a major step forward toward the twenty-first century, one that will benefit American consumers, business, and the national economy for years to come." Phil Gramm was next: "We are here today to repeal Glass-Steagall because we have learned that government is not the answer." Finally, Clinton spoke. "You heard Senator Gramm characterize this bill as a victory for freedom and free markets, and Congressman LaFalce characterize this bill as a victory for consumer protection," Clinton said, name-checking the House Democrat John LaFalce of upstate New York and citing new provisions protecting consumer privacy. "And both of them are right. And

I have always believed that one requires the other." Glass-Steagall worked pretty well in its day, he said, but "is no longer appropriate to the economy in which we live." One legislator who was very much not present was John Dingell, the longtime Michigan representative. The week before on the House floor, he had warned, "What we are creating now is a group of institutions which are too big to fail. . . . Taxpayers are going to be called upon to cure the failures that we're creating tonight, and it's going to cost a lot of money, and it's coming."

Did Glass-Steagall repeal really lead to the financial crisis? To some extent, but not as much as some contend. David Leonhardt, the *New York Times* economic columnist, noted in a column right after the meltdown that the bill led to many mergers that did leave banks with more capital, some of which ended up in the subprime mortgage market that drove the crisis. However, he noted that many big investment banks did not pursue the kinds of mergers the law allowed. Bear Stearns and Lehman Brothers, the two houses that quickly went belly-up, remained investment banks to the last. Leonhardt pinned the blame for the meltdown instead on "many of the same people who were behind Gramm-Leach-Bliley. The Clinton administration and Congressional Republicans failed to create a strong framework in place of Glass-Steagall. Democrats pushed for riskier mortgage lending, in an effort to expand home ownership. But surely the bulk of the blame lies with the policy makers and regulators who were on duty while the housing bubble inflated and Wall Street went wild—the Bush administration and Alan Greenspan's Federal Reserve." Gramm, he noted, was also the driving force behind a law that unleashed the derivatives market, which increased both opacity and risk in the subprime mortgage market.

Even if Glass-Steagall repeal isn't "to blame" for the meltdown, it was, I think it's fair to say, a very neoliberal solution (deregulate, trust the free market) to a perceived problem (anachronistic rules holding the market back). And of course its passage was driven by millions of dollars the banks spent on lobbying over many years to have these chains lifted, as well as millions in campaign contributions. The fevered race for political donations fueled much of the Democrats' 1990s pivot toward Wall Street. But it wasn't all about money. By this point, the dominant culture, very much including most Democratic economists, had simply decided that Milton Friedman and his colleagues and promoters had been correct—that is, the people on top (Wall Streeters, hedge-fund titans, and so on) and the people who described and interpreted the market (leading media figures). The old Keynesian ideas were seen as from another time, as out of date in the age of the electronic economy as an Underwood manual typewriter. Au courant liberals in positions of power, understanding what was necessary to maintain those positions, picked up the hymnal, quickly thumbed their way to the right page, and sang along. They were progressive on social issues, but when it came to money, and dirty things like labor unions, they tended to side with the right. An editorial appeared in a major American newspaper on January 14, 1987, under the headline "The Right Minimum Wage: $0.00." Under that provocative banner, the editorial argued that "there's a virtual consensus among economists that the minimum wage is an idea whose time has passed." It continued: "A higher minimum would undoubtedly raise the living standard of the majority of low-wage workers who could keep their jobs. That gain, it is argued, would justify the sacrifice of the minority who became unemployable. The argument isn't convincing." *The Wall Street Journal*? Nope. That was the Reagan-era *New York Times* talking.

BARACK OBAMA AND THE MELTDOWN

Eight years on, the national mood had shifted—a bit. George W. Bush had run the economy into the ditch. The go-go free market had led, as John Dingell and so many others predicted, to catastrophe, driven by greed, dogmatic faith in markets, and the unchecked conviction of people at the big banks that they could get away with anything. Barack Obama, with a mere four years in the Senate under his belt, didn't boast a résumé that suggested he was just the man to handle the crisis. But during the 2008 campaign, he addressed it more smartly than John McCain did, and McCain hurt himself with his comic vice presidential choice, and so Americans entrusted their hobbled nation to the first African American ever to hold the office and a man whose record and philosophy were probably more straightfor- wardly liberal than any president in a very long time.

Everyone knows what happened. He surrounded himself with economic advisers largely plucked from the establish- ment. He proposed—and passed, with no Republican votes in the House and three in the Senate—a stimulus that was the largest in history, at $787 billion, but was also less than half the size his adviser Christina Romer had originally estimated it ought to be. She proposed $1.2 trillion; Larry Summers called that figure "non-planetary"; the political team was largely with Summers; and they ended up where they ended up. The debate over the Obama stimulus—which can still get people very worked up more than a decade later—is sym- bolic of a number of arguments about how Democratic eco- nomic policy has embraced neoliberalism, ever since Jimmy Carter adopted certain conservative/neoliberal policies later in his term (deregulation, cutting capital gains taxes).

Among these: Could Obama have been more aggres- sive about public investment? His political team balked and warned that they'd lose votes—even a number of Democratic votes—if they pressed for a stimulus package higher than $1 trillion. Likewise, Obama's economic advisers wanted him to do more on relief for people with underwater mortgages, but the political team was terrified that many voters would resent the government bailing out people who (as these voters would have seen it) borrowed an irresponsible amount of money. That's what started the Tea Party movement, so we do know that that rage was out there. Finally, Obama's refusal to allow the prosecution of any of the big banks has often been savaged by progressive critics. Eric Holder's Department of Justice talked big about taking on the banks, but it in fact did little. A 2014 audit by the department's Office of the Inspector General found, for example, that the department wildly overstated the number of people in the banking business it had prosecuted.

Obama was politically cautious by nature, and after the Republicans captured the House in the 2010 elections, signed on to Republican priorities, especially deficit reduction. That was "fucking disastrous," as the economist Brad DeLong said to me. Jared Bernstein, who was advising Vice President Biden at the time, told me that "it was the Tea Party that forced us to pivot to deficit reduction too soon, but we too willingly walked through that door."* Jason Furman, who served as the deputy director of the National Economic Council during Obama's first term and as chairman of the Council of Economic Advisers during the second, defended the pivot to me as part of a broader ten-year deal that would have included some infrastructure spending up front. Furman's point underscores the reality of having to deal with a Republican Congress, which was openly and fla-

---

* This quote also is from our interview conducted before Bernstein joined the Biden administration.

grantly hostile to everything the White House wanted to do and would have opposed curing cancer if the idea had originated with Obama. Even many Democrats in Congress are cautious about spending and preoccupied with the deficit. Furman said to me, "I would just not understate that when I go to Congress, I mostly get pushed back on the fiscally responsible side, not on the other side." And Sperling told me a story about going to testify before the House in 2010 to promote a small business loan program that was going to cost $1.5 billion—nothing, in federal budget terms. *Democratic* staffers were panicked, he said, that he didn't propose a way to pay for it. "That was the mentality," Sperling said.

So Obama's hands were tied to a considerable extent by a tough fiscal reality, a ferocious Republican opposition, and Democrats in Congress who were shattered after they lost sixty-three seats in 2010. But I think it's totally fair to criticize him for not doing enough rhetorically to get Americans to think differently about the economy, and to educate people about, for example, why it's actually a good idea for the government to spend, temporarily putting aside concerns about the deficit, when the private sector is crippled as it was in 2009. He had the goodwill of a majority of the country and enough moral authority and political capital to do it. The potential was there, that first year, for Obama to make the crisis into an immensely teachable moment, and he didn't use it. Later, in 2013, he briefly adopted the phrase "middle-out economics." The journal I edit, *Democracy: A Journal of Ideas*, was a major promoter of this idea, so naturally I was pretty jazzed, as were Nick Hanauer and Eric Liu, the coiners of the phrase, when Obama started talking like this. It might not have changed the world, but it's just the kind of reframing of economic assumptions that people need to hear. But for whatever reason, Obama didn't stick with it.

All that said, though, I don't think it's accurate or fair

to dismiss Obama and Clinton as nothing more than pro-gressive neoliberals. Both made a number of high-profile and sometimes courageous Keynesian moves. Clinton raised income taxes on the well off in 1993 and increased public investments in education, infrastructure, and science. He raised the minimum wage, created the Children's Health Insurance Program, strengthened the Community Reinvest-ment Act, expanded community development banks; these were all initiatives that depended on and strengthened the public sector. He created Americorps, a brand-new govern-ment agency, which is still going strong with some 250,000 volunteers. And of course he let the government be shut down rather than agree to Newt Gingrich's proposed sharp domestic spending cuts. That was risky and brave; there was absolutely no guarantee at the time that he'd end up winning that showdown as he did. While discussing proposed GOP Medicare cuts, he said to congressional Republicans, "Even if I drop to 5 percent in the polls, if you want your budget, you'll have to get someone else to sit in this chair!" Which, of course, they later tried.

Obama, too, was no mere neoliberal. The stimulus might have been too small, but it was, according to the jour-nalist Michael Grunwald, who wrote an entire book that persuasively detailed the many ways it reshaped the Ameri-can economy, "more than 50 percent bigger than the entire New Deal, twice as big as the Louisiana Purchase and the Marshall Plan combined." It was, he argues, a transformative energy bill, a transformative education bill, a transformative health-care bill, and more. Then there was the Dodd-Frank financial regulatory bill. And of course he signed the Afford-able Care Act, which Jared Bernstein described to me as "the most equalizing piece of legislation in decades." Bernstein thinks it's unfair to dismiss Clinton and especially Obama, in whose administration he worked, as closet conservatives.

"It's too sweeping," he says. "It just doesn't feel like what we were doing day to day, right? I mean, we were so obsessed with market failure. That's what we were doing. That's just kind of pure Keynesianism. And even when the economy was recovering, it was such a weak recovery initially that we kept just trying to push more and more interventions."[*]

What's more important now is understanding what factors held Clinton and Obama back from doing more. I'd cite four main reasons. One involves donors: Democrats did become too beholden to large donors, on Wall Street, in the tech sector, and elsewhere. A second is that, well, the Republican Party exists, and the Constitution exists with all its various choke points that the Republicans are adept at exploiting. A third factor that made Clinton and Obama hesitate was their fear, and that of their top advisers who had largely embraced neoliberal precepts, of how the markets would react to more interventionist policies. And the fourth and likely most powerful reason is conservative fearmongering about the deficit. Everyone I interviewed for this book who worked in either the Clinton or the Obama administration said, as Jason Furman did above, that many Democratic members of Congress are terrified of being branded as big spenders who don't care about the deficit. After Gene Sperling told me the story about the $1.5 billion small business program, he said, "There's a real lesson in here, I think, which is that the public does not understand Keynesian economics. And so when you spend a lot and it doesn't appear to work, their view is not that you should spend more. Their view is you're a guy at the gambling table who has lost all the money. And now you're saying, 'If you just give me $50,000 more! I can tell a hot streak's coming!'"

Some of these impediments have softened a bit (although

---

[*] These quotes, too, are Bernstein speaking as a private citizen.

not Republican obstructionism, which has gotten far worse). With respect to my first reason, while big donors still control the party's money flow, internet-based small donor money is countering that influence to some extent. On the third reason, attitudes about the market have changed since 2009–2010, in part because of the influence of progressive economists, which we'll cover later. But suffice it to say here that the Biden administration went bigger and bolder on public investment than Clinton or Obama, and the markets were fine (so had Trump, by the way, with the CARES Act after the pandemic hit, when the country was obviously in deep crisis). But that fourth reason is the key. Many congressional Democrats are still terrified of deficit politics, and Biden himself often emphasized that his proposals were paid for and wouldn't increase the deficit.

The newish school of economic thought called Modern Monetary Theory (MMT) has been seeking to change that. Stephanie Kelton, a leading MMT proponent, published a book called *The Deficit Myth* in 2020 arguing that large federal budget deficits not only were not a problem but were in fact a sign of healthy and responsible economic management. At the heart of MMT is the idea that the government, as the monopoly issuer of currency in a post-gold-standard era when money "is conjured into existence from a computer keyboard each time the Federal Reserve carries out an authorized payment on behalf of the Treasury," can basically spend all the money it wants to spend, provided necessary steps are taken to safeguard against inflation. The currency issuer can't run out of money or go into default. Ergo, the federal government can spend whatever it has the political will to spend. MMT turns much economic thinking completely on its head. For example, we are taught to think that for a government, taxing and borrowing come first and spending second. Kelton writes that while that's true for you and me and businesses, it is, for the currency issuer, backward. The currency issuer spends first and taxes and borrows later. It's interesting stuff and in some ways eye-popping. Its implications for policy should be obvious (it's no accident that Kelton advised Bernie Sanders).

I suspect that explaining MMT to Democratic members of Congress from purple districts, let alone to the American people, might turn out to be a pretty heavy lift. But progressives and Democrats must figure out how to teach Americans the basic principles of Keynesian economics. Because as long as people have in their minds that the market makes wise decisions and the government poor ones, and that the government should "tighten its belt" during bad times rather than the other way around, nothing Democrats say about the economy will really make sense.

CHAPTER FIVE

The Legacies of Neoliberalism: Inequality, Monopoly, and Private Education

•

ECONOMIC INEQUALITY: NO, IT'S NOT INEVITABLE

Having shown in the previous chapter how neoliberal ideas completely took over Republican and conservative economic policy making and gained a substantial foothold in Democratic and liberal economic policy making, in this chapter I want to write about the broader destructive legacy of neoliberalism. Tragically, the key tenets of neoliberal thought—deep suspicion of government, faith that the market always knows best, conviction that any public economic intervention will ultimately crush political freedom—have bored their way into many aspects of our social and political lives well beyond the realm of economic policy making. I want to focus here on three manifestations that I think are particularly insidious.

The first of these is inequality. To me, and to most liberals, perhaps the central economic fact of life in the United States of the past four decades or so has been rampaging inequality. Statistic after statistic, study after study, shows that from 1945 to about 1975 this was a much more equal society. We still had rich and poor, obviously, but the rich just weren't nearly as rich, and there weren't nearly as many of them; nobody outside a few families had the kinds of fortunes, even adjusted for inflation, that Jeff Bezos and Bill Gates and Michael Bloomberg and so many others have today (there were 161 billionaires in the United States in 2020, according to the Bloomberg Billionaires Index). There were, during that postwar period, as there are now, upper-middle-class people, and middle-class people, and working-class people, and poor people—in, say, my hometown of Morgantown, West Virginia, as in all American towns. But there simply weren't as many rich, and there wasn't as much space between the upper middle class and the rest as there is today. Yes, our houses were different. But they weren't *that* different. My family had some money—not wealth, but my father was a successful trial lawyer. When he built our house in 1966, it was an attractive four-bedroom home of around twenty-six hundred square feet. I'd imagine he had the money to build something bigger and showier, or to throw in a pool or something. But in those days, by and large, people didn't do that. There were limits, imposed by taste and social norms and even zoning laws, that helped define the bounds of how much house a family needed.

There is a measure of inequality in economics called the Gini coefficient, which covers a range from 0 to 1.0, or sometimes 0 to 100. As in golf, lower scores are better. The United States got its best-ever Gini score, of 35, in 1968. It has climbed a lot since then, hitting 40 by the late 1980s, then the mid-40s by the mid-1990s; more recently it's been in the high 40s—49 in 2020, for example. To give you some perspective on this, the most equal countries, typically the Scandinavian nations, register in the mid-20s; the least equal, a list topped nearly every year by South Africa, are in the mid- to high 50s. In other words, in 1968, we were close to the best. Now we're close to the worst.

You wouldn't think it even needed to be argued that inequality is a bad thing. Relative economic equality should be as preferable to relative inequality, common sense tells me, as wellness to illness, sunshine to rain, love to loneliness, *Goldfinger* to *Octopussy*. If you thought that, you might have common sense, but you wouldn't be much of an economist, or at least a neoliberal one. What neoliberal economics succeeded in doing for much of the past forty years, until just recently, has been to build a rough consensus in elite opinion that inequality is just not a problem. Indeed conservatives generally go so far as to say that trying to confront inequality would be both a fool's errand and harmful. "The Perils Awaiting Conservatives Who Seek to Reduce Inequality," blared a headline over an early 2020 essay by a scholar from the libertarian Cato Institute. To the extent that conservatives have even considered the matter, it has usually been to aver that inequality is either inevitable, a healthy sign inasmuch as it is a by-product, and indeed evidence, of robust overall growth; or, most of all, that it is always, always made worse by government attempts to intervene and address it. These arguments have largely carried the day in public discourse, until recently. But these are caricatures at odds with reality.

As to the inevitability of inequality, yes, of course some inequality is inevitable; some is even desirable. As Binyamin Appelbaum put it in his book *The Economists' Hour*, "Capitalism is a competition; money is the prize." In his *General Theory*, Keynes acknowledged a "social and psychological justification" for "significant" income and wealth disparities—noting, for example, that some "valuable human activities . . . require the motive of money-making." But he believed, according to two scholars writing in the 1980s, that nothing justified "the 'large disparities' which characterized industrially developed capitalist societies circa the 1930s." The right has tended to caricature such views, bleach them of any subtlety, and conjure to life a straw man against which it is far easier to argue. Milton Friedman used to say that inequality was inevitable and good by criticizing what he called "a belief in equality of income" in Western countries. This is dishonest. No serious person thinks a janitor should be paid the same as a cardiac surgeon. The idea that "collectivists" want everyone to end up equal is likely a willful perversion of John Rawls, the most important American liberal political philosopher of the last half of the twentieth century. Rawls's theory of a good society was one in which he asked citizens to imagine that there were indeed different social classes, but they couldn't know whether they would wind up at the top of the society or the bottom; thus, knowing that they might be in the bottom, they should design a society with that possibility in mind (that is, a society in which those at the bottom didn't live lives of perpetual hardship). Rawls acknowledges the legitimacy of different classes but attaches one key condition to accepting them. In his essay "Justice as Fairness," he writes that "inequalities are arbitrary unless it is reasonable to expect that they will work out to everyone's advantage." Because he argues for a lessening in the differences among the classes, a tenet that he called the difference principle, this gets turned into an assertion that he wanted equality of outcomes. He did not. He argued that the least advantaged members of a good society would have to be better off than under any alternative system. Today, virtually everyone accepts the inevitability of some inequality. The question that we argue about is how much inequality is acceptable in a free democratic society until it curdles into being an oligarchy that is effectively unfree for millions.

On the idea that inequality is the by-product of growth,

this conservative view has been winning the argument for some time. Democrats have not found a convincing way to argue to the public that excessive inequality is bad not just for individuals but for the economy overall. But the balance is shifting (more on this in the next chapter). Conservative dominance of the debate began to be challenged in the first decade of the twenty-first century, notably through the important work of Thomas Piketty, Emmanuel Saez, Gabriel Zucman, and other economists who used vast amounts of data not available to earlier generations of researchers to show the extent of inequality and its ill effects. Their work and that of others opened up a fresh debate about all this. Piketty's highly influential *Capital in the Twenty-First Century* was published in English in 2014. Also that year, the Organisation (spelled the British way) for Economic Cooperation and Development (OECD), the intergovernmental group formed in 1961 to facilitate trade and cooperation that now has thirty-eight member nations—and is not exactly a breeding ground of radical thought—published a paper arguing that yes, as income inequality goes up, economic growth falls. "The impact of inequality on growth," the author writes, "turns out to be sizeable. . . . [L]owering inequality by 1 Gini point would translate in an increase of cumulative growth of 0.8 percentage points in the following 5 years." Interestingly, the paper also concludes that "redistributive policies achieving greater equality in disposable income has [sic] no adverse growth consequences." An International Monetary Fund paper from the following year reached a similar conclusion: "Raising the income share of the poor, and ensuring that there is no hollowing-out of the middle class, is actually good for growth." Sounds like an endorsement of middle-out economics.

As for the idea that government interventions can only

ever make things worse: this is an article of faith in right-wing circles, but, like Mr. Laffer's curve, it is simply not true. Just as the Gini number shows that American society was more equal back when we had a more Keynesian economy, it's also the case that poverty fell dramatically in the late 1960s and early 1970s in the wake of the introduction of Great Society programs (Medicare, Medicaid, greater housing aid, and more), affirmative action, and broad unionization of public employees. After the Great Society kicked in, the poverty rate for adult Americans under age sixty-five was less than 10 percent for twelve years running, from 1968 through 1979 (inclusive), something that didn't happen before and hasn't come close to happening since. Similarly, child poverty went down in that period (from 27.3 percent in 1959 to 14 percent in 1969), and poverty among seniors dropped even more dramatically (35.2 percent in 1959 to 14.6 in 1974). The poverty level crept back up during the early Reagan years before declining again, and went up again after the Great Meltdown of 2008–2009, which bankrupted families and devoured jobs. But it has never gotten close to where it was before the Great Society programs. These were government interventions that undeniably worked to alleviate poverty without destroying overall prosperity.

The above summarizes the Republican view. Among more mainstream economists, the emphasis since the 1990s has been different, and a more serious conversation has unfolded. They have not denied that inequality has grown worse. They acknowledge inequality and acknowledge that it's a problem, but they have tended to look mainly to market forces as the main drivers of inequality: automation, perhaps first and foremost; the increasing demand for skills in the workforce, and the failure of the educational system to adapt to this change; globalization, and the attendant rise in competition to U.S. workers from their counterparts in China, India, and elsewhere; immigration trends, which have brought in more unskilled than skilled workers and put downward pressure on low-end wages; the decline of labor unions; and the advent of meritocratic competition that rewards some and punishes others.

All these are obviously factors in inequality. But there's a more interesting school of thought among some liberal economists, which is that inequality isn't chiefly about market forces at all. Notable here is Joseph Stiglitz, whose 2012 book, *The Price of Inequality*, forcefully rebuts the conventional wisdom and pins the blame for inequality not on the market, but on politics: "While there may be underlying economic forces at play, politics have shaped the market, and shaped it in ways that advantage the top at the expense of the rest." Stiglitz also argued, as his title suggests, that extreme inequality hampers growth and more. "Lack of opportunity," he wrote, "means that [society's] most valuable asset—its people—is not being fully used. Many at the bottom, or even in the middle, are not living up to their potential, because the rich, needing few public services and worried that a strong government might redistribute income, use their political influence to cut taxes and curtail government spending. This leads to underinvestment in infrastructure, education, and technology, impeding the engines of growth."

The economists Claudia Goldin and Lawrence Katz also rejected the standard explanations about globalization and technology and focused on the American educational system as a major reason for inequality. Their argument, in sum, was that educational attainment in the United States ran ahead of technological change during the golden age and that since the 1970s that balance has flipped. The solutions they offer are political and policy solutions: get more people to graduate from college (and make college more affordable), invest more in early childhood education, especially in poor areas, and so on. Their work, and Stiglitz's, and that of many others, shows convincingly that stark inequality isn't inevitable at all. It reflects choices we've made.

As I'll describe in more detail in the next chapter, economics has become more open to the idea that economic outcomes reflect not just market forces but political power. Since Biden became president, the neoliberal hold on economic discourse has loosened. I'd say the vast majority of Democrats in Congress now accept this kind of thinking (not Joe Manchin, though). But neoliberalism is hardly dead and buried. Majorities of Americans tend to agree in polls that there's too much inequality, but the issue just doesn't rank as a first-order concern for most people. And if Republicans retake power, whether Donald Trump or someone else, we'll be right back to tax cuts for the rich, regulations being slashed, and—the topic of the next section—no constraints on monopoly power.

MONOPOLY POWER: ROBERT BORK'S REAL LEGACY

Everyone learned in school that monopoly power is bad (or at least they did when I was in school; Lord knows what they're learning now, especially in business schools that take so much money from right-wing interests). Monopolies can fix prices. They can also depress wages, since if workers can't offer their labor to a range of employers that must compete for them, the worker has to take what the employer will pay. They distort the free market by stifling competition, and they're simply bad for democracy; concentration of power is inherently antidemocratic. Concern about monopolies—about the concentration of power and wealth in the hands of so few—occupies a special place in history. Indeed it goes back centuries, and critics of it ranged across the ideological spectrum.

In the early seventeenth century in England, Charles I granted monopolies in such areas as production of coal, soap, and woolen clothes. These were protested by a group that called itself the Levellers, a political movement committed to popular sovereignty and natural rights. They saw monopoly *economic* power as being not unlike a monarch's *political* power: absolute and oppressive. They were radicals for their time, and over the course of history they have sometimes been seen as progenitors of the modern left, but interestingly, the 1970s libertarian theorist Murray Rothbard once called them "the world's first self-consciously libertarian mass movement." Indeed it was believers in free markets who generally opposed monopolies the most, arguing that they suffocated competition. None other than Adam Smith wrote famously of the "wretched spirit of monopoly," and in the early 1770s he inveighed heatedly against the British East India Company and argued that its "monopoly should be revoked . . . and the company left to the mercy of the market."

In colonial America, antimonopoly sentiment was strong. The Boston Tea Party, the famous uprising Americans all learn about in grade school, was in essence an antimonopoly action, carried out against that very same British East India Company, which held a crown-granted monopoly to import tea to the colonies, before the indictment was broadened to the more universal "taxation without representation." Some scholars have argued that if one examines history through a chiefly economic rather than political lens, it was the havoc wreaked in the colonies by British monopolies—the high prices, the constraints they placed on American industry—

that drove the American Revolution. The Founding Fathers had robust debates about monopolies. The leading voices here were James Madison's and Thomas Jefferson's. Jefferson wrote to Madison in late 1787, summarizing what he lamented was missing from the Constitution, chiefly a bill of rights that expressly provided a "restriction on monopolies." Madison wrote back to Jefferson in 1788 that monopolies are "justly classed among the greatest nuisances in Government." Madison reckoned, however, that since they had just written a Constitution that put the power in the hands of the mass of people and not the few (Madison had helped write it; Jefferson was in Paris at the time and thus missed the Constitutional Convention), the threat of monopoly was not great (oh, well).

At that time, "monopoly" meant power granted to a corporation by the state, whether it be king or Congress. There were a few monopoly controversies in the early republic, for example over the charter the federal government gave to the Bank of the United States. Andrew Jackson, who despised government-granted monopolies, vetoed the bank's renewal. But after the Civil War and the Industrial Revolution, the problem began to shift from public monopolies (government chartered) to private monopolies (great concentrations of economic power in private hands). Changes in the law made this possible. In the early republic, corporations were created, mostly at the state level, one charter at a time. But with industrialization came general incorporation laws. Private corporations proliferated, and monopolies dominated in a number of areas. The railroads were perhaps most conspicuous here, and indeed it was a case involving a railroad, *Santa Clara County v. Southern Pacific Railroad* (1886), that led the Supreme Court to extend Fourteenth Amendment rights of equal protection to corporations ("corporations *are* people, my friend," Mitt Romney taunted a heckler in 2011 on the campaign trail).

The Gilded Age eventually gave way to the busting of many large trusts. Everyone associates the breaking up of the trusts with Teddy Roosevelt, and with good reason; he did take several important actions against the railroads, for example. But the real hero of the era to today's antimonopolists was Louis Brandeis, first as adviser to Woodrow Wilson and later as Supreme Court justice. Brandeis criticized TR and his Bull Moose Party in 1912 as taking a soft and selective antimonopoly position, whereas "the Democratic position . . . is that private monopoly in industry is never permissible; it is never desirable, and is not inevitable; competition can be reserved, and where it is suppressed, can be restored." It was the Wilson administration that passed the Clayton Act, a tougher antitrust act than the more famous predecessor Sherman Act of 1890. And it was Wilson and Brandeis who broke the "money trust" of large banks in 1913–1914. As Matt Stoller writes in his book, *Goliath*, "The elder J. P. Morgan died in March of 1913, just as the new rules he hated were enacted. In January of 1914, Morgan partners resigned from boards of thirty powerful corporations, and a dozen railroads. The money trust was being broken apart." From there, the fortunes of antimonopolists waxed and waned; the latter happened under the three Republican presidents of the 1920s, after which FDR and key congressional allies like Wright Patman revived antitrust. Through all this time, most economists right and left agreed with Adam Smith: monopolies distorted the market and should be broken up to foster more competition. Interestingly, the aggressive antitrust posture of the New Deal era was championed "by Chicago-school economists—Henry Simons, Jacob Viner, and Frank Knight—who argued that economic planning was not getting the United States out of the Depression and that antitrust enforcement was needed to deconcentrate American industry."

When the Mont Pelerin Society was formed, its principals were antimonopolists. "Classical liberals," wrote one scholar, "were wary of monopoly as inherently inimical to democracy because in their view it undermined a necessary condition for democratic politics to flourish, namely, a competitive market." Through Hayek's efforts, the University of Chicago established the Antitrust Project headed by Aaron Director, who happened to be Milton Friedman's brother-in-law. They were all antimonopolists in the late 1940s and early 1950s. At a meeting in 1947, Friedman spoke in support of corporate policies that would "retard the tendency (if it exists) toward increasingly large and monopolistic organizations and stimulate the breakdown of existing giant corporations."

Then something changed: their funding. The Antitrust Project was bankrolled by the Volker Fund, the charitable project of a Kansas City home furnishings magnate who quite generously gave most of his fortune away, in part because he didn't want the government to get it. The Volker Fund was free market and libertarian, and by 1950 the fund's principals made it known to Director that if he was interested in receiving continued funding, he might want to rethink his position on monopolies. And over the next few years, they all, and neoliberalism with them, switched. They "no longer regarded monopoly as the great enemy of democracy. . . . Rather, they argued that not only was monopoly not deleterious to the operation of the market but also that it was a negligible symptom attributable to ill-functioning ham-fisted activities of the government"; they also "characterized corporations—even behemoth corporations—as relatively benign entities that naturally gave rise to the market conditions that would eventually undermine them." And by the time he wrote *Capitalism and Freedom* (1962), Friedman was writing dismissively about the "over-estimation of the importance of monopoly" and averring that private cartels "are generally unstable and of brief duration unless they can call government to their assistance."

The Antitrust Project took in a fairly large group of affiliated young scholars, one of whom was a recent Chicago Law School graduate named Robert Bork. Most people know Bork because of the Senate's famous rejection of him for a Supreme Court seat in 1987. But nine years before that episode, and more than two decades after his Chicago experience, Bork did something that, in the words of the antimonopoly advocate Barry Lynn, "ended up having a far more revolutionary effect on the political and social structure of the United States than even the most influential of justices." Bork's 1978 book, *The Antitrust Paradox*, kick-started a legal and economic (and eventually political) process that turned antitrust law on its head. Until then, American antitrust law had been built on the same concepts of dispersal of economic power that drove the founders to distrust monopolies. Now Bork posited—in, according to Lynn, "a long, intentionally arcane, often contradictory, and historically erroneous argument"—that the only goal of monopoly law should be to safeguard the welfare of the consumer and that the way to achieve this was to promote efficiency.

Bork's argument revolutionized the American approach to antitrust. He asserted, along with conservative legal scholars like Richard Posner, that since the purpose of the law was to promote efficiency, it should encourage mergers and other actions that could permit corporations to lower costs and offer consumers more products. The concept of market competition, and the diffusion of economic power, had been the dominant strain in the American approach to these questions (to varying degrees) from Madison through Brandeis through FDR and Lyndon Johnson, who ran a very populist antitrust administration. Now it was completely reversed. As Lynn said to me in an interview, "You could not find a more anti-Madisonian statement."

It wasn't just Republicans and conservatives who adopted the consumerist view. The Carter administration went light on antitrust enforcement, opening the door to the still-ongoing era of ever-larger corporate mergers. Ralph Nader (!) was on board, as was (to some extent) the eminent liberal economist John Kenneth Galbraith, who argued that bigness was an inevitable fact of modern life and that therefore big government and big labor provided a "countervailing power" to big business. So again, this initial impetus was bipartisan to some extent. But it was driven by Bork and Posner and then pushed to warp speed in the Reagan administration. William Baxter, the first head of Reagan's Antitrust Division, directed the Justice Department to rely on an "efficiency test" when it assessed the concentration of economic power. Baxter did take some antitrust actions, for example against American Airlines, but mostly his legacy advanced concentration of corporate power. The department established new "Merger Guidelines" (completed after Baxter left) that overrode the old LBJ-era guidelines that decreed there must be four competitors in any line of business. Under the new guidelines, "as long as executives could make the most rudimentary case that a merger would result in efficiencies that might eventually lower the price of some good or service, they had a license to consolidate, no matter what the political or social effects of the deal." Thus the era of huge mergers that cost many thousands of workers their jobs in the name of efficiency commenced. The term "merger mania" was coined in the 1980s by the notorious corporate raider Ivan Boesky.

Once these were the new rules, it proved impossible to unwrite them. As with tax policy, neoliberal monopoly policy quickly became dogma, a change helped along by the fact that at this exact same time in our history, the 1980s and 1990s, money swallowed our political system, in terms of both campaign contributions and lobbying expenditures. In addition, it was a time when the Democratic Party suffered three straight presidential losses, something that hadn't happened in postwar America. The combination of these developments led many in the Democratic Party to decide the party had to modernize and become more pro-business, less reflexively tied to labor. So arose the Democratic Leadership Council, which was actually formed in 1985 (before that third loss) but which didn't seize power until Clinton's victory in 1992. In that year's platform, the party dropped language that had been in previous platforms expressing opposition to monopolies.

Clinton's Justice Department and Federal Trade Commission (which also brings antitrust actions) did pursue some high-profile cases, notably against Microsoft, Intel, and American Airlines. But the 1990s were a decade of major mergers across industries ranging from media and telecommunications to energy—the administration approved the Exxon-Mobil merger and that of Chevron and Texaco—and farming. In essence, from Clinton's time through George W. Bush's and Obama's, the Bork paradigm was never fundamentally challenged. Donald Trump's Justice Department, surprisingly enough, did bring a couple of major antitrust cases, against the Time Warner–CNN merger and, just before Trump's term in office ended, against Google. But there was no principle at work here. He despised "fake news" CNN, and, as I noted previously, conservatives saw Google as a liberal enterprise. In particular, Trump's old friend Rupert Murdoch told him that Google was destroying the media.

Today, monopolies control so many aspects of the market and our lives that most of us literally don't go a day, or even a few hours, without relying on monopoly or at best oligopoly providers. Google, Facebook, and Amazon dictate vast portions of our lives. We all use one of two computing systems. In many cities, hospitals are now owned by one corporation, which have a monopoly on beds and can set prices accordingly. The beer industry is a near monopoly under Anheuser-Busch. Mars controls the candy business. All manner of medical supplies and equipment are produced under monopoly enterprises. Chicken farmers, as Zephyr Teachout writes in her book *Break 'Em Up*, must answer to three producers—Tyson, Perdue, and Pilgrim's Pride—that operate regionally and don't compete with one another and impose impossibly rigid contracts on the farmers, 70 percent of whom make less than poverty wages. Even our innocent amusements aren't immune. As the antimonopoly advocate Sarah Miller wrote in the journal *Democracy* in 2020, "Even the cheerleading 'industry' is monopolized: Bain Capital–owned Varsity Brands controls everything from equipment to apparel to the National Cheerleading Association itself."

Awareness has grown in recent years, through the work of people like Lynn and Stoller and Teachout and Miller and Phil Longman and Lina Khan (whom Biden appointed to head the Federal Trade Commission), about the extent of monopoly's ill effects. The word "antitrust," after disappearing from the Democratic platform in 1992, finally reappeared in 2016. Biden made serious appointments in this realm. In addition to Khan, he named Jonathan Kanter, a former corporate lawyer who had a see-the-light moment and formed a law group that advertises itself as "an antitrust advocacy boutique," to head the Justice Department's Antitrust Division. Timothy Wu, who advocates reining in the power of dominant telecom and online platforms, is a special assistant to the president. Finally, several Democrats in Congress today, notably the Rhode Island representative David Cicilline, have pledged aggressive action. It's a long-overdue correction, forty years after Robert Bork's book and seventy years after the neoliberals made their intellectually corrupt flip-flop on monopoly policy at a funder's behest.

PUBLIC SCHOOLS: THE VOUCHER HOAX

A third area of American life in which neoliberal principles have left a malign footprint is public education. Here, the overall legacy is not as aggressively hideous as on income inequality and monopoly power; "school choice," as the movement spawned by neoliberal precepts is broadly known, has not been all bad. But it was advertised by neoliberals and their enthusiasts, with their typical insouciance, as a panacea that it plainly has not been. The idea, again, was freedom. Give children more choices, make schools compete and they will improve, and we will end the scourge of the monopoly that government has over the schools (yes, they cursed this particular public monopoly, even as they cheered on the rise of private monopoly). They said it would help poor students especially. In fairness, school choice has done some good in certain poor communities where decent charter schools operate. But it has been more beneficial to children from well-off families. And one can't help but wonder how our most challenged public schools might be doing if conservatives had spent forty years, and untold millions of dollars, trying to improve them rather than undermine and replace them.

School choice has existed in one form or another since schools have existed, which, in many parts of this country, isn't as long as one might assume. It was 1918 before all (then) forty-eight states had passed laws requiring all children to attend elementary school. But the modern school choice movement started in the mid-1950s. Milton Friedman, that busy fellow, was instrumental here too, with a short 1955 essay called "The Role of Government in Education." If the date of the essay raised your eyebrow, good—you're paying attention. It was only in the mid-1950s that a lot of parents, for some mysterious reason, became suddenly unhappy with the public schools. These were of course white parents, and the reason wasn't mysterious at all: after 1954's *Brown v. Board of Education* decision, they awoke to the threat that their darlings might have to go to school with "colored" children. As for Black parents, they were unhappy well before 1954, because their schools were vastly inferior to the white children's schools. One of the Black high schools that was a plaintiff in *Brown* was a Virginia school with no cafeteria or gymnasium and no proper heating system. But no one paid them much attention.

So it's an interesting, er, coincidence that it was after *Brown* that Friedman turned his attention to education. There is a long and grimly hilarious footnote in this essay in which Friedman addresses the racial ramifications of his suggestions, which he writes were brought to his attention after he completed his first draft. As we saw in chapter 2, Friedman announces himself a mortal foe of racial prejudice, after which he quickly goes on to assert that he finds both coerced segregation and coerced desegregation to be abhorrent before reluctantly concluding, "So long as the schools are publicly operated, the only choice is between forced nonsegregation and forced segregation; and if I must choose between *these evils* [italics mine], I would choose the former as the lesser." Forced nonsegregation, evil. But cheer up! Private schools, he writes, "can solve this dilemma," because people would persuade other people to see reason and create desegregated schools: "The appropriate activity for those who oppose segregation and racial prejudice is to try to persuade others of their views; if and as they succeed, the mixed schools will grow at the expense of the nonmixed, and a gradual transition will take place." This is not merely a naive thing to say; it is so detached from reality as to be monstrous.

In any case, he wrote in the essay that it was justifiable for the state to order a certain minimum level of education for all, and even for the state to pay for it. What he frowned on, though, was the idea of the state *running* education: "the actual administration of educational institutions by the government; the 'nationalization,' as it were, of the bulk of the 'education industry.'" His idea instead was that the state should subsidize education in another way: by giving parents vouchers so they could pay to send their kids to the school of their choice. These schools could be run by the government or by religious organizations or nonprofit groups or for-profit concerns. Of course, this exact thing happened across the South after *Brown*. Vouchers *were* made available, but to white students only, so they could attend "segregation academies" that opened up across the region after *Brown*. A number of southern counties went so far as to close their public schools entirely or stop levying the taxes that typically supported them. So initially at least, the voucher system of Friedman's dreams was used solely to enforce educational apartheid in this country.

School choice was also interesting to a number of people on the left, owing to their deep frustration with the state of education in poor communities. Actually, the idea of Black schools went back to Reconstruction, when in some states as many as half of all schools were started by now-free Black citizens, funded mostly by the Freedmen's Bureau (established by Congress in 1865 to assist former slaves) and various northern benevolent associations. In the civil rights era, a movement arose on the left in the early 1960s aimed particularly at helping minority children. "Freedom schools" sprang up across the South, a project of the Student Nonviolent Coordinating Committee. By the end of Freedom Summer in 1964, there were forty-one such schools in Mississippi alone. Next up were the so-called free schools that came into being in the late 1960s and early 1970s. These schools appeared not just in the South but all over the country. They were founded by progressives and radicals for Black and other minority children and were guided by principles such as smallness of scale, participatory democracy, and a general rejection of many conventional forms of education. As the name suggests, they were free to students and parents, funded by wealthy individuals and foundations, but they were run on shoestrings, and pay for teachers and staff was very low. The free schools didn't last long. They led activists to return to the public schools to seek "community control" over their schools by breaking up large urban districts into smaller community districts.

At this same time, in the late 1960s, progressive voucher programs were initiated in a number of cities. The Harvard social scientist Christopher Jencks was a key architect of these programs. Though they shared with Friedman's scheme a retreat from the public schools, the motivations and sensibilities were, as you might imagine, quite different. The conscious goal here was racial and class integration; the idea was that half of each class at these private academies would be admitted based on standard criteria, and the other half by lottery. In addition, "bonus vouchers" would entice parents to send their children to such schools. The Johnson administration funded an experimental program along these lines designed by Jencks in San Jose, California. But results were inconclusive. The Nixon administration stopped funding it, and the plan died.

Over the course of the 1970s and into the 1980s, school choice became much more identified with conservatism, as Ronald Reagan pushed vouchers and conservative foundations and think tanks poured millions into the issue. Reagan's first education secretary, Terrel Bell, commissioned a 1983 report given the dramatic title *A Nation at Risk*, which sounded the alarm about the supposedly dire state of American education. Reagan praised the report's call for vouchers, as well as for prayer in schools and the abolition of the Department of Education. The report in fact "hadn't said a word about any of these things." His second education secretary, William Bennett, pushed vouchers and charter schools aggressively. After Reagan, in the late 1980s, the Wisconsin-based Bradley Foundation helped finance the nation's first-ever voucher program in Milwaukee, ultimately providing more than $3 million.

If all this activity produced clearly superior results, that would be one thing. But the outcomes have been ambiguous. *The Wall Street Journal* did a comprehensive study of the Milwaukee program in 2018, nearly thirty years after it started. At that point, fully one-quarter of Milwaukee students, about twenty-nine thousand children, were using vouchers. The *Journal* found that students using vouchers "have performed about the same as their peers in public schools on state exams." Some voucher students did do better: those whose enrollment numbers were limited in comparison to fee-paying students. In other words, private schools accept some students who pay with state-subsidized vouchers and other students who pay full freight. Generally, the tipping point is around 20 to 30 percent; that is, if the percentage of voucher students is kept low, the results can be better. But even many voucher advocates acknowledge that the differences between public schools and privately run schools aren't great. Mike Ruzicka, who heads a Milwaukee realtor group that has backed the voucher program, told the *Journal*, "We've come to the realization that it's not going to be a panacea."

Charter schools have a somewhat better reputation among educators, but they too have not consistently produced better results than public schools. One prominent study, from Stanford University in 2009, looked at 70 percent of all students enrolled in charter schools in the country and found that 17 percent of the schools showed significant improvement over public schools, but 37 percent were worse, and 46 percent were statistically about the same. This study has been oft cited and sometimes criticized by charter school defenders (how the study defines the word "significant," for example). But other studies have found similar results. Some studies find a lot of variation within charter schools; the really good ones serve students very well, but the not-so-good ones don't, and alas there are plenty of the latter.

That's at least thirty years of school choice, with results that are inconclusive at best. If this were a private enterprise, all these conservatives would look at this mixed track record of three decades and declare the whole thing a failure. But their ideological commitments are stronger than evidence. So the push has continued. Betsy DeVos, Trump's education secretary, was relentlessly pro-voucher. She tried to expand voucher programs in several ways, rebranding them (perhaps inevitably) as "education freedom scholarships" and even using the cover of the pandemic to redirect millions Congress passed in emergency education relief to private schools. People who try to argue that Trump was no neoliberal because of his position on trade conveniently forget about DeVos, who pursued this central neoliberal priority zealously.

DeVos is an ideologue. There are other supporters of school choice who are more credible. But they all ignore the philosophical problem at the heart of the school choice movement. Education is the greatest collective good that we have. We as a society decided many decades ago that school should be universal and free. We agreed to impose taxes to support it. The proof that we still see education as a common good is found in the fact that everyone in a given community pays taxes to support public education. If you send your children to private school, or have no children, you still pay the taxes. This is because an educated populace benefits us all.

The overall state of American public education is about the same as it was twenty years ago, or if anything is somewhat improved. Most of our public schools are actually pretty good. Some, of course, are bad. They need help. Children who grow up in poor neighborhoods face many challenges that middle-class children don't: maybe reading and learning aren't valued in their homes as much, so they fall behind very early; maybe they face nutritional issues; the legacy of lead paint that still exists in too many apartment buildings in poor areas, and lead pipes carrying water, has been found to have damaged young people's brains. I'm no expert on education policy, but it's always been my view that a far more imaginative and holistic approach is needed that doesn't wait until a child is six years old. More radically, there is a case for breaking up school districts as they currently exist. The education expert Kevin Carey of New America recommended this in a piece he wrote for the journal *Democracy* in 2020. Basically, school districts as currently drawn reinforce class and racial divisions and implicate everyone in "a series of structured choices—where to work, who to know, how to live—that leads, unavoidably, toward crushing injustice." And this, too, is a problem that liberals have helped create, not just conservatives. A lot of liberals are impressively liberal until it comes to their kids.

So figuring out what to do isn't easy. But privatizing our most deeply held public good has not worked in practice and is dangerous philosophically. Jason Blakely, a political philosopher at Pepperdine, wrote a bracing essay on this in *The Atlantic* in 2017, which is worth quoting:

> What much fewer people realize is that the argument over "school of choice" is only the latest chapter in a decades-long political struggle between two models of freedom—one based on market choice and the other based on democratic participation. Neoliberals like DeVos often assume that organizing public spaces like a market must lead to beneficial outcomes. But in doing so, advocates of school of choice ignore the political ramifications of the marketization of shared goods like the educational system.

Markets, he writes, create winners and losers. If a business goes belly-up because it didn't serve consumers' wants, the social harm is minimal. But what happens when Schumpeterian "creative destruction" is applied to a social good like schools? Blakely writes,

> In Detroit (where DeVos played a big role in introducing school choice) two decades of this marketization has led to extreme defunding and closing of public schools; the funneling of taxpayer money toward for-profit charter ventures; economically disadvantaged parents with worse options than when the neoliberal social experiment began; and finally, no significant increase in student performance. Indeed, some zones of Detroit are now educational deserts where parents and children have to travel exorbitant miles and hours for their children to attend school.

This is not freedom. It's freedom's opposite. And conservative neoliberals' obsession with privatizing education has done harm to public education that is well-nigh irreparable. If the rich conservatives who've spent all these millions on vouchers and charter schools had instead, say, financed early-reading programs in poor neighborhoods for the last forty years, we'd now be raising at least our second generation of poor children—urban and rural, Black and white—who started reading earlier in life, which study after study has shown leads to greater confidence and success.

I focused this chapter on these three consequences of neoliberalism—inequality, monopoly, and education—because they're among neoliberalism's most damaging legacies, but more than that because they all tell a story of policies that were allegedly designed to expand freedom but have actually and considerably constricted it for millions of people. Workers whose incomes haven't kept pace with certain costs of living like medical care and higher education; chicken farmers who must contract with one of three firms and do everything precisely as they say and still live in near penury; consumers whose choices are restricted by monopoly power; poor students who aren't among the very few lucky ones who get to attend a great charter school—these people deserve freedom, too. They will be more likely to attain greater freedom through collective action. But that is the one choice neoliberalism will not allow under any circumstances.

Part Two

DIGGING OUT OF THE MESS

CHAPTER SIX

How Economics Has Changed

•

"WHY DID NOBODY NOTICE IT?"

On November 5, 2008, Queen Elizabeth II paid a visit to the London School of Economics to help open a new building. This was a year or so after the emergence of huge losses in the subprime loan business, and a little more than six weeks after the collapse of Lehman Brothers set off a massive financial panic. Not surprisingly, as she was hobnobbing with a bunch of economists at one of the world's top academic institutions, conversation turned to the meltdown then engulfing the global economy. Her Majesty took her audience by surprise with a simple, disarming, and embarrassing question: "Why did nobody notice it?"

It's the most important question about economic policy of this century, probably. The Great Recession wiped out trillions of dollars of wealth, sent the world's leading economies into a tailspin from which they had only just dug out when the pandemic hit, cost millions of people their jobs and their homes. And though experts naturally disagree on the causes, and the right tried to pin it all on Freddie and Fan-

nie and those irresponsible (that is, mostly nonwhite) mortgage borrowers who put 5 percent down, the main causes
were rooted in the free market itself: excessive deregulation,
way too much risk taken by corporations and financial firms,
excessive borrowing, a U.S. administration that was asleep at
the wheel, central bankers who took a hands-off approach on
banking regulation, and "an erosion of standards of responsibility and ethics," in the words of the Financial Crisis
Inquiry Commission. All that and—perhaps most important
of all—just plain unwillingness to consider even the possibility that the global financial system could crash. Many
came to believe that a shock like the meltdown was simply
impossible in the modern world, and they were blinded by
their hubris. Or, as some prominent British economists put
it to the queen several months after she posed the question,
"In summary, Your Majesty, the failure to foresee the timing,
extent, and severity of the crisis and to head it off, while it
had many causes, was principally a failure of the collective
imagination of many bright people, both in this country and
internationally, to understand the risks to the system as a
whole."

Not every economist missed it. A handful smelled
trouble coming. Three notable figures who did were Nou-
riel Roubini of New York University, Peter Schiff of Euro
Pacific Capital, and Dean Baker of the Center for Economic
and Policy Research. Baker published a paper in November 2006 titled "Recession Looms for the U.S. Economy in
2007," correctly predicting a collapse in the housing bubble.
But by and large, people like Baker were pooh-poohed.

The good news is that this state of affairs has led to
some measure of self-reflection and internal criticism in
the economics field, which has attracted wide audiences.
No post-meltdown critique of macroeconomics was more

scathing than a lecture* the economist Paul Romer, former chief economist at the World Bank, delivered in January 2016. Romer opened his lecture, called "The Trouble with Macroeconomics," like this: "Lee Smolin begins *The Trouble with Physics* by noting that his career spanned the only quarter-century in the history of physics when the field made no progress on its core problems. The trouble with macroeconomics is worse. I have observed more than three decades of intellectual regress."

Romer goes on to describe the mistakes he believes macroeconomists made in their assumptions and models that led to the profession being divorced from the reality of the economy as it existed and operated in the real world. Many sections are quite technical and beyond the grasp of the layperson (this one included). He deals at length with something economists call the "identification problem," which has to do with how economists determine things like supply and demand curves for the purposes of making economic models. But no one could miss the meaning of a sentence like this, of which there are many: "The noncommittal relationship with the truth revealed by these methodological

---

* There is some confusion as to whether this was a lecture or a paper, and the answer is a bit complicated. Romer explained to me that he originally delivered this as a talk in January 2016, sponsored by Sigma Xi, the scientific research honor society, at the annual meeting of the American Economic Association. He was all set to publish it in Sigma Xi's journal, and it was set into galleys, but he says he got cold feet at the last second. He was torn, he says, between his "sense of duty to say honestly what I thought was true" and his "sense of personal pain" that his remarks would cause some people he liked personally. He wrote to me in an email: "In a sense, it was a 'shot across the bow,' my way of saying that they had gone too far and needed to change course. But one that stopped short of a declaration of total war that might not have been the best way to get economics back on track." He also emphasized to me that he may yet publish it.

evasions and the 'less than totally convinced . . .' dismissal of fact goes so far beyond post-modern irony that it deserves its own label. I suggest 'post-real.'"

Romer wasn't the only economist to train his sights on macroeconomics. Paul Krugman did so at great length, and without mathematical formulas, in *The New York Times Magazine* shortly after the meltdown. Krugman gave his readers a terrific primer on the history of economic thought and policy making: that until the Great Depression, economics generally held that the market left to its own devices would always find equilibriums and fix problems; that with the advent of the Depression, Keynes and his ideas about public investment, demand, and full employment took over; that Keynesianism lost credibility during the era of stagflation in the 1970s, and the Friedman/Chicago school of thought took over. He covered the debate in more recent years between the "freshwater" economists (in Chicago, at the University of Minnesota, and elsewhere) and their faith in markets and the "saltwater" economists (along both coasts, at UC Berkeley, MIT, and Princeton, chiefly) who still advocated for some measure of Keynesian policies.

In the end, the "freshwater" economists largely won. Their models claimed to show that markets naturally self-adjust to shocks and inevitably return to "full employment equilibrium" and that government intervention through spending and tax policies was likely to do more harm than good. However, they did allow that central bank policies could help smooth the transitions between shocks. Their models came to dominate in both academia and the policy world, and a broad consensus settled in the 1980s through the first decade of the twenty-first century that government should generally limit its role to reducing "frictions" in the market and correcting "market failures": wise central bankers could steer the economy by tweaking interest rates. Those on the Clintonite left saw more market failures to be corrected through some government action on matters like environmental protection (air pollution is a classic example of a market failure, a negative external cost created by inefficient allocation of resources). Those on the right saw more "frictions" (anything that interferes with the free flow of capital or goods) to be eliminated through deregulation or removing other barriers to trade. But the broad consensus seemed to be borne out by the low inflation and general stability of the period.

But that feeling of consensus also led to hubris. Krugman quotes a 1980 statement by the freshwater icon Robert Lucas, who said that "at research seminars, people don't take Keynesian theorizing seriously anymore; the audience starts to whisper and giggle to one another"; also, Lucas's (in)famous assertion from a 2003 address that the "central problem of depression prevention has been solved." This belief, Krugman wrote, was the key issue, and the reason most economists missed the signs that the bubble was going to burst: macroeconomists came to place too much faith in their models and "mistook beauty, clad in impressive-looking mathematics, for truth." Or, as the great economic historian Robert Skidelsky put it in his slim and readable *What's Wrong with Economics?*, "The authority of economics derives in no small measure from its opacity."

Romer, in an interview for this book, said his real target was the Chicago school and freshwater economics. "I started to see there were these dimensions of almost like this thuggish kind of behavior around these people who coalesced in this freshwater coalition," Romer said. "I got very discouraged about that part of economics. I just thought it wasn't behaving like a science." The word "thuggish" may seem strong, but he meant it. He used it twice, along with "gang-like," "pathology" (with respect to Milton Friedman), and "pseudoscience." But none of those quite ranked with this quotation, when Romer was talking to me about how passively too many economists swam with the freshwater tide for too long. "I think you could characterize their response as 'Look, we have no choice,'" he said. "'There are these powerful guys in charge. And we tried to do the best we could do under difficult circumstances.' You know, it's kind of like the collaborators in France, and my attitude is, you didn't have to work in the area, you could've just quit. Done another part of economics, or quit economics."

Let's pause here to discuss Romer's work briefly. His main focus has been on economic growth. He helped change the profession's understanding of growth by asserting that technology and innovation are at the heart of growth and that technological change doesn't just happen but is a result of a host of factors and decisions relating to innovations that originate within market economies. It was ideas, he argued, as much as the concrete things a society produced, that generated progress and growth. There's a whole school of economics now called endogenous growth theory that is based in no small part on his pioneering work. Romer—the son of the 1990s Democratic Colorado governor Roy Romer—was in essence studying why markets become inefficient; the policy upshot of his work was that governments need to intervene in areas like research and development and intellectual property law to produce sustainable and equitable growth.

He shared a Nobel Prize for this work in 2018 with Yale's William Nordhaus, whose work focused on economic approaches to climate change. Though they worked on different topics, the pairing made sense, tweeted the economist Justin Wolfers at the time, because "they each point to contradictions at the heart of capitalism. It's all about market failure. Left alone, markets will generate too much pollution (Nordhaus) and too few ideas (Romer)." The prize was nice payback for his rocky departure earlier that year as chief economist at the World Bank, where he resigned under fire for saying in an interview that a bank report criticizing the socialist government of Chile might have been biased. He also ruffled feathers by asking the economists working for him to write clear, concise sentences and shorter reports. He celebrated the Nobel in part by going to Burning Man.

A trip to Burning Man may sound like a lark, but in Romer's case it wasn't. He had some theories about cities and organization, and he wanted to visit America's most conspicuous instant city—a patch of desert that goes from a population of zero to seventy thousand in a matter of days and then back again when the festival ends—to see if observable fact bore out his ideas. As I read about his Burning Man excursion, it meshed well with the person I'd interviewed a few months before. At Burning Man, he was seeing if the facts fit the theory; he was, in short, doing science. And in our talk, he emphasized over and over again that science was his first-order concern. This is why "pseudoscience" is about the worst term of opprobrium Romer can deliver. He applies it to the economists who missed the meltdown, who Romer believes constructed the bubble they lived in, from which contemplation of a potential meltdown was simply impossible. "Science is the greatest thing humans have ever invented," he said. "It's a very unusual social system, and it's, I think frankly, maybe a lot more fragile than a lot of people realize. You know, people could be looking back in a thousand years and saying, 'Oh yeah, western Europe spawned this era of science, but it kind of burned out after four or five centuries, just like Babylonian math. And then it just kind of collapsed.' So I'm really driven more than anything by trying to preserve science." And preserving science, he said, is "consistent with trying to protect democracy as well." Democracy needs science, data, agreed-upon facts. To the extent that neoliberal macroeconomics strayed from that, it did enormous damage not only to the global financial system but to democracy as well.

THE GOOD NEWS: ECONOMICS CATCHES UP WITH REALITY

Back in chapter 3, I mentioned the economists David Card and Alan B. Krueger and their pioneering 1993 study of the minimum wage. Two years after that, they published a book expanding on the paper called *Myth and Measurement: The New Economics of the Minimum Wage.* They were doing an event at the Brookings Institution, the famous Washington think tank, and were laying out their basic argument that they found no evidence to support the idea that a higher minimum wage led to reductions in employment. A hand shot up from an economist in the audience who objected to all this talk about evidence, saying, "Theory is evidence, too."

Card and Krueger's work presented a challenge to their field precisely because it was based on evidence and data. They looked at what actually happened in low-wage workplaces around the New Jersey–Pennsylvania border when New Jersey raised its minimum wage, and they found that there was in fact no resulting reduction in low-wage employment in New Jersey relative to Pennsylvania. In the argot of economics, what Card and Krueger conducted was called a "natural experiment." Their method was a challenge to the way most economics was done at the time, which was that most research was based on theoretical modeling rather than real-world evidence. And their conclusion flew in the face of the prevailing theory, which had held for a century or more that when a price (here, a wage) is raised, demand (for workers) falls. So it was highly controversial, and a lot of people, particularly Republican politicians, still don't accept it.

If you're a regular human being, you may think it kind of obvious that real-world evidence and data should be at the heart of any kind of analysis in either the hard or the social sciences. But economics, as Krugman wrote in his essay, became in the latter part of the twentieth century more based on theories and models than on evidence. The models were alluring to many people, Krugman writes, because they were elegant and based on increasingly complex mathematical calculations. They won their creators Nobels. And they were reassuring because they tended to proceed from the long-held assumption of neoclassical economics that actors behaved rationally—that is, people never behaved irrationally, made poor decisions, and so on—and the system was insulated against undue risk.

At the time, there was some justification for this faith in theoretical models, explained Jesse Rothstein of UC Berkeley, one of the leading economics departments in the United States that has challenged traditional thinking. "Prior to the '90s, in general, if the theory conflicted with the empirics, you would ignore the empirics and focus on what the theory said," Rothstein told me. "And that was probably the right thing to do because the empirics weren't very good. We didn't have much data. We didn't have very good methods of disentangling all the different causal factors. And so you were probably more right to do that than not."

But in the 1990s, something changed, Rothstein said, something that has only grown more pronounced since then: "We have better data. We have better computers. We have better empirical methods. Economics kind of became known as a field that really took causal inference very seriously." This idea of causality is key, as Heather Boushey wrote in an essay in the journal *Democracy* in 2019 in which she explained for lay readers the sea changes that had taken place in economics. The techniques pioneered by Card and Krueger and quickly adopted by others "allowed economists to estimate causality—that is, to show that one thing caused another, rather than simply being able to say that two things seem to go together or move in tandem." Causality meant that, based on all this newly available data, economists could look for explanations for problems like inequality or wage stagnation or global poverty in a way that wasn't possible in previous eras. It was mostly driven by access to new data, and it was a profound change. As Boushey wrote, "Whereas in the 1960s about half of the papers in the top three economic journals were theoretical, about four in five now rely on empirical analysis—and of those, over a third use the researcher's own data set, while nearly one-in-ten are based on an experiment."

The most prominent example of work in this new empirical realm that has had a huge real-world impact is that of Thomas Piketty, and of his sometimes collaborators Emmanuel Saez and Gabriel Zucman, as well as the inequality research pioneer Tony Atkinson. Piketty's most famous work, the book *Capital in the Twenty-First Century*, sold millions of copies worldwide and was made into a movie. He argued that the return on capital (profits, dividends, incomes, rents, and so on) is greater than the growth rate of national income (total economic output), which has the effect over time of wildly concentrating wealth in the top 1 percent, the top 0.1 percent, and even the top 0.01 percent. His conclusions were driven by mounds of income-tax data from the United States covering decades, data that showed how the rich were running away from the rest, and how the superrich were running away from even the rich. The book's impact is difficult to overstate. It moved economic inequality to the white-hot center of economic debates and the political conversation. Writing together, Piketty, Saez, and Zucman have looked at tax and other data all the way back to 1913 to compare pretax and post-tax growth rates for different segments of the U.S. population (the pretax/post-tax distinction is important because it tells us whether the government's policies on income tax and other matters help to shift wealth in one direction or the other). They found that since 1980, eight percentage points of national income shifted from the bottom 50 percent of the population to the top 1 percent. They also found that "government redistribution has offset only a small fraction of the increase in pretax inequality." In other words, tax rates are not keeping up with the shift in wealth toward the rich.

Another high-profile example of the impact of data analysis comes from the realm of what's called development economics—the study of global poverty. Here, Esther Duflo, Abhijit Banerjee, and Michael Kremer are among the best-known practitioners. They introduced the idea of randomized controlled trials (RCTs) into the study of various aspects of global poverty—essentially, a way to assign people or whole villages to either a "treatment group" or a "comparison group" at random to try to determine the impacts of particular interventions. This practice earned development economists the moniker the Randomistas. The trio won the Nobel Prize in 2019 for their work. Another development economist wrote upon that announcement, "Over the last fifteen years, Abhijit, Esther, and Michael's work has truly revolutionized the field of development economics by changing our view of what we know—and what we can know—about when and why some policy interventions work and others do not." RCTs have come under some strong criticisms: that they can't be generalized upon, and that by focusing so intently on small questions, their adherents ignore important big ones. But RCTs have helped development efforts figure out how best to improve education or health-care outcomes, for example, in many poor parts of the world.

There is much more work that I could cite. Raj Chetty, one of the youngest tenured professors in the history of Harvard University, founded a group called Opportunity Insights that uses what it refers to on its website as "big data" to look at differences between neighborhoods, educational opportunities, racial disparities, and other matters. Suresh Naidu of Columbia is a development and labor economist who has done a wide range of work on labor markets, wages, inequality, and mobility. Mariana Mazzucato of University College London has done really interesting work that calls into question the assumption that only the private sector creates value. Her books *The Entrepreneurial State* and *The Value of Everything* scrutinize the way value has been defined in economics and boldly argue that the public sector, through various scientific research and development investments, has sometimes been a bigger risk taker than the private sector. And there is the work being done under the rubric of Modern Monetary Theory, which I mentioned in chapter 4.

All of this work and more has pushed economics in two directions: toward a more data-based approach, and toward the political left. Saying this is not the same thing as saying that all empiricists have been on the political left. They have not. Neither has all this research happened since the meltdown. Martin Feldstein was a political conservative who notably used data to study unemployment and health economics going back to the 1970s. Remember, as Boushey wrote above, in the 1960s papers in the top journals were about half theoretical and half empirical. So I don't want to leave an impression that it never occurred to anyone to look at data until this century. But the new emphasis on empiricism is real. People are looking at newly available data and reporting what they show, which happens to be what our own layperson eyes and ears have been telling us for decades: that the game has been rigged for the rich for the last forty years. Economics has finally caught up with reality.

Eric Beinhocker, an American behavioral economist who is a professor at the University of Oxford and the director of an important research center called the Institute for New Economic Thinking at the Oxford Martin School, told me that after the meltdown he saw academic economics split into three camps. First was the status quo school centered on the freshwater institutions that didn't want to admit that anything had gone terribly awry. Second was a more center-left camp that willingly acknowledged market failure but sought incremental reform. Then there was the third camp, in which he included himself, that believed "we need a real paradigm shift in economics. We need to chuck out the nineteenth-century model, reject its false assumptions of perfect rationality and perfectly efficient markets, and rebuild something from scratch much more empirically that takes human behavior seriously, takes real-world institutions seriously, looks at economics as a true system, one that is deeply intertwined with other systems, such as politics or the physical environment."

Beinhocker's center is pursuing this agenda in collaboration with important places like the Santa Fe Institute, one of the world's leading independent scientific research centers, whose economic scholars focus chiefly on "complexity economics," which rejects the neoclassical idea that the economy naturally exists in a state of equilibrium created by the market. "Where equilibrium economics emphasizes order, determinacy, deduction, and stasis, complexity economics emphasizes contingency, indeterminacy, sense-making, and openness to change," wrote W. Brian Arthur, one of the institute's scholars. The complexity economics school of thought also seeks to understand the economy as an evolutionary system, where the coevolution of technologies and institutions drives both prosperity and progress, but also disruption and inequality. Complexity economics scholars have thus also teamed up with evolutionary theorists, anthropologists, historians, political scientists, sociologists, and others to better understand these long-term dynamics, helping economics break out of its disciplinary silo.

Some of the newer economic research has forced economics to consider factors that the profession didn't take seriously in years past. Take the question of how wages are determined. Classical economics held that wages were determined by marginal productivity; this means, in essence, that employers will hire workers as long as the workers produce more than they cost. Wages are set by supply (the number of workers available) and demand (the number of workers needed). This has a name: the market theory of wage determination. The skills involved matter, of course, as do some other factors like location (employers in Alaska generally have to sweeten the pot to get people to consider moving up there). But the point is, it's all down to impersonal market forces. Relatedly, the thinking was that if workers wanted to increase their pay, they just needed to be more productive, because higher productivity would naturally lead to higher pay.

But many economists, like Joseph Stiglitz, now challenge this way of seeing things and argue that while the above factors do still matter, wages in many cases are also determined by something else: political power. As my friend Nick Hanauer, the progressive-minded Seattle venture capitalist whom we'll learn more about in chapter 8, likes to say, "People earn what they have the political power to earn."

Economics had rarely acknowledged factors like political power until recently. "Now it's changing, but this is such an interesting difference that I think was not well understood," the labor economist Heidi Shierholz, the chief economist at the Department of Labor under Obama who in September 2021 became head of the Economic Policy Institute, told me. "That [to] an economist, the idea is that the market naturally pays people what they are worth. That's just the natural functioning of an unimpeded market. We'll just pay people what they are quote-unquote worth. Essentially, it's the value of your work. Period. Neoliberal economic theory would say, no, the social and political context isn't driving this. In an unimpeded market, you are paid your value to the firm. And that, I think, is changing. The economists are starting to finally catch up with the rest of the freaking world, that is, to understand that the social and political context totally matters."

Shierholz co-authored a 2018 paper with EPI's Josh Bivens on exactly this topic. They found that since 1979 worker bargaining power has been vastly eroded, driven by concentration in both monopoly and monopsony power (monopsony power refers to a market in which one employer has an unusual amount of power to set wages), union decline, higher unemployment levels, and trade with low-wage nations. They further found that "collapse of worker power" has been "overwhelmingly" caused by conscious policy decisions by lawmakers. In other words, the changes I just listed didn't happen by the power of some invisible hand. They were driven by national policy—trade policy, anti-union laws, and more.

These changes predated the Great Recession. As noted, the move toward empiricism started in the 1990s with the advent of more powerful computer technology. But the recession changed a lot of things. First, it damaged (how could it not?) the credibility of the people who said such an event was impossible. Alan Greenspan, who'd been fawned over by Congress for twenty years, looked foolish when he appeared before a House committee the month after the Lehman collapse and admitted, "Those of us who have looked to the self-interest of lending institutions to protect shareholders' equity, myself included, are in a state of shocked disbelief." He admitted, under questioning from the Democratic representative Henry Waxman of California, that he had "found a flaw" in his ideology.

The market meltdown also helped the arguments of reality-based economists. It gave their critiques and new approaches more of a foothold both in economics departments ("empirical research is now the route to join those in the top echelon of economics," Boushey wrote in that *Democracy* essay) and in economic policy-making positions. Of the president's Council of Economic Advisers, of which Boushey is now a member, Jesse Rothstein told me, "Now you just don't see theorists going there. You see empirical people."

If you're wondering why Joe Biden is pursuing more progressive economic policy than you'd thought he would, these shifts are a big part of the reason why. The world of economics has undergone massive changes since the last time a Democratic president was staffing up an economic team, in 2008–2009; changes that began in the 1990s and took root in the 2010s are finally forcing Democratic policy makers pay attention.

ECONOMICS AND GENDER: THE CHALLENGE TO HOMO ECONOMICUS

Now I want to turn attention to two areas in which most scholarship is fairly new—race and gender. Economics has grappled with racial discrimination, as we'll see below, since the 1950s, although peer-reviewed journals devoted to the study of race and political economy didn't start popping up until the 1970s. Serious engagement with feminism has been more recent still. Both of these areas are important to the idea of shifting the economic paradigm because arguments that emanate from both fields are having a direct impact on economic policy making; these aren't stories that are only about the academy. As I wrote in chapter 1, a new liberal prosperity has to be different from the one Roosevelt and Truman built, the one Jefferson Cowie described as creating "a sort of 'Caucasian' unity." Women and people of color must be included in the project this time around.

As we have seen, neoclassical economics, which dates to the late nineteenth century, was built in large part around the idea that individuals are rational actors who have perfect information and always act in their own self-interest and make choices that optimize their gain. There is a name for this rational actor: *Homo economicus*, or "economic man."

The rational actor, in other words, was a man. People didn't necessarily say this out loud, and of course those were the days when people used "mankind" to mean humanity, but it's pretty doubtful that when most economists conjured in their minds an image of what *Homo economicus* might look like, the image was of a woman. First of all, men ran the economy, the world, and households. And second of all, economics was almost certainly the most male dominated of all the social sciences. A well-read layperson, if asked, could name a few famous female sociologists and anthropologists who predated the second wave of feminism (Jane Addams and Alva Myrdal; Margaret Mead and Dian Fossey, to name two in each category). But one would be hard-pressed to look through history and find many prominent women in economics. There's Joan Robinson, the noted British Keynesian and socialist. And that's about it.

Nobody examined this or thought it was any sort of problem until women started entering the field in larger numbers in the 1970s and 1980s. Nancy Folbre, who took her PhD from the University of Massachusetts Amherst in 1979 and is today one of the country's leading feminist economists, recalled to me what things were like in those days. The American Economic Association, which ran a big annual conference, at one point established a committee on the status of women in the profession, "but it was very oriented toward how to dress for success, how to publish in the right journals, how to do a good job interview." There was almost no focus, she said, on the actual content of economics. This problem is apparently not merely a twentieth-century one. As recently as 2018, Alice H. Wu, then a doctoral candidate in economics at Harvard, studied the language used by economists in a prominent online conversation platform about the economic job market. Posts about men tended to use words like "adviser," "supervisor," and "Nobel"; posts about women used words like "hot," "attractive," and "pregnant."

Although early feminist economics texts began to appear in the late 1960s, it wasn't until the 1990s that the discipline really grew. The peer-reviewed journal *Feminist Economics* published its first issue in 1995. So what *is* feminist economics—not the journal, but the actual thing? It's the study of economic questions through a feminist lens, examining persistent economic inequalities between men and women. This discipline has developed in far more directions than I will attempt to cover in this short section of this book, but I want to emphasize two contributions of feminist economics that are important and, to my thinking, directly relevant to American politics and to the point of this book (changing the economic paradigm). First and foremost, feminist economics has taken seriously the question of women's labor, which male-dominated economics hadn't done: their reproductive labor, their caregiving labor, and so on. Economics hadn't given any of this work a value or price. Feminist economics has. Maybe even more important, feminist economics has provided a bold critique of the neoclassical rational-actor theory by arguing that we're not all self-interested rational actors: we are not always motivated by greed in our economic decision making. We're sometimes motivated by generosity, kindness, reciprocity. How does economics account for that?

On the first point, about women's labor, the world of economics has undergone a sea change in the last forty years. One example is the critique feminist economists have made of Gary Becker's work on the economics of the family. In 1981, Becker, a University of Chicago free marketeer, published a paper in the journal *Economica* titled "Altruism in the Family and Selfishness in the Market Place." He followed that paper with a book on the topic and various other journal articles. Becker argued that while selfishness guides our behavior in the marketplace, altruism governs how we behave within families. The altruist, for Becker, is the breadwinner—that is, usually the husband, though he allows that this may not always be the case—while the spouse (usually wife) and chil-

dren are what he called the "beneficiaries" of the breadwinner's altruism. He asserts that people behave altruistically in
families not because it's nicer or it makes them feel better
(which to me makes the behavior by definition not "altruistic," but let's leave that aside), but because altruism is a more
efficient way to maximize families' collective happiness. In
his concluding section, Becker writes on the possible ramifications of his idea: "If I am correct that altruism dominates
family behavior, perhaps to the same extent as selfishness
dominates market transactions, then altruism is much more
important in economic life than is commonly understood.
The pervasiveness of selfish behavior has been greatly exaggerated by the identification of economic activity with market transactions."

That may sound reasonably progressive. At least Becker
made the profession take the family seriously as a unit of
economic production (economics had mostly looked at the
individual and the market, and, later, the state). But feminist economics spotted a gaping hole in the argument. As
Folbre put it to me, "He treats families as though they're
just one unit, and there's no internal conflict. There are no
individuals, they're just families as units, [with] no conflict
at all." She started her career, Folbre said, by writing about
"bargaining within the family," treating the household not
as one undifferentiated and altruistic unit but as an arena of
conflict in which men typically had the upper hand. That
Becker didn't account for this made him "a very, very visible
target of a lot of early feminist economics." One example
of such a criticism of Becker is Barbara Bergmann's paper
"Becker's Theory of the Family: Preposterous Conclusions,"
which appeared in the very first issue of *Feminist Economics*. Bergmann argues that "the traditional family has never
served everyone's interests equally and has served certain

groups very poorly"; of Becker's truly bizarre soft spot for polygamy, she drily notes that "Becker concentrates most attention on the Victorian ideal of the family, although it appears he would judge the harem, an even more retrograde version of the family, to be even more praiseworthy."

Feminist economics has accomplished something vital and tangible in this realm: it got the federal government to acknowledge and start measuring household work. This happened, oddly, during the George W. Bush administration, although it was the result of efforts begun within the Bureau of Labor Statistics under the Clinton administration. It's called the American Time Use Survey, and it measures what the government calls "nonmarket production" activities like housework and child rearing and caring for elderly parents. For anyone who scoffs at "diversity" and thinks that having women and people of color being full participants in the workplace doesn't help change the way we see things, I point out that the survey was first proposed by Barbara-Rose Collins, an African American congresswoman from Michigan—and a community organizer and single mother—who served in the House from 1991 to 1997. And inside the government, the economist who pushed to get this done was Katharine Abraham, now at the University of Maryland. It was around the time, Abraham recalled to me in an interview, of the 1995 Fourth World Conference on Women in Beijing, the one where Hillary Clinton famously declared that "women's rights are human rights." The conference gave the drive to measure household work extra impetus in the Clinton administration. "[Secretary of Labor] Robert Reich was very supportive. Both he and [his successor] Alexis Herman were very supportive of the need for good information," Abraham told me. It took seven years of planning before the first survey came out. It now appears annually.

Though the survey just measures nonmarket production in hours and types of labor without placing a dollar value on it, the way to do so is pretty straightforward, Abraham told me: "The most sensible way to do it is to value the productive tasks performed at the price that you would have to pay somebody else to do them." The dollar value is enormous. Two analysts writing in *The New York Times* in 2020 estimated that if women in the United States were paid the minimum wage for all the household work they performed in a year, they'd earn $1.5 trillion. Comparatively few people are arguing seriously that all housework should be paid, but the mere recognition that domestic work has a market value has already changed our politics, lending legitimacy and authority to the impressive work done by the organizer Ai-jen Poo, whose National Domestic Workers Alliance has passed Domestic Workers Bills of Rights in ten states and brought more than two million domestic workers under minimum wage protections.

The critique of Becker and the household survey are salutary contributions of feminist economics. Another is the way the field has challenged the supposed rationality of *Homo economicus.* I should note that feminist economics is hardly alone in contesting *Homo economicus;* critiques of the concept go back to the 1930s at least. In our time, the charge has also been led by the field of behavioral economics, which emerged in the 1990s specifically to challenge long-held assumptions about why people make the economic decisions they make. The behavioral economics critique of neoclassical rational man is grounded in psychology and ideas about what most people regard as "fair." There's a famous behavioral economics experiment in which a person is given $10 and told to specify an amount to give a second person, who must either accept or reject the first offer (no negotiating). If the second person rejects the offer, no one gets anything;

if he or she accepts, both people keep their share. The first person usually offers around $4, sometimes even $5, which is more than one might think at first blush, proving that people are less selfish than we'd assume and that they fear being turned down more than they desire all the money for themselves.

Feminist economics has made a different critique: that rational man is just a fallacy, invented by men, based on an utterly false view of human nature. Julie A. Nelson of UMass Boston wrote in a 1995 journal article of *Homo economicus*, "As in our Robinson Crusoe stories, he has no childhood or old age, no dependence on anyone, and no responsibility for anyone but himself. The environment has no effect on him, but rather is merely the passive material over which his rationality has play. Economic man interacts in society without being influenced by society: his mode of interaction is through an ideal market in which prices form the only, and only necessary, form of communication." This is nonsense, Nelson argued. People are deeply affected by their pasts and their environments. Further, we aren't just selfish; most of us consider factors like fairness, and most of us are, to one degree or another, "other-oriented" as well as self-interested. But while recognizing the maleness baked into the conception of the rational actor, she called not for an explicitly feminine redefinition of human economic decision making but for one that transcended gender: "What is needed is a conception of *human* behavior that can encompass both autonomy and dependence, individuation and relation, reason and emotion, as they are manifested in economic agents of either sex."

We don't have that conception yet, certainly not in the realm of our political dialogue, which is my concern in this book. On cable television, when talk turns to what motivates individuals' behavior in the marketplace, the old assumption about self-interested behavior still dominates. It does so because Democrats and progressive thought leaders don't do enough to challenge it.

A perfect example of what I'm talking about played out over the course of 2021 in the debate about whether the government checks issued under the CARES Act and the American Rescue Plan made people not want to work. Literally every week on cable news, especially on Fox, someone could be heard thundering about the indolent people who'd rather sit at home and collect a check. Conservatives railed against these people, and liberals mostly stammered as some Republican governors cut the checks off before the official end date over the summer of 2021. Then, in September, the renowned MIT economist David Autor challenged the conventional wisdom in a *New York Times* op-ed under the headline "Good News: There's a Labor Shortage." Autor wrote that just maybe people were refusing to return to menial, low-paying jobs not because they were lazy but because the work didn't pay enough and wasn't rewarding enough. Perhaps, Autor wrote, "Americans are less eager to do low-paid, often dead-end service and hospitality work, deciding instead that more time on family, education and leisure makes for a higher standard of living, even if it means less consumption." In other words, he believed people were choosing to accept less paid work in exchange for other things that they valued more. This is a decision millions of Americans made that neoclassical economics had no way of explaining or comprehending.

Establishing in the public mind that people are not just selfish and competitive but reciprocal and cooperative and motivated by factors other than profit maximization is a vitally important project. As I hope to persuade you in the last chapter, it's essential to changing the economic paradigm.

ECONOMICS AND RACE:
PUTTING A PRICE ON DISCRIMINATION

Just as the economics profession has been inhospitable for women for most of its history, it's been no great home for people of color. Sadie T. M. Alexander, the first Black woman to earn a PhD in economics in the United States back in 1921, left the profession and moved to the law because of the racism and sexism she encountered. According to one 2017 study, just 3 percent of economics faculty members nationwide are Black—a few more than in the hard sciences like chemistry and biology, but fewer than in English and sociology. The profession isn't entirely blind to this as an issue. In January 2020, at the annual meeting of the Allied Social Science Associations (the largest meeting of economists in the country), the American Economic Association hosted a panel called "How Can Economics Solve Its Race Problem?" The panel was convened by Janet Yellen, the former Fed chair who became President Biden's Treasury secretary. She was AEA president at the time. That June, Yellen did something even more striking: the AEA issued a statement in response to the murder by Minneapolis police of George Floyd. "The officers and governance committees of the American Economic Association are deeply saddened by the killings of Black men and women by police officers, and we condemn those acts in the strongest possible terms," the statement began. It went on to commit to "improving the representation and experience of Black Americans in our profession" and investing in "programs, policies, and practices that bring students from underrepresented groups into economics."

The economics profession has attempted to put a price on racial discrimination for longer than this might suggest. Gary Becker is again a key figure here. In 1955, at the very dawn of the civil rights era, Becker wrote his doctoral dissertation about racial discrimination. It was published in 1957 as the book *The Economics of Discrimination*. Though he was a devout Chicagoan, Becker did at least take racial prejudice seriously. His argument, boiled down, is that discrimination of any sort by employers (in hiring, say) reduces the incomes of the discriminated-against minority, which is unsurprising; more interestingly, he posited, discrimination reduces the income of the employer doing the discriminating because they will have to pay higher wages to the preferred employees. For example, if I ran a pizza parlor and wished to hire only people with blond hair, I might pay a premium for blondes, and it would eat into my profits.

Thus, many economists would argue, the market does in fact punish discrimination. And yet it happens anyway, a fact that Becker acknowledged. We all see the government bring numerous lawsuits against business for violations of federal hiring laws, so we know that it happens. But Becker acolytes would say that while the government punishes discrimination visibly, the market punishes it in ways we don't as easily espy. Becker's thesis was theoretical; finally, in 2016, in the new empirical age, the sociologist Devah Pager put the theory to the test and found that Becker might be right: businesses that engaged in such discrimination were "less likely to remain in business six years later."

It wouldn't be accurate or fair to say that economics hasn't paid attention to race. It has. And yet, to this lay reader's eyes, in the literature I read while researching this book, something felt a bit off. Bigotry is emotional, and economics doesn't have a good way to understand or measure human emotion. That may not be economics' fault; emotion is probably impossible to measure. But that elusiveness speaks to the limits of mathematical formulas and even empirical evidence: Since very few white people will admit to being racist, racism can't be "measured." It is felt. And obviously, it is felt a lot more by some people than by others, and the nonscientific testimony of those who feel it seems more relevant than the scientific efforts of white social scientists who don't feel it. Which is not to say that their work is meritless, just that it has limits.

But don't ask me. Ask a Black economist or two. Which I did. William "Sandy" Darity of Duke University is probably our country's most prominent African American economist. In the middle of the first decade of the twenty-first century, he did something not a lot of people do. He developed an entirely new field of study: stratification economics, which is the study of intergroup inequality (that is, it's about not just race but gender and ethnicity and religion and even caste) and how it is shaped by power dynamics and social relationships. It combines elements of economics, sociology, and psychology, and it looks not solely at income inequality, which is the form of inequality that gets the most attention in the media, but wealth inequality, which is a bigger and thornier and even more difficult-to-solve issue because it's rooted in historic and systemic racism (for example, the fact that Blacks were barred from buying homes in most neighborhoods in the United States for generations, preventing them from building home equity—the main form of wealth most of us have—and passing it down).

Darity has a pretty grim view of his profession. The dramatic changes that Heather Boushey described above have not, to Darity, extended to the profession's treatment of race. In fact, he asserted to me that to this day the top economics journals publish papers that traffic in stereotypes about Black people's aberrant behavior. He said it was "very difficult" to publish on race in the top peer-reviewed journals "unless you do research that says that the kinds of inequalities that we observe are due to dysfunctional behavior on the part of Black people." He added, "There is still research that's published in the economics journals that is predicated on some forms of genetic determinism of disparities, not only within a country, but across countries."

Darity also offered an interesting critique of Becker's work on discrimination, of which he's not a fan. "The big problem with the Becker model is that ultimately it takes the position that discrimination cannot be a persistent phenomenon in competitive markets," Darity said. He explained that according to Becker if one group of workers is being paid lower wages but has roughly the same level of productivity as the other group, some employers will hire those workers, and over time the wage differential will be eliminated. In other words, some employers will choose profits over prejudice, and this will lift the wages of the out-group. But to Darity, life doesn't work that way. "Empirical research indicates pretty strongly that discrimination continues to be pervasive, especially in employment," he told me.

Darity has focused his recent work on reparations, the compensation of today's Black Americans for government-sanctioned discrimination in the past. With A. Kirsten Mullen, he is the co-author of the 2020 book *From Here to Equality: Reparations for Black Americans in the Twenty-First Century*. Writing that the racial wealth gap is *"the most robust indicator of the cumulative economic effects of white supremacy in the United States"* (their italics), they argue that Black Americans who can prove that they had at least one ancestor held in slavery should be entitled to restitution. They summarize the existing literature on how reparations might be structured, and they conclude with a call for payments in the range of $15 to $20 trillion to be made over a period of several years.

Our present-day Congress is highly unlikely to embrace such an idea, but that hardly means that people shouldn't press for it. The wealth gap is an extremely serious problem that has gotten more attention in recent years, and given the history of racial discrimination in this country (and the present reality of it, especially with respect to housing), some kind of repayment scheme is justified. Darity is also associated, along with Darrick Hamilton of the New School, another prominent African American economist, with the idea of baby bonds—giving every newborn American child $1,000 at birth and up to $2,000 per year through age eighteen, with the highest amounts going to the lowest-income children. This would be a race-neutral and universal policy, but it would obviously benefit poorer children more. Hamilton put it this way in an interview: "Baby bonds offer you a chip that helps you play the game of capitalism. It affords you the ability to get into the market. So baby bonds are a birthright to capital that ensures that everybody at birth has some access to capital. It fits into my larger nomenclature of making sure that people have the necessary goods and services so that they can have authentic agency." That birthright to capital, Hamilton argues, would go a long way toward narrowing the racial wealth gap. Incidentally, Hamilton, too, takes a starkly negative view of the economics profession. He tied the lack of diversity within the profession to the substance of how race is often discussed in economics: "Compared to other social sciences, economics lags far behind, and they're not bastions of equality either. And I think that part of the lagging has to do with the rhetoric of the profession. The way in which economics explains inequality, particularly along racial lines, often is reduced to some human capital deficit."

It's now a given in liberal politics in ways it wasn't even a few years ago that racial equity must be built into economic policy. I've noticed this change personally as a writer and especially as an editor. A few years ago, if one were writing about certain programs of the New Deal, it was enough to throw in one "to be sure" paragraph noting that these programs weren't available to Black people, and that was bad. In more recent years, though, systemic racism in the United States has come under much more thoroughgoing scrutiny.

Three recent books—none of them by economists, incidentally—have been particularly important to this shift. I mentioned two of them earlier. The first is the journalist Richard Rothstein's 2017 *The Color of Law*, which devastatingly lays bare how the federal government—mostly Democrats and liberals—facilitated discrimination in the residential housing market for decades by allowing developers and lenders to bar Black families from home ownership. Rothstein noted that while "most of these policies are now off the books, they have never been remedied and their effects endure." Heather McGhee's 2021 *The Sum of Us* does a brilliant job of showing how racism imposes costs not just on people facing discrimination but on society as a whole. It's both a personal story (she traveled across the country interviewing people) and a work of deep policy analysis. Finally, *The Whiteness of Wealth*, also from 2021, by the tax law professor Dorothy Brown, shows in unrelenting detail how the tax code is in effect a tool of white supremacy—how loopholes and deductions that mostly benefit well-off white people didn't just happen but were in many cases litigated into being by wealthy whites. These books and many others have changed the conversation about racial economic equity.

More than ever, rendering economic justice to the middle class means doing so for women and people of color. By definition, around half the middle class is women, and about half the U.S. workforce was female before the pandemic (it has probably dropped a bit). The middle class is also racially diverse: roughly 59 percent white, 18 percent Latino, 12 percent Black, and 10 percent other. Diverse and broad-based prosperity is a goal of middle-out economics.

In sum, President Biden's progressive agenda didn't happen in a vacuum. Early on, he proclaimed advancing racial equity as one of the four core goals of his administration (along with tackling COVID, changing the economy, and addressing climate change). People debate how much progress the administration has made on that front, but that he has even identified it as a core problem is something that happened in part because writers and scholars like the ones cited in this chapter pushed these issues to the fore. This is how change happens—over years and years, and then, to those who haven't followed the story, suddenly.

CHAPTER SEVEN

How Politics Has Changed

●

THE OUTSIDE GAME: AFTER A TWENTY-YEAR DELAY, THE EXPLOSION

A little more on how change happens: Yes, it happens over years and years, but how, exactly? As I wrote in the last chapter, the academy and the thinkers within it play a role in making change. But then, and I'd say mostly, change happens through a complicated and often wary dance between activists and pragmatists; between outsiders and insiders; between those who take to the streets to demand change and those who carry those demands into the halls of power and negotiate change.

On the broad left side of the political spectrum, where I sit, I would call these two groups "leftists" and "liberals." Others will use other labels. The mainstream media tend to label Congresswoman Alexandria Ocasio-Cortez and her progressive cohort the "liberal wing" of the Democratic Party, but that has always felt off to me. True, Ocasio-Cortez has opted to enter the halls of power, to battle from within, but there is an insurgent quality to her politics and that of the

Squad that simply isn't there for the vast majority of liberals in Congress (their vote against the bipartisan infrastructure bill in November 2021—the wrong vote, in my view—is a case in point). She's there to fight the powers that be, including the leading Democrats when necessary.

And that, to me, makes AOC more of a leftist than a liberal. What are the differences? Leftists want bolder and faster change, while liberals tend to accept that change happens gradually and incrementally. Whether the issue is economic justice or civil rights or climate change, leftists want more and have a systemic critique of society that liberals share only up to a point. That's a constant, but it reflects, I think, a broader point having to do with their attitudes toward power. If I may phrase it as a kind of apothegm, liberals believe that power is something to be shaped, and leftists see it as something to be fought. All the particular policy differences, to my mind, flow from those different attitudes toward power. These differences, I believe, are to some extent pre-ideological; that is, they originate not in developing an intellectual analysis of the world and its power relationships (that comes later, in college or grad school) but in people's temperamental and emotional predisposition. Some people are more comfortable, feel more vital, out in the streets marching, and other people feel more at home in a conference room striking the compromise that becomes written law.

If change is to be made, the world needs both types. When I call AOC a leftist, I mean that in no sense pejoratively, as I know some will take it. The history of the left in this country is one of much honor and accomplishment. Sure, not entirely: there were Soviet fellow travelers in the 1930s, extremist Maoist sects in the 1960s; today, there are some tendencies on the far left that think of liberalism as a bigger enemy of progress than conservatism, which is historically wrong and destructive of coalition building. And on international affairs, there is a deeply frustrating left that blames everything on America, as if no one else in the world—not even Vladimir Putin—had any agency or power. But the vast majority of left-wing activism since the Industrial Revolution has been courageous and constructive: on behalf of trade unions, working men and women, African Americans, women, poor people, immigrants. The only people who gave a damn about Black sharecroppers in the 1930s were American communists, who organized the Sharecroppers' Union, which was a great victory. Of course they also took their marching orders from Stalin, especially on foreign policy and with respect to his endorsement of the "popular front" in 1935. Life is complicated. But very little would have changed in this country without the demands of impatient radicals.

At the same time, very little would have changed without the more mainstream liberals who work the system—who, for example, earn the law degrees and write the legislation that makes the change real. No one ever makes a movie about the person who, after hours invested in convincing skeptics, finally gets subparagraph 83(b)4(F) inserted into a bill, but sometimes subparagraph 83(b)4(F) makes all the difference. Every progressive law that is passed requires a small army of experts to craft its specifics and sweat over its implementation, and despite the reputations of bureaucrats most of them carry out these tasks with meticulous care and perform their jobs very well (no one knows this because people know only what they read, and no newspaper will ever carry the headline "Things Running Beautifully at Interior Department"). I hate the fact that these people are overlooked in our political culture. Michael Lewis's *Fifth Risk* was a brilliant intervention in this area that showed readers that government employees actually do good and important things, and Timothy Noah did a big *New Republic* cover story defending and celebrating the work of career bureaucrats, but these are exceptions to a very lazy rule.

As praiseworthy as these people are, it is clear that change *starts* with activists. Their degree of success depends on a lot of factors, most of them out of the activists' control. Does some tragedy occur that makes reform possible, the way the Triangle Shirtwaist Factory fire made labor reform possible? There are many factors like this. One of the most important has to do with which party is in power. This goes a long way toward determining what activists do. In general, it's fair to say that when a Republican administration is in office, activists on the left are mostly playing defense, fighting the administration's plans: against the Iraq War, against the push to privatize Social Security. But during the time of a Democratic administration, activists play offense: now is the chance to get something passed, they reason, and to push the administration toward boldness. And so, as is often said on the broad left, "space opens up" for activism during Democratic administrations that just isn't there during Republican ones. This is what happened with respect to health care early in the Obama administration. Foundations put millions of dollars into the goal of passing major health-care reform. The most prominent effort was led by the advocacy group HCAN (Health Care for America Now, pronounced AITCH-can), which spent $40 million ($26.5 million of it supplied by the Atlantic Philanthropies, a private foundation that shuttered in 2020), most of it on field organizing to build support for reform. A multitude of grassroots organizations sprang up to push the administration to embrace single-payer health care (a government-run system), or at least to include in its proposal a public option (a government-run provider as an alternative to private insurers). That neither of those was included in the final bill was definitely frustrating to activists, but most everyone agreed that passing something was an accomplishment.

Health care is a good example of the space-opening-up model of activism. There were other fronts in those early Obama years, though, where activists felt little or no space opening up. The most frustrating of these was economics, where activists wanted a far different approach from the one Obama delivered (the failure to prosecute the Wall Street banks, which I discussed in chapter 4; an inadequate response to the foreclosure crisis; the generally nonconfrontational rhetorical stance toward large capital that Obama adopted, with occasional exceptions). Combine this with the grim economic reality of the day—by mid-2010, the recession had killed off nearly eight million jobs—and there was much unhappiness, especially among the young.

It's worth thinking for a moment about the perspective of young people in the Obama years. Say you were born in 1990. As a child, you would have experienced the tech-driven economic boom, so that's to the good. But everything else you watched unfold in the realm of politics would have been negative. The culture wars. The Clinton sex scandals. The contested 2000 election. The 9/11 attacks. The two wars we declared afterward and their associated horrors (Abu Ghraib, CIA torture). The near collapse of the world economy. Then Obama was elected, and maybe you felt a jolt of optimism. But things didn't change quite as much as you'd hoped. On top of all that, you watched as our politics became more and more polarized. I, too, came of age in a time of serial horrors—war, riots, assassinations, stagflation. But at least in my day, polarization wasn't a factor. The political system worked fairly well. Those glorious thirty years of chapter 1 lasted into my teens. But if you were born in 1990, your idea of the United States of America was of a country that started needless and costly wars, that worshipped excessive wealth and the free market, and that had a government that was fundamentally dysfunctional. Small wonder socialism is popular among the young.

The frustration on the left about Obama's reluctance to go after the people who gave us the meltdown was deep and real, but most Democratic honchos didn't take their displeasure seriously. The left hadn't mattered much as a political force within the Democratic Party since the early 1970s. Jesse Jackson's presidential campaigns in the 1980s were important in the sense that Jackson reminded the party of its class obligations to working and poor people; they also pointed to a fairly sizable constituency for progressive policies. But inside the Democratic tent, the 1980s was far better known as the decade of the avowedly centrist Democratic Leadership Council and of the then congressman Tony Coelho's cementing of party ties to big-money donors. There had been a strong left in the 1930s during the New Deal, and again in the 1960s; so it was time in the 1990s, according to the cycles of history, for a left to emerge. But it never happened. The left had very little influence in the Clinton years. This continued into the Obama era, and it might have remained so had not an Estonian-by-way-of-Canada left-wing provocateur had an idea. Kalle Lasn, a sixty-nine-year-old filmmaker, had co-founded the anti-consumerist magazine *Adbusters* back in 1989. Sometime in the summer of 2011, *Adbusters* issued a call for people to "flood into lower Manhattan, set up tents, kitchens, peaceful barricades and occupy Wall Street for a few months." The date chosen was September 17, which is Constitution Day in the United States, a fact known to about 1 percent of the American population (perhaps the Canadian *Adbusters* staff thought the date had more significance to Americans than it does). In any event, an estimated thousand or so people came that first day. The pithy and effective catchphrase "We are the 99%" had actually debuted a few weeks before when a blog under that name was launched, encouraging posts from readers about the manifold ways in which said 99 percent were getting the economic shaft. By October, Occupy demonstrations had spread to other cities. On October 13, the word was passed in lower Manhattan's Zuccotti Park that the property's owner, Brookfield Properties, planned to clean and perform maintenance the next day, and that protesters, hundreds now encamped on a permanent basis, would have to leave. The protesters cleaned up the park themselves, an act of civic munificence not normally associated with protesters. Brookfield canceled the cleaning. The 99 percent won one.

The protests petered out after a couple of months, with occasional "reoccupations." At the time, Occupy was broadly judged a failure. It was by design a bit on the anarchic side: it was leaderless, and the movement issued no demands, which was odd. Andrew Ross Sorkin, the *New York Times* business columnist, wrote on the one-year anniversary of the movement that Occupy "will be an asterisk in the history books, if it gets mentioned at all." A decade-plus later, though, I think things look different. Occupy was the first in a series of protests—against the Keystone XL Pipeline; against policing in the wake of the 2014 shooting of Michael Brown in Ferguson, Missouri—that drew many thousands and have had a big impact on policy. President Biden canceled the Keystone pipeline. Consciousness about police shootings of Black Americans is higher than ever, and Congress actually passed a decent criminal justice reform bill on a bipartisan basis that Donald Trump signed. And the economic grievances that Occupy highlighted are still driving the Biden agenda. Another important effort of the 2010s was the Fight for $15 movement, dedicated to a $15 minimum wage. It got started in November 2012 when a hundred or so fast-food workers in Manhattan walked off their jobs at McDonald's, Pizza Hut, KFC, and the like. Over the next few years, coordinated nationwide one-day strikes were held in cities across the country. While there's been no change in the federal minimum wage, states and cities all over the country have raised their minimums, and more and more large employers are doing so of their own volition, no doubt partly in response to this movement. The National Employment Law Project estimates that Fight for $15 has helped win $150 billion in raises for twenty-six million workers. The Sunrise Movement, which grew out of meetings starting in 2015 by young activists seeking an aggressive response to climate change and incorporated itself two years later, would have been considered too left-wing by most Democrats a generation ago, but in 2020 sixteen of the Democrats running for president endorsed its Green New Deal.

It's probably not a coincidence that all these movements took shape during the Obama years. True, they all came into being for different reasons. Occupy was a reaction to the Great Recession and Obama not being more aggressively populist. Black Lives Matter was formed in response to the acquittal of George Zimmerman in the shooting death of Trayvon Martin in 2012 and then grew after the Michael Brown shooting and other tragedies. The Fight for $15 was rooted in frustration that the federal minimum wage hadn't been raised in so long. But the fact of a Democratic administration gave these movements room to grow, because if there had been a Republican administration, most activist energy would have been directed at opposing the GOP agenda. With a Democratic administration, activists on the left had room to make demands. And even though they didn't win every fight in Congress, they shifted politics considerably. The cycle of history got delayed by twenty years, but once the left reasserted itself, it exploded.

THE INSIDE GAME: HOW ELIZABETH WARREN CHANGED THE DEMOCRATIC PARTY

The story, a famous part of the lore of Elizabeth Warren's rise, goes that when Harry Reid called her to ask her to lead the commission that oversaw the spending of the Troubled Asset Relief Program (TARP) money in 2008, she said, "Who?" and he had to explain that he was the Senate majority leader. The tale somewhat overstates the extent to which Warren was a political naïf. Back in the 1990s, after she had already made a name for herself as a specialist in bankruptcy law, she was appointed a top staffer to the National Bankruptcy Review Commission, named by President Clinton and congressional leaders. But the story does get at something about her personality: she knew the world of politics, but she wasn't overly impressed by it.

When Warren first decided to specialize in bankruptcy law, according to the journalist Ryan Grim in his book *We've Got People*, a thorough account of the rise of this new left, she was fairly conservative, and she "approached the research from a right-wing angle, expecting to prove that people filing for bankruptcy were trying to bilk the system." But burrowing into the specifics made her see that banks were penalizing working people confronted with emergencies; it changed her approach to bankruptcy law, and to politics. She made her national mark as that TARP overseer, becoming famous for grilling Obama's Treasury secretary, Tim Geithner, on matters like why the administration hadn't insisted on new leadership at some of the big banks that made the mess.

This is in a sense forgotten history now because of the way Bernie Sanders thundered into the national picture in 2016 and became the über-hero of the left, followed by AOC and the Squad after the 2018 election. But Warren was among the first national political figures to point Democratic politics in a new, more economically populist direction. The first augury that there was room in the high levels of government for people with a decidedly non-neoliberal economic worldview (notably on trade) appeared when Sherrod Brown won his first Senate race in Ohio in 2006. Brown, a congressman whose politics were recognizably to the left of your typical House Democrat, bested the two-term GOP incumbent Mike DeWine by twelve points in a state that went twice for George W. Bush. In 2012, conservative PACs put a target on him, perhaps more than any other incumbent Democratic senator, and he still won by seven points. He was, and remains, one of the most important economic spokespeople in the Democratic Party.

But Brown didn't barrel into Washington quite the way Warren did. After she finished tussling with Geithner, she aggressively lobbied Congress and the Obama administration (including one frosty hour-long meeting with Obama himself) to make sure that the Dodd-Frank financial reform bill included her pet idea of the Consumer Financial Protection Bureau, which she had first promoted in the journal *Democracy* in 2007 (note: before I became editor). When that became law, and she was denied the job of being its first director (Republican senators agreed not to block it as long as Obama did not name Warren to run it), her national profile was high enough that a political future began to feel more natural. And it just so happened that in her adopted home state of Massachusetts, Democrats were desperate for Warren to reclaim Ted Kennedy's Senate seat and start leading the party to progressive Valhalla.

It was early in that campaign, in September 2011, that she spoke the words that made her a first-rank star, delivered to a living room full of supporters and caught on a video that instantly went viral:

> There is nobody in this country who got rich on his own. Nobody. You built a factory out there? Good for you. But I want to be clear. You moved your goods to market on the roads the rest of us paid for. You hired workers the rest of us paid to educate. You were safe in your factory because of police forces and fire forces that the rest of us paid for. You didn't have to worry that marauding bands would come and seize everything at your factory and hire someone to protect against this because of the work that the rest of us did. Now look, you built a factory and it turned into something terrific, or a great idea? God bless! Keep a big hunk of it. But part of the underlying social contract is you take a hunk of that and pay forward for the next kid who comes along.

I remember well the electric reaction to that among both mainstream liberals and people on the left. Here was someone who, in a colloquial and understandable way, expressed the core principle of a liberal economic philosophy about the common good that so many Democrats seemed afraid to verbalize.

I pause here to emphasize an important point about political rhetoric, and how powerfully it defines the way most of us think about our leaders. It's also, often, a key dividing line between liberals and leftists. Warren is not someone I would call a leftist. In July 2018, as she contemplated her presidential run, she told the New England Council, a nonpartisan regional alliance of businesses and other organizations, that she was "a capitalist to my bones." She's a liberal. But so is her Senate colleague Michael Bennet of Colorado. Bennet, as he was preparing to run for president, put together a PowerPoint presentation about what had happened to the American economy over the previous four decades, which he once shared with me. Warren would have agreed with it close to 100 percent. Yet their approaches to politics are different enough that in mainstream press shorthand Warren is always lumped with Sanders ("the Sanders-Warren wing of the party") while Bennet is called a moderate.

Why are they typically identified as being in opposite camps? Certainly they take different positions with regard to solutions even when their analyses of what's gone wrong may be similar. But the answer also has to do with rhetoric—specifically, with a willingness to talk smack on the rich and on corporate America. Only a handful of Democrats (plus Sanders, who isn't a Democrat) are willing to do this. In fact, Democrats have always been careful about this. People on the left frequently invoke the famous line from FDR's October 1936 campaign speech laying out the second New Deal, the phrase that ends this little section:

> We had to struggle with the old enemies of peace—
> business and financial monopoly, speculation, reck-
> less banking, class antagonism, sectionalism, war
> profiteering. They had begun to consider the gov-

ernment of the United States as a mere appendage to their own affairs. We know now that government by organized money is just as dangerous as Government by organized mob. Never before in all our history have these forces been so united against one candidate as they stand today. They are unanimous in their hate for me—and I welcome their hatred.

One will often see pundits (including myself) yearn for Democrats to talk like that. But not many of them do. Even FDR didn't as often as that famous quotation might suggest. He spoke regularly of the "common man" and the "forgotten man," but that kind of rhetoric is aspirational. It's positive, uplifting, and it's not threatening to anyone in the sense that it never states outright that for the forgotten man to gain, the rich capitalist has to lose something. All Democrats do aspirational. Not many do confrontational: outright telling the overclass that they're going to have to pay. As Faiz Shakir, Bernie Sanders's 2020 campaign manager, with a long career of working for top Democrats like Harry Reid and Nancy Pelosi, put it to me in an interview, "Biden carrying out maybe the same paid leave policy as Bernie would is only half the battle. You're also trying to let people know that you're going to take people on in order to do it. . . . There's something to the way Elizabeth Warren and Bernie Sanders go about their politics, right? Identifying a Wells Fargo CEO, or Elon Musk or Jeff Bezos, or whoever it might be, saying, 'Hey, you know, this is a symbol, this is an emblem of what we're up against.' "

Joe Biden, who rarely if ever did it as senator or vice president, does a fair amount of it as president, maybe not with respect to specific individuals, but certainly with respect to saying that corporations and the rich have to pay more.

But he's an exception. Since the 1990s and the rise of the New Democrats, very few Democrats speak that way. A big part of the reason for this was the corporate campaign donations on which the party became so dependent once Senate campaigns started costing in the tens of millions of dollars. When you go fishing often enough in Manhattan, Beverly Hills, Silicon Valley, Aspen, and Jackson Hole, you learn pretty quickly which lures attract and repel.

So Democrats tread carefully on these grounds. But Warren did not. She didn't care if she offended corporate donors. Indeed she seemed to take delight in it. And *that* is what made her a star. Warren jolted the party. She communicated to a hungry rank and file that there were still Democrats who could talk in the old class warfare terms (Sherrod Brown also did it sometimes, in addition to a handful of House members in safe liberal districts with a taste for populism). So people watched her closely when she entered the Senate in 2013. She made it known to Harry Reid that she wanted a spot on the Banking Committee. The banks made it known to Harry Reid that he could put anyone except Elizabeth Warren on the Banking Committee. Harry Reid put her on the Banking Committee.

All this predates what has come to be called the "resurgent left." The left seemed no more relevant in Democratic politics in 2013 than it had been in 2009, when Obama's chief of staff, Rahm Emanuel, spoke contemptuously of the free-spending "libtards" pushing the administration toward perceived disaster. At the same time, though, and with the Democratic president safely reelected, little auguries, suggestions that rank-and-file progressives were dissatisfied with the status quo and were going to make noise about it, were beginning to appear. In late 2013, Obama was mulling a new Fed chair. It came down to Larry Summers, Janet Yellen, and the former Fed official Donald Kohn. Summers had the inside track for a job he was known to hunger for. Two years earlier this quintessential Democratic neoliberal would likely have been waved through. But now things were different. There was a major anti-Summers grassroots mobilization, with petitions from MoveOn and other such groups, and this time those groups had a real voice in the halls of power: Warren, along with Brown and Jeff Merkley of Oregon, all sat on the Banking Committee, which would vote on a Fed chair nomination. They announced they'd oppose Summers, which meant Obama would have to go through the embarrassment of relying on Republican support to get Summers through. Summers withdrew, and Yellen, the activists' choice, got the job.

Another sign of an aborning left, and specifically of Warren's power, occurred in late 2014 when Obama nominated Antonio Weiss to be an undersecretary in the Treasury Department. Weiss had good progressive credentials both politically and culturally; he'd stepped in to back *The Paris Review*, the esteemed literary quarterly started by George Plimpton, in the period of uncertainty after Plimpton's death. His beneficence wasn't the problem. His fortune was. He was a partner at Lazard, the investment bank, which specialized in corporate inversions, whereby an American corporation buys a foreign corporation, then declares itself foreign to avoid U.S. taxes. Warren announced her opposition to Weiss and made Lazard's role in these inversions a huge issue, highlighting Burger King's purchase of the Canadian Tim Hortons chain, on which Lazard, and Weiss, advised. The base mobilized. Importantly, in that November's midterms, Republicans captured the Senate, meaning they'd be gunning to water down the Dodd-Frank financial regulation bill. Warren tied this grim new reality to Weiss's nomination, saying that Treasury needed people whose credentials did not include helping American corporations dodge taxes. "Enough is enough with Wall Street insiders getting key position after key position and the kind of cronyism we have seen in the executive branch," she said that December. In January 2015, Weiss withdrew. He got a consolation job that didn't require Senate confirmation. Score another victory for Elizabeth Warren.

SANDERS AND AOC:
THE DEMOCRATS MOVE LEFT–TO A POINT

Right before Antonio Weiss withdrew his nomination, Warren bluntly told the editors of *Fortune* magazine, "No. I'm not running for president." Left progressives were desperate for someone to challenge Clinton. Everyone knew she'd be the nominee, but the lack of enthusiasm on the left for Clinton was palpable, and activists wanted someone to say the things the cautious Clinton wouldn't say. By April, Bernie Sanders stepped in. He'd been mulling it for a year or more. He probably would have deferred to Warren, but when she demurred, the slot opened up. Bill Press, the radio host and former chair of the California Democratic Party, was among those advising Sanders to get in. "It's obviously a real uphill battle—you're going to be up against the biggest political machine in the country, and one of the best and most experienced people in the country, Hillary Clinton . . . it's a way, way, way long shot, but it's not crazy," he told C-SPAN in early 2016. Sanders, for his part, told the Associated Press at the time of his announcement, "People should not underestimate me."

It's not my purpose here to repeat the blow by blow of the acrimonious Clinton-Sanders primary. That's been done thoroughly in other books. My point here is to discuss how Sanders shifted the political discourse, especially on economic policy. That could only have happened through the vehicle of a presidential campaign. As Press said in that same interview, "You can be a senator and you can yap and yap and give speeches, and, you know, it's just another senator. If you're a presidential candidate, there's some aura about that that people listen." And this much has to be acknowledged, even by his critics, of whom I was one in 2016 (much less so in 2020): He rose to his historical occasion. Not everybody can do that. Presidential primaries are littered with the political corpses of people who, for whatever reason, just couldn't pull it off with the unremitting national spotlight shining on them. Sanders did pull it off. He raised tens of millions, which took him and his team completely by surprise. He drew crowds of twenty thousand and thirty thousand. He said pretty much the same things he'd been saying for forty years, allowing for the addition of certain new issues like climate change. He did not have a politician's charisma in the conventional sense: he couldn't tell a joke or be self-deprecating to save his life. I'll never forget when a bird landed on his lectern during a March 2016 rally and stayed there for about twenty seconds. For those seconds, he couldn't think of anything witty or extemporaneous to say. It didn't matter. After the bird left, he told the crowd solemnly that the bird was "a dove, asking us for world peace. No more wars." The crowd was rapturous.

What he did have was the authenticity of consistency. On the one hand, saying basically the same things for forty years can mean that a person isn't capable of growing and learning. On the other, given that most politicians "grow" and "learn" in the direction of their big donors, Sanders's sameness was evidence of his incorruptibility. His provenance also figures into his authenticity, a fact that isn't often mentioned in discussions of his belief system. He represents probably the only state in the country where a politician can take his positions without fear of penalty. There are no large corporations in Vermont. The state has one Fortune 1,000 company, an insurance business. Not a single billionaire lives there. No investment banks are based there. And so on. The transition of this historically moderate Republican state— the first Democratic Vermonter ever elected to the Senate was its current senior senator, Pat Leahy, in 1974—into a major lefty redoubt has made the place uniquely hospitable to one with Sanders's views.

Still, he showed in 2015 and 2016 that his views resonated far beyond Vermont. And his rhetoric. Did Sanders ever have enemies! He named them over and over and over. The big banks, the corporations, the billionaires, the corrupters of the political system—they were all going to be set straight when he became president. What a contrast he made to Clinton. When he raised the matter of her paid speeches to Goldman Sachs, it seemed to encapsulate everything that separated 1990s-style mainstream liberalism from the new leftism. This is another key dividing line between the two camps today: attitudes toward corporate power. Clinton took the traditional mainstream liberal view that Goldman is a legitimate stakeholder in economic debates. But not only would Goldman Sachs never have invited Sanders to give a speech; if somehow it did, he would have operatically refused.

I admit that I didn't recognize the staying power of what Sanders was building in 2016. I failed to see that the anger was as broad and as deep as it was. I was for Clinton. I'd known her for a long time, since 1999, when I started covering her 2000 Senate run; she had moved left on some important matters, notably her support for a financial transactions tax, which indicated a willingness to make some enemies among a group she'd been cozy with. And mostly I thought it would be great if the United States followed the election of its first Black president by elevating its first woman. Beyond all that, I thought she was clearly the more electable of the two. She lost, of course, although she won the popular vote, so I ended up being wrong about her electability. I also underestimated the right's success at getting a big chunk of America to hate her (and, of course, she made her own mistakes; and, of course, there was James Comey). But I still think Sanders could not have won a presidential election. His main electoral problem was his lack of support among Black voters above thirty. A Democratic nominee can't win without high levels of Black turnout. Sanders had fine credentials in terms of his civil rights positions, but coming from such a white state, he never had to build the relationships senators from more diverse states did—those years of going to Black churches, working with local civil rights leaders after a police shooting, and more. Also, his reach into the white working class was limited. So was Clinton's, and so was Joe Biden's in 2020, but according to Nate Silver, Sanders benefited heavily in several primaries from the votes of "Never Hillary" voters, many of whom were Republicans and independents voting in open primaries; it's doubtful many of these voters would have gone for Sanders over Trump. Finally and most important, I think a Sanders candidacy would have tied the party in knots. Democratic House and Senate candidates in swing districts and states would have been asked every day: Do you support Bernie Sanders? Do you support Medicare for All? The complete elimination of private insurance companies? Are you for socialism? Do you back a total ban on fracking? And so on. For an adroit politician, these aren't terribly hard

questions. But most politicians aren't that adroit in the pressure cooker of a campaign when they're being defined by
the other side's thirty-second attack ads. These candidates
would have been on the defensive, and it would have been
exactly the kind of defensiveness that Donald Trump would
have known how to exploit to drive the narrative. I suspect
that by November 2016 the Democratic Party would have
been bitterly divided.

Sanders did not become the nominee, but there's no
doubt about how dramatically he changed our economic
conversation, especially around the $15 minimum wage and
the idea that health care is not a privilege of employment
but a right that inheres in the mere fact of being alive. And
in the wake of Sanders's 2016 performance, groups sprang
up to influence congressional elections that were decidedly
on the antiliberal left—something not seen, I don't think,
in my lifetime. Justice Democrats. Brand New Congress.
Our Revolution, which grew directly from Sanders's campaign. Justice Democrats started as an effort to elect many
progressives to the House, but by crunch time in 2018, as
Ryan Grim writes in his book, it "converted itself . . . into
a weapon wielded solely" on behalf of one candidate, Alexandria Ocasio-Cortez, the next breakout figure in the left's
ascent.

In high school, Ocasio-Cortez finished a very impressive second in an international science fair. At Boston University, she graduated cum laude in 2011. But she assumed
no particularly aggressive career path out of college. She
volunteered for the Sanders campaign in 2016. In 2017,
she decided that she would challenge the incumbent congressman Joe Crowley of Queens in a district that included
parts of Queens and the Bronx, where she lived. Crowley
was a powerful member of Congress, but for local purposes

he was far more importantly the chairman of the Queens County Democratic Party. Long past the time when most of the old urban Irish-dominated political machines had withered away, the Queens machine remained powerful, controlling endorsements, cautiously bringing Blacks and other groups into a share of power provided they were loyal to the machine, guarding against insurgencies. Crowley was first elected to the state assembly in 1986. He got to Congress in 1999. He'd faced his last primary challenge, before Ocasio-Cortez in 2018, in 2004.

She thumped him, 57 to 43 percent. She just outworked him, caught him asleep at the wheel, completely unalert to the existence of this new insurgent infrastructure that powered her win. The three other insurgents who with AOC became known as the Squad also won that year: Ayanna Pressley of Massachusetts and two Muslim women, Rashida Tlaib of Michigan and Ilhan Omar of Minnesota (the latter representing, interestingly, one of the most storied Jewish districts in the country, an area that produced Al Franken, Tom Friedman, Norm Ornstein, and the Coen brothers). A couple more joined their ranks in 2020: Cori Bush of Missouri and Jamaal Bowman of New York. The House Progressive Caucus had mushroomed to ninety-five members by 2021, while the centrist Blue Dog Coalition had shrunk from nearly sixty members in 2010 to just nineteen by 2021. Those numbers are a bit deceptive. With respect to the Blue Dogs, they were decimated in the 2010 midterms, when they lost about twenty-five seats, so their losses since 2011 have been incremental; still, they're a small fraction of the Democratic caucus, and given the fact that it's mostly GOP state legislatures drawing districts in swing states, there's only so much room for growth. The Progressive Caucus's far more impressive number comes with the asterisk that a number of members of that caucus are not insurgents of any sort but are mainstream liberals completely loyal to Nancy Pelosi who for reasons of local politics think it wise to be affiliated with the caucus (Carolyn Maloney, Jerrold Nadler, Rosa DeLauro, and many veterans like them). Still, the numbers are the numbers. It's pretty clear which direction the wind is blowing.

It will be interesting to see, in future elections, how left insurgent candidates fare and just how many can win congressional seats. The record is mixed. So far, for a candidate of this profile to win, a certain combination of factors has been required: an energetic and charismatic candidate; an open seat or an aging incumbent who quit paying attention and didn't take a primary challenge seriously (as well as AOC, this applies to Pressley, Omar, Bush, and Bowman); a heavily Democratic district (through 2020, Justice Democrats had not flipped a seat from red to blue); and within that category, a certain *kind* of district, with not just a large population of people of color but a large population of *young* people of color. Outside those kinds of districts, such candidates have had more difficulty. For example, in Ohio's Eleventh District, which takes in downtown Cleveland but runs through some exurbs down to Akron, the more mainstream Shontel Brown defeated Sanders firebrand Nina Turner not once but twice, in 2021 and 2022. The first race was close-ish; the second was not. And in Nebraska's Second, a left-leaning Democrat lost narrowly to the Republican in 2018 but by a larger margin in 2020.

In addition to that, in 2020, there were eight straight-up general election contests between mainstream liberals and left insurgents—in other words, eight direct test cases of which platform had more appeal in an overwhelmingly Democratic district. How did this happen? Because two states, California and Washington, have so-called jungle primaries, where every candidate runs in one primary irrespective of party, and the top two vote getters face off in the general, setting up the possibility that two members of the same party can square off in the general. This happened in seven different California districts. The more mainstream candidate won six of those races, in most cases handily: one was single digits, while the other five ranged from fourteen to fifty-six percentage points (the fifty-six was Speaker Pelosi). In the one race won by a Sanders-endorsed candidate, the opponent didn't appear to run an active campaign, failing, for example, to respond to a local newspaper's request "seeking information and a photo." Meanwhile, in the single Washington district, the more mainstream candidate won by fifteen points.

The win by Eric Adams in the New York City mayoral primary in 2021—Adams unabashedly emphasized curtailing crime rather than defunding the police—and the defeat of left-leaning candidates who ran on police defunding in even very liberal Seattle suggests certain limits to how left Democratic voters are prepared to go. In some contested congressional primaries that took place in 2022 as this book was going to press, more mainstream Democrats defeated left challengers in North Carolina, Nebraska, and Kentucky. At the same time, progressive insurgents beat a couple well-financed moderate incumbents or narrowly won some open seats in districts that do not fit the AOC-district profile, districts that are more swing-ish. If these candidates can win in November, the left will have evidence with which to rebut the longstanding "electability" arguments of centrists. If they lose, they'll have trouble making that case.

For all that, two points are important and true. One, while the Democratic electorate as a whole prefers more mainstream liberal candidates, on an issue-by-issue basis that electorate is well to the left of where it was a generation ago. Consider these numbers from Pew: In 2000, 28 percent of Democrats identified as liberal. By 2018, that was up to 46 percent. The percentage identifying as moderates dropped from 44 to 37 percent, and those calling themselves conservative dropped from 23 to 15 percent. That's a real shift. The Democratic rank and file, I should note, is still far less ideological than the Republican rank and file, Pew found. Among Republicans, 68 percent said they were conservative, 27 percent moderate, and 4 percent liberal (those 31 percent don't have much, if any, representation in Congress these days). But it's a very different Democratic base now from the one that almost elected Al Gore: younger, more racially diverse, more educated, far more left leaning on cultural issues, more skeptical of the market economy, and more geographically concentrated in cities, select suburbs, and university towns.

The second point is that congressional Democrats, reflecting this change in the electorate, are to the left of where they were during, say, the George W. Bush years. This is partly because, as I noted above, many moderates got wiped out in 2010, and they've never really come back from that. In addition to that, some suburbs that in prior eras would barely have elected Democrats, let alone progressive ones, have changed enough demographically that such outcomes are now possible. Most emblematic here is Orange County, California. For decades, it was one of the most reliably conservative counties in the country, and indeed one of the birthplaces of the modern right in the 1950s. It was represented largely by Republicans in Congress for most of its history. Today, of the seven congressional districts wholly or partly within Orange County, five are represented by Democrats, most of them quite liberal.

So the changes in the Democratic Party include but go well beyond the impact of Warren, Sanders, and Ocasio-Cortez. And more dramatic changes loom. Soon, the three House leaders—Pelosi, Steny Hoyer, and James Clyburn, all above eighty—will retire. It's very likely that the new leadership will be at least somewhat to their left, as will new committee chairs and so on. This doesn't mean the Democrats are going to become a left-wing party like Jeremy Corbyn's Labour Party was. This is a different country with a different (i.e., non-parliamentary) system. The Democrats can't hold a majority in the House without winning a number of purple districts. But it does mean that certain issue positions taken during the years of neoliberal, New Democrat hegemony are dead for the foreseeable future: free trade, banking deregulation, demands on poor people such as those made in 1990s welfare reform, and more.

Is all this movement entirely positive? Not necessarily. I think a taxation-financed system of public health care is the right way to go someday, for example, but the political reality is that we'll get there incrementally, and even when we do get there, it won't look like the Medicare for All discussed at the 2020 Democratic debates. Under currently existing Medicare, recipients pay various out-of-pocket costs, and they can still buy (and about 80 percent do) supplemental private insurance, so private insurers would still exist even if Medicare were expanded to all Americans. Taxes would be extremely high under any plan that was not offset by premiums, deductibles, and co-payments. Recall that Bernie Sanders's own state of Vermont, the most liberal state in the country, once tried to implement statewide Medicare for All and dropped it when it saw what the tax hikes would be.

Beyond this, it is important to note that the Democratic Party *does not support* Medicare for All. In the 2020 presidential election, Democratic primary voters had the chance to vote for four candidates who backed M4A: Sanders, Warren, Kamala Harris, and Julián Castro. They lost. The guy who supported more modest change won, by a lot.

Critics say the Democrats have moved too far left of the American people. On economic questions, I don't think it's true at all. Nearly all the elements of Joe Biden's Build Back Better plan polled quite well. Indeed, some of the most popular elements—expanding Medicare to include dental and vision coverage, for example, which polls through the roof—were dropped by Democrats in Congress out of fear of the price tag, which suggests that the broader public may be ready for economically populist initiatives that congressional Democrats don't yet have the gumption to undertake. Cultural issues are another matter. While cultural politics are largely outside the scope of this book, I will note that cultural elitism is a very real problem for Democrats, especially as our political divide becomes more and more defined by levels of education. The party has a dilemma here. Its leaders tend to be from elite universities and navy blue cities and states where listing one's preferred pronouns is something people do, while its rank and file is, as I noted above, pretty liberal (46 percent), but still with plenty of moderates and a respectable dollop of conservatives. Democrats can't even speak to their own base, let alone swing voters, with a blanket embrace of activists' positions on cultural leftism. But on economics, the polling data suggest that populist positions are winners.

FINALLY, THE PANDEMIC

The rise of the resurgent left, from Occupy to AOC, over the last decade is important. But there is no doubt that the main event that created space and support for new government interventions in the economy was the pandemic. The reason is simple: At a time of true crisis, people expect the government to do something. In fact, they know that it is *only* the government that can do something.

Even the Republicans recognized this. The pandemic was declared on March 11, 2020. Just sixteen days later, Congress passed the CARES Act, a $2.2 trillion stimulus bill to try to keep the economy from cratering too severely. The final version of the bill passed by voice vote in the House; one House Republican tried to demand a roll call vote, but his colleagues were having none of it. This was after the Senate passed it 96–0. It just goes to show: when there's a real crisis, everyone's a Keynesian. (That, and the fact that if it's a Republican president requesting the spending, it's allowed.)

The pandemic has changed our society and the world in so many different ways. Three are particularly germane to this story. First, it revealed more starkly than before the existing inadequacies and inequities in the American economy. It showed us how precarious life is for so many workers. It exposed our massive gaps in health-care coverage and the social safety net. It revealed the racial chasm that haunts the country in areas of health and income security and with respect to exposure to the virus itself. A Kaiser Family Foundation study in 2020 found the following hospitalization and death rates per 10,000 population for Black, Hispanic, and white Americans, respectively: Black, 24.6 and 5.6; Hispanic, 30.4 and 5.6; white, 7.4 and 2.3. I can't say that this new awareness has resulted in a sea change in American politics, but it has focused most of the Democratic Party on the idea that these disparities have to be addressed through policy.

The second change is that the pandemic has given workers more leverage than they had before. Millions of people left the workforce. That has meant fewer workers, which in turn means that employers have to compete for them. Interestingly, this has been more true for blue-collar workers than for white-collar. Some fast-food chains, struggling to hire enough people, started offering signing bonuses, education benefits, and other perks to get people to fill their jobs. A study by the Federal Reserve Bank of New York found that the "reservation wage," which is what economists call the lowest wage an unemployed person would be willing to accept for a given job, was 41 percent higher for people without a college degree in March 2021 than before the pandemic—from $43,405 to $61,483. That was actually more than the increase for college-educated workers, which was just 22 percent. A 2021 report from the Conference Board found that 49 percent of employers of "industry and manual service workers" said it was hard to retain workers, while only 28 percent of employers of office workers agreed.

This is all still shaking out as I write, but it could have profound economic consequences. Republicans and right-wing commentators worked furiously to establish it as conventional wisdom that all those "Democrat" relief payments (which were of course bipartisan as long as a Republican was president) were making Americans lazy and proving that certain people don't want to work for a living. But maybe people weren't being lazy at all. Maybe they were, in essence, on strike. Maybe, as David Autor wrote in that *Times* column I quoted in chapter 6, they decided that difficult, menial work just wasn't worth doing for $7.25 an hour. This has shifted some degree of political power from employers to workers, something that has been all too rare since the paradigm shift of the 1970s.

The third big change, and probably the one that mattered the most politically, happened within one man. If you look back over the way Joe Biden was covered in 2019, after he announced his presidential candidacy via a video built around criticism of Donald Trump's response to the 2017 white supremacist rally in Charlottesville, you will see that he was slotted as the candidate of "restoration." The video had some powerful rhetoric about Trump, direct and blunt; what it didn't have was rhetoric about the change he wanted to bring to America—a staple of Democratic campaigns since FDR. When he said in the video that "the core values of this nation, our standing in the world, our very democracy, everything that has made America America, is at stake," he seemed to be saying, "Let's just go back to what we were before Trump, and things will be okay." His plans were more incrementalist than those not only of Sanders and Warren but of most of the twenty candidates. On health care, for example, while six candidates backed some version of Medicare for All, Biden stuck with building on Obamacare by adding a public option. He took many opportunities to position himself as the Obama candidate: if you were happy with Obama, as the vast majority of Democrats were according to polls, you'll be fine with me.

Democratic voters weren't buying at first; after the disastrous false start that was Iowa, where officials couldn't manage to count the votes, Sanders won the first two contests. Then Biden carried South Carolina by a huge margin and won all the most important races in the March 3 Super Tuesday voting by large margins. That week, the grim new reality of the pandemic started to set in. I remember being at a small academic conference at Stanford that Wednesday and Thursday; the fifteen or so of us sat around a conference table during the day and went out to dinner at night as normal. But that Friday, as I was flying home, Stanford officials announced that in-person classes were canceled for the rest of the semester. The next Tuesday, March 10, Biden again cruised in a slew of primaries, crucially including Michigan, where Sanders had narrowly upset Clinton in 2016. The next day, March 11, the World Health Organization declared the pandemic.

I'm convinced that it was this cosmic timing—Biden securing his party's nomination at precisely the moment people started dying en masse and the economy began to collapse—that persuaded him that he had to be more ambitious. His campaign, via Ron Klain and Anita Dunn, began talking to Faiz Shakir and Jeff Weaver of Sanders world about how the two sides could cooperate; what pieces of the Sanders agenda Biden might be willing to adopt. He never embraced any Sanders positions outright, but he did announce his support for lowering Medicare eligibility to age sixty, a potentially important step toward Medicare for All, and he also unveiled a version of Warren's free-college plan (Biden's capped the "free" part for families earning under $125,000, whereas Warren's had no income limits). Biden's rhetorical change was even more striking: he began comparing what the country faced to the Great Depression, and his task to the one confronted by FDR in 1933. I quoted him in a *New York Review of Books* article I wrote that summer: "I think it may not dwarf, but eclipse what FDR faced. . . . We have an opportunity . . . to do so many things now to change some of the structural things that are wrong, some of the structural things we couldn't get anybody's attention on."

Then, in the wake of the murder of George Floyd by Minneapolis police, Biden doubled down. Not only was it now time to expand the social safety net and renew a commitment to public investment. It was now clear, he announced in a remarkable June 2 speech in Philadelphia, that "the moment has come to deal with systemic racism."

That summer, he began regularly using the now well-known phrase "Build Back Better," with its unmissable implication that he was aiming for far more than restoration. The four planks of Build Back Better were more boldly progressive than any presidential candidate in history (more than FDR, because he never addressed environmental and racial issues): (1) substantial commitments to investments in clean energy; (2) the same with regard to caregiving (child care, pre-K, and so on); (3) proposals to promote the manufacture and government purchase of products made in America; (4) efforts to address the racial wealth gap and other manifestations of systemic racism.

This turned decades of campaign conventional wisdom on its head. That wisdom had always said that candidates run to the left (or right) during the primary and tack toward the center in the general. But nearly as soon as Biden became the nominee, he began moving left. And it worked! This is partly, sure, down to the fact that most swing voters wanted Donald Trump out. It's also a function of how the electorate has changed in polarized America; there are fewer swing voters and more base voters. But it's also a function of the fact that most of what Biden campaigned on was popular. And it is a function of the decade of political changes this chapter describes, and the economic changes the previous chapter described. But in the end, I would argue, the pandemic opened the door. If the pandemic had never happened, could a candidate have won campaigning on Biden's agenda? We can't know, of course. But the pandemic and the summer of racial protest changed his approach. And once he changed, his party, or the vast majority of it anyway, changed. The fact that Build Back Better didn't pass shows that the political system, given the Democrats' wobbly majorities, balked at making change this dramatic; but even if Biden never passes them, the fact that someone campaigned on these positions and won, and probably would have passed them if he'd had just one more Democrat in the Senate, shows that these policy positions, which Democratic presidential candidates would have been afraid to embrace a generation ago, have broad support now, having been incubated for years by the work of thousands of people.

Intellectual ferment and activism are crucial elements of social change. But they need a catalyst. The pandemic was a devastating tragedy, but politically speaking, it gave American liberalism an opening.

CHAPTER EIGHT

The Role of the Nonprofit World

•

"THE KING IS NOT DIVINE"

The 21 Club, the posh Manhattan restaurant that was a famous speakeasy during Prohibition where the eighty-four-page wine list recently featured a 2011 Opus One red blend for $825 a bottle, would seem an unlikely launching pad for a progressive economic insurgency. Just down the street from Rockefeller Center, it was (the restaurant closed in 2021, another pandemic victim) one of New York's most exclusive restaurants, with a renowned clientele stretching from Humphrey Bogart (table 30) to Henry Kissinger (table 7) to, yes, Donald Trump (table 11, along the wall), who became a habitué during the 1980s and who would sneak away from Trump Tower during the transition, when he was president-elect, and have a meal there. The low ceiling of the dark main dining room was festooned with toys, bric-a-brac, mementos brought by celebrated regulars: a toy torpedo ship from President Kennedy, one of John McEnroe's (real) tennis rackets. The famous hamburger would have set you back $31 at the bar. Twenty-eight lawn jockeys—their riding silks painted in different colors, but their faces a safe, uniform white—adorned the wrought-iron facade. "I walked up and saw those lawn jockeys, and I went, 'What?!'" recalled Felicia Wong, the president and CEO of the Roosevelt Institute, a liberal think tank.

But it was here, in one of the ten private dining rooms, that about two dozen liberal intellectuals gathered on the evening of July 19, 2017, to begin plotting an economic insurrection. They were brought together by Larry Kramer, the president of the William and Flora Hewlett Foundation, based in Menlo Park next to the campus of Stanford University. William Hewlett had co-founded Hewlett-Packard in 1939 with his friend David Packard. Within a year, they had developed an audio oscillator and sold seven of them, at $71.50 a pop, to Walt Disney for use in the groundbreaking film *Fantasia*. They got rich in a hurry, and deserved to; beyond the wealth, Hewlett seems to have been a kind and generous man who never put himself above menial tasks. One day in 1967, an office phone rang; it was a precocious eighth grader looking for parts. Hewlett spoke to the youngster himself, and Steve Jobs's life was changed forever, he later said, by that conversation.

Hewlett and his wife, Flora, endowed the foundation in 1966. Today, it's one of the country's largest philanthropic institutions, awarding more than $450 million in grants in 2019 in education, the environment, the performing arts, and more. Kramer became the foundation's president in 2012. Before that, he was dean of Stanford Law School. He's a constitutional scholar and a brilliant polymath—a member of the American Academy of Arts and Sciences, the American Philosophical Society, and the American Law Institute. A native of Chicago who went to Brown as an undergraduate and returned to his hometown and its eponymous university to earn his law degree, he knows a little something about almost everything, and a lot about a lot of things.

Kramer is personally progressive in his politics, and most of Hewlett's giving can reasonably be described as tilting toward liberal-ish ends. But the sections of the IRS code that govern charitable giving call for groups like Hewlett to be nonpolitical in the partisan sense: they are allowed to seek to advance either progressive or conservative goals, but they are not allowed to lobby for particular legislation or endorse candidates for office. People who work in this vast nonprofit realm tend to take these rules very seriously, not just for the sake of legal compliance, but as a matter of principle, or a few principles: that solutions to social problems will be stronger if rigorously tested; that they are more enduring if they're the result of a rough consensus; that bipartisanship remains a laudable goal of policy making.

Attempts to adhere to these principles can make for some sadly comical situations in today's Washington, where I live and work. I've attended countless seminars and meetings arranged by nonpartisan but basically liberal organizations where the panel includes a token conservative (and yes, conservatives do the same in reverse; I've been the token liberal on several conservative-arranged panels) who politely agrees that if just the right kind of groundwork is laid, then, yes, a compromise on, say, a universal pre-K program, or a new Authorization for Use of Military Force to replace the Iraq War–era one, or a new campaign-finance regime is well within the realm of the possible. The liberals on the panel nod along, and the audience does the same, because to do so is the proper way to behave at such conclaves, but deep down everyone knows that this is utter bullshit, because today's Republican Party will never compromise with Democrats on any of these things. But people have to pretend they will, which in some ways is silly but in others has its uses: someone has to try. And very occasionally, even in this rancidly polarized age, something of value does pass Congress on a bipartisan basis, such as the 2021 infrastructure bill, which had the backing of nineteen Republican senators and thirteen GOP House members.

So Kramer, and Hewlett, are committed to bipartisan solutions and trying to find some Republicans to enlist in their causes. Kramer, who is in his early sixties and speaks in full sentences that are fast and aggressive, learned this general lesson at a young age. I asked him at one point to tell me a formative story about himself, and the story he chose was not about his commitment to social justice or to a set of ideological convictions; it was a story about listening to both sides. In the fourth grade, he read a book called *A Dog on Barkham Street*, about a boy tormented by a neighborhood bully: "I read it and cried and cried." Then he discovered a sequel to the book, but told from the perspective of the bully: "I read it and cried and cried." He continued, "The lesson I took from it—not self-consciously at the time, but in retrospect it has been incredibly formative for me—is that idea that there really are always two sides, that what might seem like unreasonable behavior to me is not unreasonable to the person behaving that way, and you need to really try to see it from that person's perspective."

This 21 Club dinner, and the more substantive meeting held the next day at the offices of the Ford Foundation near the United Nations, represented the start of a project that of necessity would not, at least at first, have room for many conservatives, who are just too deeply locked into their worldview on this matter. The point of this gathering was emphatically progressive: to see if the group could, and should, embark on the project of trying to turn the country's baseline economic assumptions and structures on their collective head; to see if the reigning neoliberal economic paradigm could be smashed and replaced with something well to its left. The question the group confronted, put simply, was this: How do you change an economy?

Kramer watched with dismay as the country slogged its way through the Great Recession and the impossibly slow recovery. But his career, and his scholarship, were in the law. That changed when he left Stanford to lead Hewlett in 2012. He began, he told me, to pay more attention to the economy and to think more deeply about the purpose of philanthropy and how philanthropy could change things.

To most Americans, political philanthropy—giving to groups working directly to influence elections or policy making—is completely invisible. Philanthropy, to your average American, is the American Cancer Society, or the United Way, or a local nonprofit group hastily put together to provide flood relief to local residents, or, in our time, to raise money for surgical masks or ventilators or a food bank. But political giving every year is massive; it is counted not in the millions but in the billions. More of it happens on the right than on the left—think of the Koch brothers, for example. And most Americans have no idea how much the priorities of donors dictate each side's political agenda. On the broad right, donors want their taxes cut and their regulations scaled back, so that's what Republicans do. On the broad left, there is concern about a much wider range of issues, but some catch fire and others do not: there are a lot of rich people who care about climate change, and comparatively few who care as much about poverty alleviation or workers' rights. And of course, no one really questions a rich person when she or he walks into a room and says, "I want to spend my money on X." People want the check. This is true of both sides. So changing what political philanthropy does, forcing upon it a new priority that doesn't spring from donors, that's hard.

Things move slowly in the foundation world, and for a while Kramer's ideas remained ideas. Then, he says, in 2016, matters became more urgent to him. "A bunch of things happened during that period," he told me. "The first one was, there was a talk that Paul Ryan gave during the election in his home district on what the world would look like if Hillary won. I haven't been able to find that talk again, but what I took away, it had language like 'your lives will be gray, crushed by the sameness of the collective.' It was like third-rate Ayn Rand. Which makes it like sixth-rate in my view. I mean, I loved reading *The Fountainhead* when I was a kid; I loved *Atlas Shrugged*. They were super-fun. But the idea of taking that seriously as philosophy in real life is ludicrous."

And yet, he realized, Ryan and millions of others did take it seriously; it's what they were taught in college, and for most people what they learn in college is what they continue to believe throughout their lives. He came to understand that "a whole generation or two of people had been taught this, whether it was neoclassical markets, the way Economics 101 is taught, or Ayn Randian philosophy, or social choice theory. This had been what they were taught. So not surprisingly, twenty years later, when they were in leadership positions, it reflected what they did."

Then Trump won the election, and "it was really clear that on the left and the right there was this shared dissatisfaction with what people had been being fed for a long time." Around the same time, Kramer was chatting with a friend, David Singh Grewal, a legal historian at UC Berkeley, about all these matters, and Grewal recommended to Kramer Angus Burgin's *Great Persuasion*, the history of neoliberal economics that I cited in chapter 2. It was after read-ing Burgin, Kramer recalls, that "a lot of lights lit up."

Kramer had just written a book on judicial review, and in it he borrowed a concept from Edmund S. Morgan, the eminent historian of the early republic: "Morgan wrote a book called *Inventing the People* in which he basically says all politics is make-believe. Right? You know, there are these intellectual paradigms. He was talking about it in politics. So at one point in time people believed that the king is divine, and that worked for them. It was make-believe of course, but it structured their reality in ways that worked tolerably well and lined up with what they experienced. But then, when social and political changes took place, that no longer worked. You've got the rise in popular sovereignty. But the idea that the people have a voice is no less fictitious or make-believe than the king is divine."

In his mind, Kramer applied the paradigm concept to economics in the present-day United States. The king is divine—until, one day, he isn't. Free-market economics reigns as the paradigm—until it doesn't. Could that day's arrival be hastened, and how?

That was late 2016. By the next July—pretty fast, in foundation land!—Kramer had organized the Ford confer-ence and that pre-conference dinner at 21 to see if this group of people could be the nucleus of a movement for a new eco-nomics. He pulled together a group of people who, in their different ways, had been thinking about these questions for a long time. Burgin was there, as was Felicia Wong. Mike Kubzansky, the head (managing partner) of the Omidyar Network, was there. The Omidyar Network was founded in 2004 by Pierre Omidyar, the founder of eBay; its giving has been mostly concentrated in various aspects of technology, but Kubzansky, like Kramer, is very keen on changing the country's economic principles. "I think we've done a decent job of discrediting" neoliberal ideas, Kubzansky told me in an interview, "but there's still this meta-narrative, which we haven't solved on our side, which is, what is the positive case" for a new economics?

Other attendees included Danielle Allen, a political philosopher at Harvard who in 2020 won the prestigious John W. Kluge prize in the humanities; Jacob Hacker, the Yale political scientist; Paul Pierson of UC Berkeley, who is Hacker's co-author on a series of books written over the last two decades showing in essence how our democracy works these days mostly for the donor class; Kim Phillips-Fein, an NYU historian who got a lot of attention for a history of business-based opposition to the New Deal; Sabeel Rahman, a professor at Brooklyn Law School (later the head of Demos, a think tank that does work on economic justice and democratic reform, now a member of the Biden administration); Eric Beinhocker, the behavioral economist; and Heather Boushey.

At the 21 dinner—and by the way, recalled Mark Schmitt of New America, "It wasn't fancy or nice. We were in a windowless, beige, very overheated room upstairs"; the chicken was dry, and the beans had "the texture of old shoelaces"—Kramer asked Allen, Hacker, and Steven Teles, a political scientist at Johns Hopkins, to make some introductory remarks. It's interesting that none of the three is an economist. Teles was an unusual choice for other reasons. He had recently published a well-received history of the rise of the conservative legal movement, so everything he learned researching that book would be relevant here; still, he would have been something of an odd man out in this assemblage because in his own politics he is centrist-to-liberal with even a bit of a libertarian streak ("liberaltarian," he sometimes calls himself).

As to what they discussed, here's Allen: "I talked about how a watered-down Rawlsianism seemed to dominate the policy landscape, how that led people to focus too exclusively on questions of distribution, and how we should resituate thinking about political economy" so that it was concerned not just with "a set of distributional results, but also the underpinnings of social systems that deliver political equality or freedom and democracy." "Rawlsianism" refers to the liberal philosopher John Rawls, discussed earlier, whose most famous work concerned how we define a just society. So by watered-down Rawlsianism, she means that the focus on economic distribution of wealth, while necessary, is insufficient by itself, and that intellectuals should not lose sight of those last three things she mentions.

Hacker says he talked about "the work that I've done with Paul about the kind of way in which the American political economy has been recast in ways that are just producing these massively unequal outcomes." Teles tossed just a spoonful or two of cold water on the proceedings. He is known in these circles as a bit of an iconoclast on a key point. As liberals try to build movements like this, they look to movements and structures the right built in the 1970s and 1980s for cues, hoping to find the answer, some Rosetta stone showing how it's all done. (Liberals tend to impute to conservatives vast organizational powers that they may or may not have, probably in part because liberals assume conservatives to be no-nonsense authoritarian types who accept the giving and taking of orders in a way liberals are constitutionally incapable of.) But Teles argues there is no Rosetta Stone—that liberals' idea of the influence of the famous Powell Memo of 1971, written by the future Supreme Court justice Lewis Powell for the U.S. Chamber of Commerce as a blueprint for saving capitalism, was overblown. He also believes the liberal stereotype is wrong. For example, as he said to the group, referring to the Olin Foundation—an extremely influential conservative foundation of the mid- to late twentieth century—it was very nonhierarchical; it was the type of foundation that "more or less sits back and waits for ideas to come to it."

The next day at the Ford Foundation, conversation covered both the substance and the strategy of trying to build a "neoprogressive" economic paradigm. According to some notes of the gathering that were shared with me, the group started out talking about the Mont Pelerin Society, which, as we've seen, was the name the group of 1940s neoliberals adopted for themselves in 1947 as they began their assault on Castle Keynes. There were no great revelatory break-throughs at the Ford meeting; there rarely are in these kinds of situations. But enough happened that most everyone felt it was worth keeping at it. "The conversation was basically, 'What is neoliberalism, and do we have a coherent critique of it?'" Wong recalled. "And then, the heart of the question was whether we could go beyond critique to alternative." On this point, the notes shared with me ask, "How might we better connect the intellectual spadework being done in different academic disciplines? How do these ideas better connect to the world of policy making? Or to the world of media, culture, and narrative?" Those are the right questions. The central challenge with any such effort is how to turn academic jargon into talk that regular people can understand and that can change the way they think.

Hacker told me he thought the meeting was "pretty amazing, actually." He elaborated: "It's just very rare for the head of a major foundation with lots of money to say we're going to put a lot of chips into the basket of changing thinking and action over the next twenty-five years or something like that. And I think that got everyone talking in a way that wouldn't have occurred otherwise. It is so rare." Mark Schmitt added, "Larry's effort to build a new funder consensus on economic policy has been one of the most remarkably successful efforts I've ever seen. . . . The dinner and meeting were significant in defining the community (with some ideological and institutional diversity) and establishing that it was going to be a serious effort."

Kramer was pleased: "The purpose of that meeting was to get some people together to say, 'Here's what I'm thinking about. What do you think? Is this plausible, doable?' That was literally what I wanted to get out of it. And what I got out of it was, yes, it's plausible and doable. There are lots of people thinking about this. They're disaggregated, but you can build the connections. What philanthropy can do is build the connective tissue."

The next spring, in April 2018, Kramer had written a memo to the Hewlett board called "Beyond Neoliberalism: Rethinking Political Economy." He wrote, "Circumstances are ripe for the emergence of a new intellectual paradigm—a different way to think about political economy and the terms for a new 21st-century social contract. Helping develop and communicate such ideas is a task well suited to philanthropy, and one in which the Hewlett Foundation is well positioned to participate." He asked the board for $10 million to be spent over ten years toward this end, as a kind of down payment, and the board approved. (I should note that *Democracy* journal has received two modest, five-figure grants from this project.)

That summer, there was a larger conference held at a resort outside Seattle called Cedarbrook (a step or two down from 21: the wine list includes several selections for $13). Boushey took the lead in organizing this two-day meeting,

and Kramer funded it. It brought together about fifty scholars across six disciplines, "to understand how each discipline
is thinking about the big questions of what is happening in
the economy, how do we think about outcomes, how do we
think about what each of these disciplines can add to the
knowledge," Boushey recalled.

Whereas the 21 Club–Ford meeting brought together
scholars and people from foundations and think tanks,
Cedarbrook was a meeting of scholars only, from different
disciplines, to get a sense of where their work overlapped,
where it conflicted, and what each could contribute to the
larger effort. "I think what came out of Cedarbrook was, on
the one hand, a greater sense of excitement and, on the other
hand, a greater awareness of just how difficult it was going
to be to create cohesion and a sense of movement," Kramer
remembered. "People were all over the place in terms of
what they were interested in."

Kramer's comment underscores a key challenge. It was
hard to call this a highly organized effort. In part that reflects
Kramer's approach to funding. He's not the type, he once
told me, to give people or groups money expecting a particular set of "deliverables," to lapse into nonprofit world
argot. He identifies people or organizations that he thinks
are doing useful work; he gives them money and tells them
to go make some flowers bloom. In part it also reflects the
fact that among the group there were and are disagreements
about both substance and tactics. For example, according
to the notes from the Ford Foundation meeting that were
shared with me, tensions arose within the group about the
meaning and importance of "freedom," about the concept of
growth, and "around the notion that bad (oppressive) outcomes can be the result of democratic processes." You have
a lot of really smart people who've devoted their adult lives

to these questions, and they're bound to have strong opinions on these matters. Finally, there is the tendency, quite pronounced in the nonprofit world, to study matters sometimes to the point of over-studying them and an associated tendency to avoid clear, firm, and direct language.

Still, there was among the group a definite sense of momentum. In 2018, Kramer hired Jennifer Harris, who had worked on global economic issues in the Hillary Clinton–era State Department, to oversee grant making in this area to keep the ideas coming. "I said, 'Here's $10 million, Jen, you can spend it however you want, but make this happen,'" Kramer recalled.

Three years later, as I was finishing this manuscript, what had become of this effort? Quite a bit and on at least four fronts. First, Kramer reported that twenty-five Hewlett grantees in Jennifer Harris's Beyond Neoliberalism program had joined the Biden administration—along with three Hewlett employees, including Harris. There was a working group, Kramer told me, of seven heads of important nonprofit organizations meeting regularly to advance this effort; six of them joined the administration. The hires are a strong sign that someone in Biden world was paying attention to the Hewlett program, that Kramer's people were not just talking to themselves and their friends. Second, the funder group, which at the beginning was just Hewlett and Omidyar, had expanded to about twenty-five donor organizations, which now meet twice a year to assess progress.

Third, Hewlett and its partners have endowed centers at four universities, with more on the way, to serve as homes for research and teaching in post-neoliberal economics, which has the potential to create a new generation of thinkers and ideas. The four are Harvard, MIT, Johns Hopkins, and Howard University. The MIT center will focus on labor;

Howard on race; the Johns Hopkins effort, which includes Teles and Angus Burgin, "is sort of center-right-ish, that's what it brings to this." When we spoke, Kramer said he was planning on adding some land-grant universities around the country, and universities in the global south, which leads to the fourth development, which is keen international interest in the project. He told me of conversations he had on a trip to Europe, first to Berlin and then to Glasgow for the COP26 climate conference. "That first memo I wrote, everybody had read it, and it moved them to start thinking about this stuff," Kramer said.

Kramer still thinks that for this project to have serious impact on thought and policy making in the United States will take a decade, "maybe even longer." In the meantime he said he was pleased with what the Biden administration was doing. "They've stayed out of the culture wars," he told me in late 2021, "and they proposed a package of pretty dramatic change that I think makes sense from the perspective of what we really know about how the economy works." He does think Biden "has not been able to tell a compelling story to explain what he's doing in ways that really sing for the American people and bring along enough of his party." And it's not just a question of policies: "You need a conception of the nature of your society."

THE INCREASINGLY AT LEAST SEMI-VAST LEFT-WING CONSPIRACY

The Hewlett-led effort is one front in a busy war. Trump's shock victory spurred a lot of commotion on the broad left, involving many of the same people and their institutions: Wong and the Roosevelt Institute; Boushey and the Washington Center for Equitable Growth, which she headed until joining the Biden administration; Kubzansky and Joelle Gamble of Omidyar; Dorian Warren of Community Change and of the Economic Security Project, co-founded by Chris Hughes, the Facebook co-founder who split with Mark Zuckerberg and now believes the company should be broken up; Rahman and McGhee of Demos; many of the academics named throughout this book.

This network of people and groups have helped change the economic conversation in dramatic ways. It's nearly impossible to draw a direct line from "think tank X produced Y report that led to Z legislation." Reports and conferences and seminars are not acts of revolution. They don't usually lead to immediate policy change. But they do shift emphasis and, over time, the thinking of the policy-intellectual community broadly, and this eventually seeps its way up to at least some Democratic politicians. And it's also tied to the activism I described in the previous chapter. Activism, which is public and generates media attention, provides the spark that gives new momentum to policy conversations. "This is what movements do best, right? They put issues on the agenda that leaders don't necessarily want on the agenda," Dorian Warren, a thoughtful younger leader with a foot in both the activist and the intellectual camps, told me. "We've been talking about increasing inequality of income and wealth for decades. We had all the data, but it didn't matter because there was no power. And then Occupy comes and it puts the issue on the agenda. And even if Occupy goes away, the issue stays on the agenda the entire decade." That, in turn, signals to the think tank and foundation worlds that there is support out there for such and such an idea, and that leads to energy and funding.

So the 2010s was a decade in which, alongside the activism I described in chapter 7, an impressive infrastructure arose to support the push for more liberal approaches to economic issues in particular. The broad left has spent years fixated on the study of how conservatives built their intellectual and activist infrastructure in the 1970s—the formation of the Heritage Foundation, the Cato Institute, and so on—and how that ferment helped produce the Reagan presidency and advance its policy priorities. Now something similar has happened on the liberal side over the past decade. Actually, taking the longer view, the project goes back to the 1980s, after Reagan and his new conservatism took over. There were, even at the height of those New Democrat years, groups that didn't swim with that tide and opposed the New Democrats on labor and trade issues most conspicuously. Probably the most important of these is the Economic Policy Institute, which was founded in 1986 with significant backing from various labor unions. EPI experts have done indispensable work over the years on inequality, CEO compensation, the minimum wage, and a long list of other issues. It was headed for a time, until she joined the Biden Labor Department, by Thea Lee, a widely respected economist who left the AFL-CIO to go to EPI. The Center for Economic and Policy Research, co-directed by Eileen Appelbaum and Mark Weisbrot and the home base of the senior economist Dean Baker, who called the 2007 meltdown, has been an important voice on these matters, with a strong emphasis on inequality both in the United States and abroad, and on issues like intellectual property. Baker's burning obsession is to get liberals to understand that creating a more just economy is a question not merely of implementing the right government programs but of paying attention to how the market is structured from jump street to favor the wealthy. Baker's Exhibit A here is patent and copyright monopolies, which, he has written many times, redistribute billions of dollars upward and inflate the prices of, say, pre-scription drugs by as much as 80 or 90 percent.

The Center on Budget and Policy Priorities was founded by Bob Greenstein in 1981—the year Reagan took office—to analyze the federal budget with an eye toward what kinds of priorities the numbers reveal, specifically with regard to programs for working-class and poor people. The group also does important work at the state level, having helped establish miniature versions of itself in forty-two state capi-tals. This is crucial for balance; conservatives have invested far more money in state-level work, chiefly through the well-known American Legislative Exchange Council. The Campaign for America's Future (CAF), headed by Robert Borosage and Roger Hickey, is another labor-funded group whose focus is on fighting inequality and working toward sustainable (that is, green) growth. For a time in the 1990s and the first decade of the twenty-first century, CAF held an annual "Take Back America" conference that grew to draw thousands of attendees. On the non-economic front, the Brennan Center for Justice is clearly among the most important liberal ideas/advocacy groups founded during this period (in 1995). Led since 2006 by former Clinton speech-writer Michael Waldman, Brennan focuses on voting rights, elections, and democracy; it spent a decade or more devel-oping many of the ideas that went into the Democrats' (for now) ill-fated voting rights bills they tried to pass in 2021.

A key moment in this history was the founding, in 2003, of the Center for American Progress (CAP), a multi-tentacled liberal think tank founded consciously to be a liberal answer to the Heritage Foundation and the Cato Institute, headed initially by John Podesta and later by Neera Tanden (and now Patrick Gaspard, who was Barack Obama's ambassador to South Africa). CAP provided an important policy counterweight to the Bush administration and was enormously influential within the Obama administration and sent numerous staffers into government. In more recent years, CAP has sometimes been criticized on the left over certain of its funding sources. But CAP's historical place is secure; it was around the time of the creation of CAP that liberal donors began to understand that they needed to invest heavily in ideas and their packaging.

The year after CAP's founding, a man named Rob Stein, an attorney who before his death in May 2022 had a long history in the Democratic nonprofit world, put together a PowerPoint presentation to show rich liberals how badly their conservative counterparts were outspending them on advocacy and organizing. Out of this was created the Democracy Alliance (DA), a consortium of wealthy liberal donors who agree to invest in organizations vetted and approved by DA staff. David Brock's Media Matters for America (MMfA) was an early recipient of DA largesse. MMfA proves the point of how consciously people on the left were trying to ape the 1970s right: Media Matters was the liberal answer to Accuracy in Media, created in 1969 by Reed Irvine to police the mainstream press for liberal bias. Media Matters does the same from the other side, as well as now monitoring the avowedly right-wing media for lies and distortions.

That's the prehistory of the 2010s, when we saw new organizations founded by people too young to carry the bruises borne by the liberals who were coming of age in the Reagan 1980s. The new activists and intellectuals were less shaped by the idea of liberalism in retreat, less on the defensive, and they reimagined their organizations for an era when the populist left is resurgent. The Roosevelt Institute, for example, was a fairly sleepy outfit that mainly provided support for the Roosevelt Presidential Library until Andrew

Rich took over in 2009. He got prominent economists like Joseph Stiglitz to affiliate themselves with the institute and quickly raised its profile. Felicia Wong, who grew up in Sunnyvale, California, and holds a political science PhD from UC Berkeley, took over in 2012. Since then, Roosevelt has become an enormously influential organization, at the center of progressive efforts to build a more democratic economy, and it has grown rapidly. "We were spending $4 million and raising $2 million, and that's not good, even I know that," Wong told me. "Now we're at about $14 or $15 million, and with a staff of about seventy people." But "what I am most proud of," she told me, "even more than the institute's growth, is the creation of a network of people who in their own worlds are influencers and important thinkers. I'm super-proud of that."

One of the main things that happened in recent years is that the very idea of what constituted "the liberal establishment" changed. It became younger and more diverse, and it shifted to the left. Not aggressively to the left—for example, Bernie Sanders's conception of Medicare for All, entailing the elimination of private insurance, is by no means uniformly embraced. But perceptibly to the left, such that it's now a given in a way it was not when Obama took office that greening the economy has to be a priority, that government has to find ways to redistribute income downward from the 1 percent, and that racial and gender equity can no longer be afterthoughts in the design of programs. The journalist Rebecca Traister wrote a valuable piece in *New York* magazine in July 2021 that described some of these networks and talked about how these people and institutions were both part of the establishment and attempting to reshape it. As Traister put it, "The approach they were taking—those looking to push the Establishment from the inside and those wondering how to make a new Establishment—functioned like the professional class's version of grassroots organizing."

This new establishment also came to include a new breed. Big-money donors, of course, have always been part of the establishment. But in post-meltdown America, there arose a new species: the activist-donor. These were rich people not content merely to write checks, or even to write checks and discreetly steer the policy conversation. These were people who wanted to be part of the conversation. Chris Hughes has been one such figure. After an ill-fated stint as owner of *The New Republic*,* he has stayed in the game and taken positions one doesn't normally associate with multimillionaires, like a call to raise his own taxes and the aforementioned plea to break up Facebook. His Economic Security Project is "organized around two fights we think we can win," according to the group's website: a guaranteed income and antimonopoly action. He's become one of the most significant funders of progressive populist economic causes in the country.

But perhaps the most interesting figure here is Nick Hanauer of Seattle. Nick inherited a successful bedding and linen business from his father, which is ongoing, but more to the point he was the first nonfamily investor in Amazon. If you google "Nick Hanauer net worth," you'll see numbers between $1 and $1.5 billion. He doles out a good chunk of it to causes and organizations he believes in (a list that I should note includes the journal *Democracy*, which I edit), he runs a nonprofit in Seattle called Civic Ventures that is devoted to state and municipal issues, and he has financed or helped finance ballot initiatives to raise the minimum wage

* I am the current editor of *The New Republic*. I have met Hughes on a couple occasions, and he has written for the journal *Democracy*, but I had nothing to do with *TNR* during his ownership.

in Seattle and establish a state income tax in Washington for the rich.

When I first met Nick, around 2005, he could fairly be described as a moderate Democrat. I'm pretty sure I first met him at a dinner hosted by Third Way, the centrist Democratic think tank (sign of the times: Third Way, too, has moved to the left of where it once stood on economic issues). But over the years, his politics shifted dramatically. He's still a capitalist, as he is always quick to note. But as inequality got worse and worse, his views changed. "At some point, I got clarity about the size of the problem, and the distance we have to travel to fix it," he says. "And that distance is a lot farther than most people want to travel."

Nick has given two TED talks, in 2014 and 2019. Both are eye-opening for people who haven't been exposed to these ideas. You can see in the body language of the audience members their intense interest in what he has to say. After opening both talks by telling his audiences that he is in not the top 1 percent but the top 0.01 percent, he goes on to deliver a message I doubt many expected to hear from such a person. From the first talk: "The problem isn't that we have *some* inequality. *Some* inequality is necessary for a high-functioning capitalist democracy. The problem is that inequality is at historical highs today, and it's getting worse every day. . . . Our society will change from a capitalist democracy to a neo-feudalist rentier society like eighteenth-century France." From the second: "It isn't capital that creates economic growth; it's people. And it isn't self-interest that promotes the public good; it's reciprocity. And it isn't competition that produces our prosperity; it's cooperation. What we can now see is that an economy that is neither just nor inclusive can never sustain the high levels of social cooperation necessary to enable a modern society to thrive."

My favorite Hanauer story, one that tells us a lot about his level of engagement on these issues, dates to early 2017. After a Seattle minimum wage ballot initiative had failed to pass, the city council passed an increase that kicked in that January 1. Eric Beinhocker was in town to visit Hanauer and was staying at the W hotel. He ordered room-service breakfast. He looked down at his bill, for $23, and noticed that $1.50 was added to it for something the hotel was calling the "MW Surcharge." A note at the bottom explained: "A 6.5 percent surcharge has been added to help offset the cost of the Seattle Minimum Wage. This is not for services provided and is not paid directly to service staff."

Late that morning, Beinhocker tweeted about it: "Shameful—@WHotels 'surcharge' for paying its workers a living wage. Where's surcharge for CEO's pay? #fightfor15." A couple hours later, Hanauer tweeted: "Hey @WHotels you charge a 6.5 percent surcharge for paying workers fairly, but no surcharge for the $4 million you pay your CEO. Why???" One of them got in touch with me, or maybe I noticed their tweets, I don't remember, and I (writing columns for *The Daily Beast* at the time) made detailed inquiries to the W Seattle and to Marriott, the parent company. My inquiries went unanswered, but it wasn't just me: Hanauer "called them up and gave them hell," he told me. His team started alerting union organizers and others. Marriott contacted Beinhocker. And by 6:28 p.m. local time that same day, the company tweeted back to Beinhocker: "We had a surcharge due to minimum wage increase. After review, we decided to end the policy."

As I wrote in the *Beast* at the time, "It's awfully telling. It wouldn't surprise me if the hotel people who made this decision to slap on this surcharge didn't even realize how aggressively ideological a move it was, how rooted in supply-side assumptions is the idea that paying their lowest-paid workers a little more is so unique a burden that they have to whine to their customers about it. And then tell them that the money from the surcharge doesn't even go to staff!" Beinhocker decided to be magnanimous about it in my column. "They did the right thing, and they did it quickly," he told me. "So good for them for fixing it." Hanauer, rather less so. "Itemizing the costs of paying workers decently is a perfect example of trickle-down-economics thinking in the Starwood corporate culture," he emailed me (Starwood owned the W chain and was in turn owned by Marriott). "The obscene salaries and bonuses we pay ourselves are 'good for the economy' and much deserved. Paying our workers a little bit more is bad for the economy and consumers. Wow. What sociopaths."

Very few people know this world like Gara LaMarche, who has been involved in liberal philanthropy in one form or another since the late 1980s. At that time, he led something called the Freedom to Write Program at the PEN American Center; it happened to coincide with Salman Rushdie's publication in 1988 of *The Satanic Verses* and with Ayatollah Khomeini's fatwa against the author. He moved from there to the Open Society Institute (now Open Society Foundations), George Soros's philanthropic organization. He headed the Atlantic Philanthropies while it was spending $26.5 million to help push through Obamacare. Most recently, he ran the Democracy Alliance for seven years until giving up his post after the 2020 election.

In an interview, LaMarche told me that yes, he has seen a notable shift among the donor class and in the liberal nonprofit world toward concern with, and funding for, issues of economics and class. "People came more or less consensually to the view that economics ought to be at the center of any progressive resurgence, and that there ought to be an answer to what are you doing to raise the living standard of middle-class and working-class people," he said. "And that that ought to be the central driving force of a Democratic message." There were dissenters to this view, he acknowledged, in the ranks of the DA and more generally—the "hedge-fund-type donors" with somewhat more conservative economic views. In my own experience, those kinds of views were once far more dominant among Democratic donors, who were plenty liberal on social issues and matters like environmental policy but less so on economics. That has changed. LaMarche cited Hanauer specifically as influencing the economic views of a number of DA partners, as well as Damon Silvers, a policy analyst who works for the AFL-CIO and is an important voice on these matters.

LaMarche told me, though, that he is less convinced than he used to be about the political benefits that will accrue from a more populist economics. "There are two premises of this kind of idea of economics, [of] doing kitchen-table stuff and really delivering stuff to people," he said. "One is that it's good for people. And the second is that it is the right politics as well. I'm not so sure of that second part anymore. We'll see. Because you can deliver things to people who aren't your natural base and change their economic circumstances and still not reap the benefits of it because of the enormous cultural bias in the country. So I'm not sure of the politics of it anymore. It's still the right thing to do."

It's the right thing to do, and anyway it is not the job of the people in the nonprofit world to make the politics work; they don't have a big enough megaphone. Only Democratic politicians have the megaphone. In the next and final chapter, I will lay out my ideas about how the Democrats can sell fundamental economic changes and reap the benefit politically.

CHAPTER NINE

What the Democrats Need to Do

•

THE FATEFUL HOUR

This book appears at a perilous time for this country. It's the fall of 2022, in advance of crucial midterm elections. The Biden administration and congressional Democrats have succeeded in passing some historic legislation. But they haven't changed the economic paradigm. It hasn't been for want of trying. Biden spoke of it many times. He staffed his administration full of people committed to changing the paradigm—from Heather Boushey, involved with those Hewlett meetings from the start, to Jared Bernstein to Cecilia Rouse to Jonathan Kanter at the Antitrust Division of the Justice Department to Lina Khan at the Federal Trade Commission to chief of staff Ron Klain, who welcomed progressives to White House meetings in sharp contrast with Obama chief of staff Rahm Emanuel, and so many more. If we agree with Elizabeth Warren's dictum that "personnel is policy," then Biden's policy is all that any progressive could reasonably ask for out of a president who has to worry about winning votes in places like Georgia and Arizona.

And yet the roadblocks the administration hit—including within its own party—show how heavy a lift it will be to change people's economic assumptions. Recall Senator Manchin's words, from late September 2021, when budget negotiations were grinding their way through the sausage machine: "I'm just not, so you know, I cannot accept our economy, or basically our society, moving towards an entitlement mentality. That you're entitled. I'm more of a rewarding, because I can help those that really need help." The sentiments expressed here tell us a lot about Manchin's assumptions about the proper role of the public sector in an economy. From a neoliberal point of view, they are perfectly reasonable sentiments. If the government's role should be limited to ameliorating severe market failure, then what Manchin says is right; one could hardly, in fact, expect him to say anything else. But if one sees a different and larger role for the public sector in providing supports for working people, supports that aren't tied to employment in an era when far fewer people are working at the same factory for forty-five years than when Manchin was growing up, then one would not talk the way he talked there. The intra-Democratic debate in the fall of 2021, excruciating as it could be to watch, showed that most congressional Democrats have embraced new economic thought to one degree or another. But not all have. And the public hasn't; yes, the particular elements of the bill, universal pre-K and so on, poll very well, but there is little evidence so far that the broader public has been persuaded that what they have been taught for the last forty years about the merits of the free market and limited government and the evil of deficits is wrong.

As Faiz Shakir put it to me in our interview, "The big fight of our times is reshaping power in the American economy." That's something that, as I write these words, the Biden administration has only begun to take on. That fight involves going after monopolies, strengthening unions, creating fair trade rules, using various tools to raise wages, reforming patent laws, and making other moves that will start to shift money and political power from corporations to workers and from the rich to the middle class. It means directly taking on some powerful lobbies. It also means changing the way people think about the economy. Recall that I wrote in the introduction that the economy, in addition to being a battery of statistics, is "a set of ideas." It is these ideas that Democrats must challenge and change.

Doing that is the work of the next decade. But in the meantime, first things first. These next two elections could determine whether this country survives as a functioning democracy. The last presidential election came within one man's (Mike Pence) wobbly conscience of being stolen; the next one could be. If Trump wins—or worse, if he loses but various state Republicans manage to reverse close results and the GOP-run Congress certifies him as the winner—we will face a fateful hour. Democracy won't disappear overnight. Instead, we will likely enter a phase of what the democracy scholars Steven Levitsky and Lucan A. Way have called "competitive authoritarianism": a regime that looks like a democracy, because it officially has a free press and an independent judiciary and so on, but that is in practice rigged for one party to prevail most of the time. Through gerrymandering (backed up by federal judges on the stacked judiciary), the Electoral College, the unequal Senate, the right-wing media that uses First Amendment protections to spread confusion and lies, and the right-wing propagandists who spread venom on a social media platform whose algorithms reward anger, Republicans hope they will manage to hold either the executive or the legislative branch, or both, for years to come as they find ever more creative ways to challenge the voting rights of Americans who vote heavily Democratic, and as the courts back them up. This is the United States that the Republicans want.

We will also see Trump, if reelected, slowly—or maybe not so slowly—destroy the executive branch, turning it from (at its best) in essence a large corporation promoting the public interest, driven by people with expertise who actually care about outcomes, into a fiefdom of unqualified lackeys who will perform his bidding, ignoring law and custom to do what Trump wants them to do. We were lucky the first time around in that he knew so little about where the actual levers of power are in the executive branch. Now he knows.

The Democrats—and activists, and foundations—have many fronts on which to fight this battle for democracy. But they simultaneously need to stay focused on economics. At the end of the day, this is still the first thought most voters carry with them into the voting booth: Am I better off, is my family better off, my community, the country? And the Republicans still have an advantage over Democrats here. In polls that ask respondents questions like "which party do you think would be better at handling" such and such an issue, Democrats these days come out ahead on most measures, since Republicans have little to offer by way of solutions on health care, immigration, civil rights, the environment, and so on. But majorities or pluralities usually say they think the Republicans will do a better job of managing the economy. Here's just one of many such polls: in October 2021, Gallup found that by 50 to 41 percent survey respondents said that Republicans were better than Democrats for prosperity.

So while the Democrats are busy trying to save democracy, they have to change this economic presumption, too.

REASON AND EMOTION: THE FOUR PILLARS OF THE DEMOCRATIC ARGUMENT

Earlier in the book I wrote this sentence: "Here is a truism of our political discourse that is not widely enough recognized: the right thinks in terms of morals, while the left tends to see matters through an economic lens." Here now is another truism of American politics, related to the first: Democrats try to win arguments with facts. This I think is partly due to liberals' natural respect for science and evidence and partly due to their belief, based on what their pollsters show them, that the facts are on their side a lot of the time, in both policy and political terms. Polls throughout 2021, for example, consistently showed that Build Back Better enjoyed the support of around 60 percent of voters, while some individual elements within the broader bill polled even higher. This being the case, many Democrats appear to think, all we have to do is state the facts, and we'll win.

But this is not how people's brains work. People are not vessels of pure reason. People reason emotionally. In love, we see someone and are smitten, or at least intrigued; we notice later that she does something we don't like, find annoying, but we reason it away as insignificant or even eccentrically endearing. From the music we like to the sports teams we favor to our reaction to the latest pop-culture craze, we have emotional responses that are instantaneous; only after that do we construct in our brains the reasoned arguments about why Olivia Rodrigo is great or the Dallas Cowboys suck. This is no less true in politics. One laid eyes on Barack Obama for the first time (as most Americans did) in 2004 when he gave a celebrated speech at the Democratic convention, and one responded favorably or not. That instant, reflexive response was not rational. It was emotional—to his looks, his voice, his smile, his cadences, maybe even his tie, and the way the whole package made one feel. Once that emotional response is registered, reason is almost powerless to dislodge it.

Republicans seem to understand this point better than Democrats do, in general. It helps that so much Republican rhetoric emanates from the wellsprings of the evangelical church. The phrase "dog whistling" entered the political lexicon during the George W. Bush years, referring to the way he smuggled certain scriptural phrases into his speeches whose scent evangelical voters would be sure to catch. Democrats no longer tap those religious wellsprings, except with respect to the Black church, and I think this is a mistake. Democratic politicians should lean on scripture more than they do, as well as making broader emotional appeals.

Don't get me wrong. Facts are foundational. But they're not enough, in the same way that a foundation isn't a whole house. Factual arguments need to be buttressed with emotional arguments. Reason and emotion need to be brought into harmony. That can be hard to do in the realm of economics (the "dismal science," after all). But as I've argued in this book, the right did it. So herewith, my best stab at doing that from a liberal perspective. My argument rests on four pillars. The first of the four is fact based and appeals to people's reason; the other three seek to prompt responses that are more emotional. These pillars can also be divided into categories that I label "attack" and "advance": that is, the first two pillars attack Republican and neoliberal economic conventional wisdom that still holds sway with most people; the last two advance new principles that replace it with a new narrative frame. So with no further ado:

1. Attack the perception that Republican administrations are better for the economy. This, as I wrote above, seems hardwired into the collective public mind. But it's not true. In fact, it's not remotely close to true. On key indicators like GDP growth, increase in the median household income, deficit management, and even performance of the stock market, Democratic administrations in recent history have a far better track record than Republican administrations.

Simon Rosenberg heads a group called NDN, a liberal think tank and advocacy organization. He has spent years advising Democrats, presidents included, on how to talk about economic matters. In 2020, he put together a Power-Point deck, which he updated in 2021, which compares the nation's economic performance in various categories over the last thirty-two years—that is to say, under sixteen years of Republican administrations (Bush, Bush, Trump), and sixteen years of Democratic administrations (Clinton and Obama). On every measure, the results were a wipeout. All these numbers are from Rosenberg's June 2020 PowerPoint, an updated version he sent me in October 2021, and a bit from my own calculations using his numbers and double-checking them against other public sources:

Jobs created during the sixteen years of Democratic presidencies versus Republican presidencies: 33.8 million versus 1.9 million. That is not a typo. Job creation per month: under Democrats, 176,093; under Republicans, 9,687. Average GDP growth: Democrats, 3.1 percent; Republicans, 1.62 percent. Dow Jones Industrial Average increase: Democrats, 185.5 percent; Republicans, 26 percent.

You read that right. Because the DJIA went in the red under George W. Bush by around 25 percent. If you google this, you'll see different sets of numbers. People have different ways of measuring these things, and different ways of calculating the increase. But you will see consistently that the stock market, which Trump loved to tout, performed okay under George H. W. Bush, horribly under George W. Bush, well under Trump, a bit better under Obama, and far better under Clinton.

As for impact on the budget deficit, it's not remotely close. Clinton took the country from a $290 billion deficit to a $236 billion surplus, for a $526 improvement. The deficit did increase under Obama by $126 billion (though he cut it by more than half in his second term). Combined, they left the country $400 billion better off. The Bushes and Trump combined to add nearly $3.5 trillion to the deficit.

Finally, median household income increase: Democrats, 9.5 percent; Republicans, 0.6 percent. Yes, that's 0.6 percent, as in less than 1. It went up under Trump by 9.2 percent, which is very good, but it went down under both Bushes. It went up 5 percent under Obama and around 14 percent under Clinton.

There you have it. Jobs, GDP, stock market, deficit, income. These are the five frequently cited indicators of a healthy economy. I don't celebrate the deficit reduction in the way I do the other measures; as discussed, fear of the deficit is something I'd love to see Democrats get over. But it is worth pointing out, in the meantime, that their deficit numbers do not line up with the stereotype of liberals as free spenders. I'd like to add reduction of inequality to this mix, but unfortunately no one has a good record on that. It went up under the Democrats, too, due to the neoliberal hegemony. But by all five of these measures, the results are not even close. The economy does far better during Democratic administrations—a reality that goes back not just to the elder Bush but to 1960 at least.

In sum, the economic record is clear. Democrats are far better stewards of the economy by every major measure. And yet they *never* talk about it. They should talk about it all the time. Some billionaire should fund a nonprofit to promote this story. The Democratic National Committee should pay to put these numbers on billboards across America. The last three Republican presidents have overseen economic carnage, each worse than the previous one. The last three Democratic presidents, the current one included, have had to clean up the messes, and they have left the country stronger. Every voting-age American should know this story.

2. Destroy the myth of *Homo economicus* and replace it with a human being. The idea that we are all self-interested and that acting selfishly promotes the common good is inherently right-wing. It tells people this: Just fend for yourself, and your family. That is your only commitment to society. This is pernicious. Besides, it doesn't reflect most people's lived reality. Most of us spend part of our lives being dependent on others: when we are children, when we are sick, when we are old. Most of us also understand and accept that we are members of a broader society and that membership carries certain obligations. We accept the idea that there is such a thing as the common good. People often act not out of self-interest but out of generosity. We are social creatures who crave not just material comfort and more stuff but friendships and love and the approval of those around us.

Even most businesses—that is to say, even market capitalism—are governed not by relentless self-maximizing but by reciprocity and cooperation. Think of the chain of cooperation required to deliver, say, a television from a factory in China to your family room. That takes a series of actors to work together—yes, all behaving in their self-interest, but all also working cooperatively to ensure that they get their share of the profit. In their 2012 book, *The Rainforest: The Secret to Building the Next Silicon Valley*, the venture capitalists Victor W. Hwang and Greg Horowitt write that cooperation is *more* important to successful capitalism than competition. "Rainforests" is their metaphor for successfully innovative firms and ecosystems. And rainforests, they write, "depend on people *not* behaving like rational actors" (my italics). They continue:

> Extra-rational motivations—those that transcend the classical divide between rational and irrational— are not normally considered critical drivers of economic value-creation. . . . These motivations include the thrill of competition, human altruism, a thirst for adventure, a joy of discovery and creativity, a concern for future generations, and a desire for meaning in one's life, among many others. Our work over the years has led us to conclude that these types of motivations are not just "nice to have." They are, in fact, "must have" building blocks of the Rainforest.

So yes, motivations "include" competition, but they include those other factors as well. There is a massive literature out there along these lines that draws on different branches of economics (as I noted in chapter 6), sociology, anthropology, cultural anthropology, and much else. The more we study, the more we learn that human behavior is not reducible to self-interest. But this innovative and important thinking has not made its way into our political discourse.

That needs to change. Democrats need to talk expressly and directly about how capitalism isn't simply about competition and how most human beings are not solely relentless self-maximizers. Today's economic discourse in the realm of politics proceeds entirely from the old neoclassical, neoliberal, and Friedmanesque assumptions. Democrats have to introduce new assumptions into that discourse.

Here's why this is so crucial. If we proceed from the neo-liberal presumption that we all should stick to pursuing our self-interest, then the only policy solutions that make sense are Republican ones. If people need only to advance their self-interest, then the state should mainly just get out of their way and let them pursue away. But if we proceed from a different set of assumptions built around the ideas that we are both self-interested *and* other-directed, and that our motivations for our economic decisions are multifaceted, then the policy solutions that make sense are more liberal.

This means Democrats need to talk not just about policies but about *the ideas behind them.* After all it's ideas, not lower prescription drug prices, that change the world. History's greatest leaders have found ways to boil high-flung ideas down into language that most people could understand, and that is what Democrats have to do here: "My Republican friends believe that all we need to do is selfishly pursue our own interests, and everything will work out fine. We Democrats have a different view. We think people are more generous than that. We think people thrive on competition, yes, but we believe they value cooperation, trust, and the esteem in which they are held by others. And we think that the way we shape economic policy should reflect this more complex view of what motivates our behavior in the marketplace." I promise you—the right would freak out if Democrats began aggressively talking like this. They would freak out because they would know deep down that most people feel this way about themselves and do not see themselves as simply self-interested creatures. If Democrats can put a fuller view of human nature back into economics—and into politics—they can put the right on the defensive and change the starting point from which debates about economics proceed.

3. Tie economics to democracy. In the early days of the 2020 presidential campaign, Pete Buttigieg was asked by NBC's Chuck Todd: "Are you a capitalist?" His answer was pretty brilliant, I thought: "Sure. Yeah. Look, America is a capitalist society. But: It's got to be democratic capitalism. And that part's really important, and it's slipping away from us. In other words, when capitalism comes into tension with democracy, which is more important to you? I believe democracy is more important. And when you have capitalism capturing democracy, when you have the kind of regulatory capture where powerful corporations are able to arrange the rules for their benefit, that's not real capitalism. If you want to see what happens when you have capitalism without democracy, you can see it very clearly in Russia. It turns into crony capitalism, and that turns into oligarchy." In a little more than a hundred words there, Buttigieg expressed a profound point. Economics and democracy are not the separate issues they are taken to be in the media. They are *the same issue.* The Mont Pelerin Society argued that once economic freedom was threatened (by a tax, or a new government program), political freedom was by definition under threat, and that as long as economic freedom—which they defined as a minimal state with low taxation—was maintained, political freedom would be safe. They were wrong. As we look around the world, from Hong Kong to Hungary, Georgia to Guatemala, we see that it is quite possible, indeed not uncommon, for countries to have economies that are essentially market based even while they clamp down on political freedoms. Buttigieg invokes Russia above, and it, along with China, is perhaps the most obvious example of a country with a basically capitalist economy (state-capitalist, in China's case) where political freedoms are severely curtailed. But there are many other such countries. In fact, by comparing the World Population Review's annual ranking of economic freedoms and Freedom House's annual survey of political freedoms (broken down into political rights and civil liberties), we can see some empirical results. The World Population Review, or WPR, ranks Hong Kong and Singapore as the world's freest countries economically; to Freedom House, though, both are just "partly free" (a score of 72 makes a country "free"; the United States scores 83; Singapore scores 47, and Hong Kong 43). Georgia is a third country that makes WPR's top ten but is ranked only "partly free" by Freedom House. In addition, within the WPR's top twenty or thirty are countries that often elect left-of-center governments that today's American right would revile as socialist; they see no diminution of political freedom when those governments replace conservative ones (New Zealand, Denmark, Chile, Canada, Ireland, and a number of others). A survey of the world casts grave doubt on the argument that economic and political freedoms inevitably walk hand in hand. In a very general sense, they do, insofar some of the most obviously repressive nations also have tightly controlled economies (North Korea being the poster child here). But among the world's capitalist countries, the range of democratic freedoms is quite wide.

Recent experience right here in the United States is also on point. Donald Trump's idea of capitalism is rapacious and almost completely unchecked by state intervention. Yet his idea of political freedom, as we have seen, is one of total disdain for concern about the rights of those who don't support him politically. Trump has decoupled the ideas of economic freedom and political freedom more aggressively than any president in the history of the United States by far. This just makes it all the more urgent that Democrats *re*-couple economics and democracy.

Democratic elected officials need to explain to Americans, as Buttigieg said, that if the economic and political systems become too controlled by the wealthy, if inequality continues unchecked, if we don't build a robust middle class, if we can't deliver to middle- and working-class people the kinds of policies on offer in every other developed democracy, and on a permanent basis, if we can't properly tax wealth, if we can't create an ethos wherein businesses understand that their long-term interests are better served by a healthy democracy to which they contribute their share than a corrupted and out-of-kilter one that asks little of them, then the impacts on democracy will be severe, and it will fail. This is a connection few politicians make. It's of vital importance that they do.

Let me conclude this section with a story. We all know what Thomas Jefferson was doing in the summer of 1776: he was writing the Declaration of Independence. But less known, and more interesting, is what he did that fall. He went down to Virginia, where he was a member of the state legislature, and led the fight to abolish the commonwealth's laws on primogeniture and "entail," which kept large estates within families across generations. This is no mere coincidence. He, and all the founders, knew that excessive inherited wealth was fundamentally incompatible with democracy. In a few months' time, Jefferson laid the foundation for our political rights in Philadelphia and went to Richmond to curtail the unfettered economic rights of the rich. The Democrats need to say and say and say what Thomas Jefferson clearly believed: a healthy democracy depends on a fair economy.

This story makes an important point. To the extent that

present-day liberals seek historical justifications for a new economics, they always go back to FDR—his Second Bill of Rights, which I discussed in chapter 1, or his Four Freedoms, which I mention below. Occasionally, they mention TR's trust-busting; a few cite Wilson and Brandeis. But the tradition I'm talking about here goes back to the founders, and Democrats have to say that. To go back to FDR tells the swing voter, "We are building on only a liberal tradition." To go back to the founders tells them, "We are building on an American tradition." The whole story is conveniently laid out for Democrats in the bracing early 2022 book *The Anti-Oligarchy Constitution*, by Joseph Fishkin and William A. Forbath. They cite numerous founders making such arguments and note that the principle of economic redistribution was embedded in many early state constitutions. They cite Jefferson, Daniel Webster, and several others, including James Madison, whom they quote as saying (and remember that land ownership in those days was the chief source of wealth accumulation): "The balance of power in a society accompanies the balance of property in land. The only possible way, then, of preserving the balance of power on the side of equal liberty and public virtue, is to make the acquisition of land easy to every member of society." The relationship between economic and political equality is not a liberal idea. It's an American idea.

Making this tie to democracy will help Democrats sell their economic program. It will blunt the right-wing criticism that they're just interested in giving people handouts. Republicans will continue to say that, of course, but if Democrats explicitly connect paid family leave and free community college and the rest to the preservation and strengthening of democracy, and the great democratic purpose of advancing human happiness, and link all that back to the nation's founding, they will put Republicans on the defensive. An argument fought on this terrain is one Democrats and the broad left can win.

4. Tie economics to freedom. Today, the right owns the word "freedom." Democrats and the broad left have to take it back and redefine it. As I noted in the introduction, it was smart of Milton Friedman to call that book *Capitalism and Freedom*—to connect a dreary topic like economics to so enthralling a concept as freedom. Democrats today must say this: It is our economic vision that will give people freedom, and the Republican vision of freedom has left millions struggling, even in many cases in misery. Freedom is not freedom if you work full time and live in poverty. Freedom is not freedom if a single medical crisis can drive you to bankruptcy. It is not freedom if child care is too expensive for you to hold a job, or if you are born poor and at every turn are blocked in your rise: by underfunded schools, overpriced colleges, and usurious college loans.

Liberals adore Franklin Roosevelt's famous Four Freedoms speech to Congress from January 1941. What were those freedoms? Actually, two of them were negative freedoms: freedom of speech and of worship. But the second two were positive freedoms, and they generated more attention and discussion—and controversy, because they were new at the time and, unlike the first two, not universally agreed upon in this country. They were freedom from want and from fear; the former meant a "healthy peacetime life" for people of all nations, and the latter sought a "worldwide reduction in armaments" such that global peace was not threatened. It was that third one in particular that has been attacked by the right, because a healthy peacetime life implies, well, exactly the kinds of things Joe Biden has been trying to conjure into reality. The second expression of positive liberty was the 1948 United Nations Universal Declaration of Human Rights, spearheaded by Eleanor Roosevelt. The declaration includes a preamble and thirty articles. While the declaration honors the traditional negative freedoms of speech and so on, most of the articles express positive freedoms, both legal and economic (including, in article 23, the right to "form and join" trade unions), and the preamble invokes FDR's Four Freedoms. That, and the fact that this was written under the auspices of the UN, with the famously liberal Mrs. Roosevelt as the chairwoman, was enough to drive the right wing of the time bonkers.

The Democrats' economic program today can fairly be described as seeking to advance positive liberties. The expanded social safety net certainly attempts to provide freedom from want. But looked at another way, the programs they advocate provide people *freedom to:* to achieve their fullest potential, to change jobs without having to worry about their health coverage, to pursue their ambitions knowing that they can enroll their kids in a safe child-care facility, to try community college without falling into debt, to move to a new part of the country because taking such chances becomes less risky, or to stay in their hometown because a certain level of public investment has made it so that there are jobs and opportunity in town again.

Here's a key point: Investment in programs that help people doesn't encourage sloth and indolence. On the contrary, these programs make most people decide *they have more freedom* to try to better themselves. Google "percent of Americans who don't like their jobs." You'll see that depending on the poll, it's between 60 and 85 percent. Now, some percentage of those unhappy people can't leave their jobs because they lack the skills or perhaps the ambition to find a better one. But it's fair to assume that most people unhappy in their jobs would rather be, well, happy in their jobs. Free community college or affordable day care would give them the freedom to try.

The right-wing responses here would be the age-old ones. First, that a spiderweb of welfare-state programs such as Biden has sought to promote would make the U.S. worker soft like her European brethren and sistren. Let's therefore turn back to the World Population Review and consult its list of Most Productive Countries 2021. The United States ranks respectably here. It is sixth. But the five countries it lags behind are all in lazy, slothful, worker-coddling Europe: Ireland, Norway (so even a Scandinavian nation leads us!), Switzerland, Luxembourg, and Germany. Denmark, France, the Netherlands, and Belgium round out the top ten. Measured a different way, by hourly productivity, the United States ranked third, but still behind Norway and Luxembourg, and not so far ahead of that symbol to the American right of everything that's wrong with Europe, France (sixth). So this idea that worker-friendly policies reduce productivity is provably not true.

The other argument, related, is about individual motivation. Here, Republicans have classic Econ 101 theory on their sides. Economics has held for decades that if the state gives people income, they choose leisure over work. Democrats have little to say in response. I say they should. There is an increasing body of scholarly research that shows that some cash transfers have no effect on the hours people work, and certain other cash transfers actually make people more likely to work; make them more likely to take a chance on starting a business; make children healthier and better students, thus improving the chance that they will grow up to contribute more to society. I'll point here to two studies. The first, from 2017, is by three scholars from MIT and one from Harvard. They analyzed the data of seven randomized controlled trials conducted in six countries in the developing world and found "no systematic evidence that cash transfer programs discourage work." From Honduras to Morocco to Indonesia and more, they found that programs aimed at poor people—some based on recipients meeting certain conditions, and some not—did not make them lazy:

> Aggregating evidence from randomized evaluations of seven government cash transfer programs, we find no systematic evidence of an impact of transfers on work behavior, either for men or women. Moreover, a 2014 review of transfer programs worldwide by Evans and Popova also shows no evidence—despite claims in the policy debate—that the transfers induce increases in spending on temptation goods, such as alcohol and tobacco. Thus, on net, the available evidence implies that cash transfer programs do not induce the "bad" behaviors that are often attributed to them in the policy space.

A second study from the World Bank in 2018 finds much the same result. These authors studied similar programs across a broader range of countries and found the following:

> The simple "Econ 101" model in which the income effect of a cash transfer results in recipients reducing work and increasing leisure is very seldom what we see happening in reality. The closest approximation to this model appears to come in the labor of the elderly when they receive government pensions. Yet this is hardly the group for whom more leisure is viewed as being a social bad, and there are few head-

lines excoriating lazy pensioners. In contrast, prime age adults tend to see very little change in either the amount they work, or the amount they earn when receiving unconditional or conditional cash transfers, or charitable grants.

Do these findings based on developing-world programs translate to more developed societies? We don't yet know. But they give us reason to believe that the traditional economics view about work behavior is wrong, just as it was wrong about the minimum wage.

This is what elected Democrats have to do: change these assumptions. As I argued above with respect to democracy, if the debate about what constitutes freedom proceeds from the existing assumptions—that less government equals more freedom, and that government assistance turns people into layabouts—then of course it will be hard to sell programs like paid family leave and subsidized child care. But if we proceed from different assumptions—that the free market has reduced people's freedoms by making their lives harder, and that smart government investments can open up options in people's lives and increase their freedom—then those programs start from a stronger philosophical foundation and become easier to pass.

In selling such programs, today's Democrats should flip the FDR formulation on its head: They should emphasize *freedom to* rather than *freedom from*. That is, instead of making arguments like "subsidized child care will free mothers from the worry about whether their children are safe," they should make arguments like "subsidized child care will give women freedom to go out in the world and achieve their potential." In fairness, some of them do this. Elizabeth Warren, the Senate's leading advocate of child care, talks this way much of the time. She tells the story of how her aunt Bee (yep, just like in Mayberry) came to care for her two small children, freeing Warren to keep her job. When Democrats emphasize freedom from, they can sound to people as if their goal is merely to build a bigger nanny state. But when they emphasize freedom to, they sound as if they are building this state as a means to an end: the freedom for more people to live happier, more productive lives. I think this kind of framing will prove much more resonant in our time.

Finally—and this is not quite a fifth pillar, but still an important point—all this needs a name. Names are important these days in politics. I sit in a lot of meetings where people refer to the "post-neoliberal moment." I'm sorry, but if you're still using "post-," you don't have a movement. A movement needs a name. The conservatives of the 1970s didn't go to the media and say, "Hey, we have a post-Keynesian idea to run by you!" They said they had this new thing, supply-side economics.

If someone comes up with some new great name, fine by me. In the meantime, I'm happy with middle-out economics. It conveys exactly what the theory is: that prosperity is built from the middle out. People who never took an economics course can make the logical connections: middle means middle class, which means not the rich, which means me. And since everyone likes to think of themselves as being in the middle class, even people who in fact aren't, it's aspirational: it speaks to everyone below the middle class who aspires to join it. Democrats need to drill this (or perhaps some other brilliant phrase someone comes up with) into the public consciousness with discipline and, yes, monotonous frequency.

.   .   .

As I have tried to show in this book, this nation's economic assumptions have changed twice in the last century, both times as a result of a crisis. The first was after the Great Depression, when we changed from the laissez-faire principles that had guided most economic policy making for decades or even centuries to the interventionist principles of John Maynard Keynes. Those worked well for forty years, until the next crisis, the stagflation crisis of the 1970s, which opened the door for the neoliberals to assert their arguments. The election in 1980 of a conservative president allowed their ideas to jump from op-ed pages and PBS to actual policy.

The things they said were never true. Tax cuts don't pay for themselves. Lower taxes don't bring in more revenue. The unregulated market not only didn't fix everything but made a lot of things worse. But Republicans and the right-wing media were so in lockstep in repeating these untruths, and Democrats so undisciplined about rebutting them at their philosophical root, that they stuck around long past their shelf life. The Great Recession should have driven the neoliberal project into the grave; it should have been a "paradigm pivot" moment like the Great Depression and the 1970s stagflation, but it wasn't, and a big part of why was that the Democrats didn't have a direct answer to supply-side economics. And part of the reason why the Democrats didn't have an answer was that the liberal infrastructure that feeds the Democratic Party energy and ideas—foundations, think tanks, academics, and activists—hadn't developed that answer. A lot of people were working on it, but there was nothing resembling a consensus, and the two Democratic administrations of the period were internally divided on the answer, too. As the old saying goes, an explanation, even a bad one, beats no explanation.

So the paradigm didn't shift after the Great Recession. But enough people were hungry for such a shift that things started happening. In the economics profession, among activists, in the foundation world, and within the Democratic Party itself, anger at economic inequality and other manifestations of rising oligarchy intensified. More brainpower, resources, and attention were focused on the problem. Meanwhile, Donald Trump got elected. The pandemic hit. The country was thrust back into crisis again—economic for sure, but not solely; this crisis, or these crises, were about democracy and public health (actually, life and death) as well as the economy. Maybe the door was open enough again, as it had been in the 1970s, for a new paradigm to charge through?

But now there was a new political reality that hadn't existed in the 1970s: deep, stark polarization. In the 1970s, there was a large, persuadable middle that had soft ideological commitments and could switch from Carter to Reagan, from more or less trusting government to fully distrusting it. That isn't true today. The persuadable middle then was approximately 20 percent. Now it's closer to 5 percent. Convincing people to rethink things now will be a lot harder than it was in the 1970s: there are fewer persuadables, less margin for error. Also today, there is an alternative right-wing media that didn't exist then, telling people that any domestic investment is socialism and will go to the (mostly not white) undeserving.

Thus will changing the paradigm be the work of many years. Can the Democrats, and the people in their orbit, do it? I think they can. They have popular policies, but they have to remove those policies from their silos and connect them to values and offer people a vision for themselves as individuals and for society at large, a vision that stirs people's souls as Americans. They have to connect their economic *ideas* to *ideals* that Americans cherish—democracy and freedom. You can't get much more American than democracy and freedom. They are core to our national project. And they are not separate from economic justice. They are inseparable. It is up to the Democrats to defend all three. And they must see this as not three fights but one.

ACKNOWLEDGMENTS

Kristine Puopolo was a brilliant editor of this book. In an early conversation, when I was talking about the link between economics and democracy, she tossed out, "How about freedom, too?" So a big part of my argument actually came from her. I thank her and everyone at Doubleday who worked so hard on this book. Chris Calhoun, my agent, provided his usual astute and invaluable guidance and advice to me as we went through the proposal process and beyond. I want to thank everyone who agreed to be interviewed for this book, from the esteemed economists to the political operatives and everyone in between; their insights, I hope and believe, made this a far richer reading experience for you than if it had all just sprung solely from my head. I want to thank some friends who read or talked me through certain sections of the book. I'll inevitably forget some people here, because I had hundreds of such conversations; but notably Dean Baker, Eric Beinhocker, Heather Boushey, Joe Conason, E. J. Dionne, Arthur Goldhammer, Jacob Hacker, Harold Meyerson, Guy Molyneux, Jo-Ann Mort, Felicia Wong, and Rich Yeselson were helpful. Special thanks are due Larry Kramer of the Hewlett Foundation. We met at a conference at Stanford in March 2020, just before the pandemic. The day I flew home, a Friday, the Stanford student newspaper carried the headline that classes were canceled for the rest of the semester. It was the day before that that Larry and I had a coffee, and he explained to me Hewlett's Beyond Neoliberalism project. Some months later, I was describing that chat to Chris Calhoun, and Chris said, "This sounds like a book to me." Larry—and later, others—graciously agreed to cooperate.

My *Democracy* journal colleagues Jack Meserve and Sophia Crabbe-Field have worked with me editing a large number of articles that enlarged my understanding of these issues. They are smart, kind, energetic—and funny, which always helps. My *New Republic* colleagues (too many to name) have been supportive and a joy to work with; Win McCormack, who owns the magazine and hired me, is incredibly well-read and committed to the principle that ideas can change the world, and I love batting them around with him.

Finally, I want to thank my sister, Susan Tomasky, who talked a lot of this through with me, from her valuable perspective as a liberal with both business-world experience and a less coastal view of America; my wife, Sarah Kerr, who listened to my ideas and for two years emailed me a steady and useful diet of "this may be helpful" links; and Margot Tomasky, who always made me remember to smile.

NOTES

PREFACE: IT'S ALL ONE ARGUMENT

xi   An ongoing Economic Anxiety survey: Janet Nguyen, "Americans on Shaky Ground Financially, Speaking Out More on Racism, Poll Finds," Marketplace-Edison Research Poll, Oct. 15, 2020.

INTRODUCTION: HOW DO YOU CHANGE AN ECONOMY?

2   "the care economy": For a description of all this activity, see, for example, Rebecca Traister, "Biden's Big Left Gamble," *New York*, July 5, 2021.

5   "He was and is acutely aware": This and other quotations in this introduction, from Bernstein, interview by author, June 24, 2021.

6   about $31.5 billion: See Diana Azevedo-McCaffery and Ali Safawi, "To Promote Equity, States Should Invest More TANF Dollars in Basic Assistance," Center on Budget and Policy Priorities, Jan. 12, 2022.

6   a little under 2 percent: Andrew Van Dam, "Is It Fair to Call Biden's $3.5 Trillion Plan Another New Deal?," *Washington Post*, Oct. 2, 2021. Van Dam put the Biden figure at 2.1 percent, but he was assuming passage of a $3.5 trillion reconciliation bill.

8   "and it lost on a party-line vote": DeLauro, interview by author, July 10, 2021.

8   "I want to change the paradigm": Justin Sink and Nancy Cook, "Biden Promises New 'Paradigm' in Economic Program Next Week," Bloomberg News, March 25, 2021.

14 higher personal freedom rankings: See "Freest Countries 2022," World Population Review, worldpopulationreview.com. The Personal Freedom Index numbers were, specifically, Sweden, 9.45; Finland, 9.27; Norway, 9.26; Denmark, 9.25; United States, 8.72.

16 "the greatest happiness of the greatest number": Adams to the

president of the Continental Congress, Oct. 25, 1781, founders
.archives.gov.

17 the top 1 percent: Carter C. Price and Kathryn A. Edwards, "Trends
in Income from 1975 to 2018," Rand Corporation, www.rand.org.

17 If you were in the 99th percentile: These numbers come from
dqydj.com (Don't Quit Your Day Job), an economics information
and statistics site.

CHAPTER ONE: THE GOLDEN AGE

22 "was much more a conglomeration": Joshua B. Freeman, *American
Empire: The Rise of Global Power, the Democratic Revolution at Home,
1945–2000* (New York: Penguin Books, 2012), 1.

23 Skidelsky compared global and Western: Robert Skidelsky, *Keynes:
The Return of the Master* (New York: PublicAffairs, 2009), 114–23.

24 "stable in the Bretton Woods age": Ibid., 122.

24 Likewise, four economists taking a longer: Andrew Glynn et al.,
"The Rise and Fall of the Golden Age," in *The Golden Age of Capitalism: Reinterpreting the Postwar Experience*, ed. Stephen A. Marg-
lin and Juliet B. Schor (Oxford: Clarendon Press, 2007), 42.

25 "I will pay no more": Amy Bentley, *Eating for Victory: Food Ration-
ing and the Politics of Domesticity* (Urbana: University of Illinois
Press, 1998), 37.

25 "which had been opened to the public": Isser Woloch, *The Postwar
Moment: Progressive Forces in Britain, France, and the United States
After World War II* (New Haven, Conn.: Yale University Press,
2019), 140.

26 "a survey of the existing national schemes": Sir William Beveridge,
"Social Insurances and Allied Services," Nov. 25, 1942, National
Archives, Kew, U.K., filestore.nationalarchives.gov.uk.

26 want, disease, ignorance, squalor, and idleness: Woloch, *Postwar
Moment*, 36.

27 "the best health services": Ibid., 145.

28 "Therefore, I propose a second Bill of Rights": Ibid., 211.

28 broadcast nationally on radio: Ibid., 218.

29 one of our great presidents: See, for example, this C-SPAN "Presi-
dential Historians Survey 2021," in which Truman ranks sixth, behind
Lincoln, Washington, Franklin Roosevelt, Theodore Roosevelt, and
Eisenhower, at www.c-span.org/presidentsurvey2021/?page=overall.

29 "as the big meatpacking companies": Woloch, *Postwar Moment*, 234.

29 All told, in 1946, about 4.6 million workers: Jeremy Brecher,
Strike! (Oakland: PM Press, 1972), chap. 6, libcom.org.

29   around 60 million people: The Bureau of Labor Statistics numbers on workforce size go back only to 1950. In 1950, the workforce was 62.2 million. See Mitra Toossi, "A Century of Change: The U.S. Labor Force, 1950–2050," *Monthly Labor Review*, May 2002, www.bls.gov.

30   crashed by 22 percent: Jonathan Levy, *Ages of American Capitalism: A History of the United States* (New York: Random House, 2021), 484.

30   GDP was 4.1 percent: See GDP growth rates at Kimberly Amadeo, "U.S. GDP by Year, Compared to Recessions and Events," Balance, April 28, 2021, www.thebalance.com.

30   5.7 percent: Source: Bureau of Economic Analysis, U.S. Dept. of Commerce, news release, January 27, 2022, www.bea.gov.

30   "an unprecedented growth rate": Glyn et al., "Rise and Fall of the Golden Age," 48.

30   as far back as 1946: See my review essay "The World Trade Center: Before, During, and After," *New York Review of Books*, March 28, 2002.

31   "total federal government expenditures": Levy, *Ages of American Capitalism*, 486.

31   "the dominant political-economic coordinating mechanism": Ibid., 517.

32   300 Major League Baseball players: Major League Baseball Salaries 2021, *USA Today*, databases.usatoday.com/mlb-salaries/page/16/.

32   5.5 million other people: Darina Lynkova, "28 Millionaire Statistics: What Percentage of Americans Are Millionaires?," spendmenot.com, July 12, 2021, spendmenot.com. Lynkova writes that 5,671,005 households earn $3 million or more a year; to allow for the decrease from $3 million to $2.8 million, I rounded down a bit.

32   For example, on dollars earned above: All these numbers are from Federal Individual Income Tax Rates History, files.taxfoundation .org.

33   30 to 40 percent range: Thomas Hungerford, "Corporate Tax Rates and Economic Growth Since 1947," Economic Policy Institute, June 4, 2013, www.epi.org.

33   "The unrivaled freedom of economic": Howard R. Bowen, *Social Responsibilities of the Businessman* (Iowa City: University of Iowa Press, 2013), 5.

34   In that same year, Truman signed: Wilbur J. Cohen and Robert J. Myers, "Social Security Act Amendments of 1950: A Summary and Legislative History," Oct. 1950, 3, www.ssa.gov.

35   "a sort of 'Caucasian' unity": Jefferson Cowie, *The Great Exception: The New Deal and the Limits of American Politics* (Princeton, N.J.: Princeton University Press, 2016), 131.

36   "incompatible racial groups should not": Rothstein, interview by Terry Gross, *Fresh Air*, National Public Radio, May 3, 2017.

37   "less than 1 percent of salaried employees": Rick Wartzman, *The End of Loyalty: The Rise and Fall of Good Jobs in America* (New York: PublicAffairs, 2017), 167.

37   "the only contribution the Eastman Kodak": Ibid., 176.

38   A *Fortune* magazine survey: Ibid., 179.

38   For example, one hundred women: Nancy Gabin, "'They Have Placed a Penalty on Womanhood': The Protest Actions of Women Auto Workers in Detroit-Area UAW Locals, 1945–47," *Feminist Studies* 8, no. 2 (Summer 1982): 386–87.

38   At the UAW's March 1946 convention: Ibid., 388.

38   Winifred Stanley introduced an act: See "Representative Winifred Stanley of New York," History, Art & Archives, U.S. House of Representatives, history.house.gov.

39   it passed the House overwhelmingly: See www.govtrack.us/congress/votes/88-1963/h29.

39   women made 82 cents to men's $1: See "Highlights of Women's Earnings in 2019," *BLS Reports*, Dec. 2020, www.bls.gov.

39   an OECD study from 2016: See Gabriela Ramos, "Gender Discrimination in Social Institutions and Long-Term Growth," OECD, March 8, 2016, www.oecd.org.

CHAPTER TWO: WHO WERE THE NEOLIBERALS?

42   25 and 40 percent of the Roman population: From unrv.com, a website devoted to Roman history.

43   Online Etymology Dictionary: From etymonline.com.

43   "*Leonato, I am sorry you must hear*": William Shakespeare, *Much Ado About Nothing*, act 4, scene 1, lines 87–94.

44   Council on Foreign Plantations: Locke's legacy was much attacked on the postcolonial left in the 1960s not only because of the described work but because he was paid for it in Royal African Company stock. But Locke was also a fierce opponent of Charles II, who dramatically expanded the slave trade and implemented policies in the colonies that rewarded large slaveholders. For a balanced discussion that mostly defends Locke, see Holly Brewer, "Slavery-Entangled Philosophy," *Aeon*, Sept. 12, 2018.

44   "pursuit of happiness": See for example Joseph Fishkin and Wil-

liam A. Forbath, *The Anti-Oligarchy Constitution: Reconstructing the Economic Foundations of American Democracy* (Cambridge, Mass.: Harvard University Press, 2022), 43.

45   "This freedom from absolute, arbitrary power": John Locke, *Second Treatise on Government*, chap. 4, sec. 23.

46   would not be excessive: Nicholas Phillipson, *Adam Smith: An Enlightened Life* (New Haven, Conn.: Yale University Press, 2010), 234.

46   keep tuition reasonable: This is a serious problem in today's America. One 2018 study found that state spending on higher education had gone down by an inflation-adjusted $7 billion after the Great Recession. Public universities increased their tuitions by 36 percent over that period as a result. I single out Jindal because he was perhaps the worst, and indeed tuition in Louisiana doubled in those years. See Michael Mitchell et al., "Unkept Promises: State Cuts to Higher Education Threaten Access and Equity," Center on Budget and Policy Priorities, Oct. 4, 2018.

46   "the liberal system of free exportation": Adam Smith, *An Inquiry into the Origins of the Wealth of Nations*, bk. 4, chap. 5, online (public domain) version of the 1905 edition published by Edwin Cannan, at libertyfund.org.

46   "'Classical liberalism' is the term": Ralph Raico, "What Is Classical Liberalism?," Mises Institute, Nov. 1, 2018.

48   "malefactors of great wealth": He used the phrase in an address he gave while president at the Pilgrim Monument in Provincetown, Massachusetts, Aug. 20, 1907.

48   "After Progressive Republicans came to power": Heather Cox Richardson, *To Make Men Free: A History of the Republican Party* (New York: Basic Books, 2014), 151.

48   "became a somewhat tainted term": A. James Reichley, *The Life of the Parties: A History of American Political Parties* (Lanham, Md.: Rowman & Littlefield, 2000), 210.

49   "I am reminded of four definitions": At Oxford Essential Quotations, oxfordreference.com.

49   called himself a liberal: Reichley, *Life of the Parties*, 210.

49   the review was headlined: William MacDonald, "Ogden Mills Defends Liberal Standards," *New York Times*, March 1, 1936.

50   "What do our opponents mean": Address of John F. Kennedy upon Accepting the Liberal Party Nomination for President, New York, Sept. 14, 1960, jfklibrary.org.

50   "It is extremely convenient": Milton Friedman, *Capitalism and Freedom* (Chicago: University of Chicago Press, 2002), 5.

52   "we no longer automatically favor": Charles Peters, "A Neo-liberal's Manifesto," *Washington Monthly*, Sept. 5, 1982.

53   Government spending as a percentage: See, for example, Michael Schuyler, "A Short History of Government Taxing and Spending in the United States," Tax Foundation, Feb. 19, 2014.

53   "rational economic man": Niall Kishtainy, *A Little History of Economics* (New Haven, Conn.: Yale University Press, 2017), 65.

55   "was forging a new set": Zachary D. Carter, *The Price of Peace: Money, Democracy, and the Life of John Maynard Keynes* (New York: Random House, 2020), 149.

55   "it is *not* a correct deduction": John Maynard Keynes, *The End of Laissez-Faire*, sec. 4, panarchy.org.

55   "lazy fairies": Arthur M. Schlesinger Jr., *The Crisis of the Old Order, 1919–1933* (Boston: Houghton Mifflin, 1957), 187.

56   "under a modified capitalistic system": Ibid., 189.

56   in Electoral College history: He won the Electoral College 523 to 8. Richard Nixon beat George McGovern in 1972 by 520 to 17, and Ronald Reagan beat Walter Mondale in 1984 by 525 to 13. Interestingly—the two states that FDR's Republican challenger Alf Landon won? This is a good trivia question for modern audiences who don't know much about the history of regional party bastions in the United States. The answers are Maine and Vermont.

57   "it is obvious that delegation": Daniel Stedman Jones, *Masters of the Universe: Hayek, Friedman, and the Birth of Neoliberal Politics* (Princeton, N.J.: Princeton University Press, 2012), 53.

57   "that the main direction": Angus Burgin, *The Great Persuasion: Reinventing Free Markets Since the Depression* (Cambridge, Mass.: Harvard University Press, 2012), 39.

57   "quite apt to score": Quoted in Lippmann's *New York Times* obituary, by Alden Whitman, Dec. 15, 1973.

58   "had difficulties identifying constructive 'revisions'": Burgin, *Great Persuasion*, 73.

58   114 percent right after the war: Kimberly Amadeo and Michael J. Boyle, "US National Debt by Year Compared to GDP and Major Events," Balance, July 30, 2020, thebalance.com.

58   it was 270 percent: "Post World War II Debt Reduction," Office for Budget Responsibility, July 2013, obr.co.uk.

58   it was above 100 percent: See this chart from the St. Louis Federal Reserve: fred.stlouisfed.org/series/GFDEGDQ188S#0.

59   enjoying a sales spike: John Carney, "The Road to Serfdom Is a Best Seller Again," *Business Insider*, Feb. 17, 2010.

59   "So while Hayek wanted to critique": Stedman Jones, *Masters of the Universe*, 68.

59   "morally and philosophically, I find myself": Burgin, *Great Persuasion*, 91.

60   "an acknowledgment of the importance": Burgin, *Great Persuasion*, 105.

60   "any turn toward propaganda": Ibid., 131.

61   "their number is negligible": Dwight D. Eisenhower to Edgar N. Eisenhower, Nov. 8, 1954, teachingamericanhistory.org.

62   "Friedman helped to pave the way": Lanny Ebenstein, *Milton Friedman: A Biography* (New York: Palgrave Macmillan, 2007), 103.

63   "a rising tide of support": Ibid., 151.

63   "far from comprehensive": Friedman, *Capitalism and Freedom*, 36.

64   "Opponents of such laws": Ibid., 113.

64   "less likely to be considered for jobs": Robert H. Frank, "When It Really Counts, Qualifications Trump Race," *New York Times*, Nov. 15, 2008. Frank's column, written in the wake of Barack Obama's victory, is an attempt to explain Obama's win by arguing that voters proved Friedman correct, which seems to me a stretch. A presidential election is not a normal job application, and Frank, in pointing to the study I cite, does acknowledge the difference.

64   "I believe strongly that the color": Friedman, *Capitalism and Freedom*, 111.

65   "to seek to persuade": Ibid.

65   "freedom of choice" plan: Readers who are really interested in this history will be fascinated to listen to an April 10, 1961, radio interview with Dure by Ray Niblack of WINA Charlottesville. It can be found at the website of the American Archive of Public Broadcasting. The twenty-eight-minute interview is revealing of how skilled orators of the day could make segregation sound palatable to the predecessors of soccer moms.

65   "freedom of association carried with it": James H. Hershman Jr., "Leon S. Dure (1907–1993)," *Encyclopedia Virginia*, encyclopediavirginia.org.

65   failed to integrate the schools: The case, a landmark civil rights case, was *Green et al. v. New Kent County Schools*. The county had two schools, one white and one Black, which were strictly segregated until 1965 (eleven years after *Brown*, notice). After that point, the county allowed children to choose which school they wanted to attend: "freedom of choice." Yet, confoundingly I'm sure to local officials, only a few Black kids choose to attend the white school, and not a single white student opted for the Black

school. See the discussion of the case at oyez.org and Justice William Brennan's majority opinion at the website of the Legal Information Institute of the Cornell Law School.

66 "He became less a social scientist": Ebenstein, *Milton Friedman*, 139.

66 "We did it. We're very sorry": Gary Richardson, "The Great Depression," Federal Reserve History, federalreservehistory.org.

67 "seemed irresistibly prescient": Burgin, *Great Persuasion*, 204.

67 "did far more harm to the country": Ebenstein, *Milton Friedman*, 188.

68 Inflation hit 11 percent in 1974: See "U.S. Inflation Rate, 1960–2022," Macrotrends, www.macrotrends.net.

CHAPTER THREE: NEOLIBERALISM OF THE RIGHT:
FROM REAGAN TO TRUMP

71 "My only question about Wanniski's version": See Arthur Laffer, "The Laffer Curve: Past, Present, and Future," Heritage Foundation, June 1, 2004, www.heritage.org.

72 "The napkin is definitely cloth": Email interview with Liebhold, Sept. 15, 2020.

72 "owes much of its contagion": Robert Shiller, *Narrative Economics: How Stories Go Viral and Drive Major Events* (Princeton, N.J.: Princeton University Press, 2019), 42.

73 Friedman and his wife, Rose: Ebenstein, *Milton Friedman*, 201.

75 a Treasury Department study from 2013: Jerry Tempalski, Office of Tax Analysis, Department of the Treasury, "Revenue Effects of Major Tax Bills Updated Tables for All 2012 Bills," Feb. 2013. This is a shorter, follow-up paper to Tempalski's original 2006 paper, which had an eight-page narrative section. It was called OTA Working Paper 81.

75 Designed to finance the war effort: Will Freeland and Scott A. Hodge, "Tax Equity and the Growth in Nonpayers," Tax Foundation, July 20, 2012.

76 "income tax revenues from the top": Arthur Laffer, "The Reagan Tax Cuts Did Too Pay for Themselves," *Investor's Business Daily*, Aug. 7, 2015.

76 But what Laffer *didn't* say: See Glenn Kessler, "Rand Paul's Claim That Reagan's Tax Cuts Produced 'More Revenue' and 'Tens of Millions of Jobs,'" *Washington Post*, April 10, 2015. Kessler writes the paper's "Fact Checker" column and awards politicians from one to four Pinocchios based on how big a whopper they just told.

The fours are reserved for items that are just flat-out lies in which there is no gray area at all. He gave Senator Paul three Pinocchios for this claim.

77 conservatives like Gregory Mankiw: See Gregory N. Mankiw and Matthew Weinzierl, "Dynamic Scoring: A Back-of-the-Envelope Guide" (Harvard Institute of Economic Research Working Papers 11000, 2005). They found that tax cuts might pay for up to 32 percent of their cost.

77 it's Republicans who've saddled the nation: See Historical Tables, Office of Management and Budget, www.whitehouse.gov.

77 deficit at $3.2 trillion: See "Federal Surplus or Deficit," FRED Economic Data, St. Louis Federal Reserve, updated Oct. 25, 2021, fred.stlouisfed.org.

78 The Bush tax cuts likewise: See, for example, Emily Horton, "The Legacy of the 2001 and 2003 'Bush' Tax Cuts," Center on Budget and Policy Priorities, Oct. 23, 2017. The Center on Budget and Policy Priorities is, admittedly, a left-of-center group, but the general economic consensus, which you know in your bones if you lived through it, was that the post-9/11 recovery of the first decade of the twenty-first century was on the sluggish side, with, for example, little median household income growth—very slow compared with such growth under Clinton. And that was before it all came tumbling down in 2008.

78 What the tax cuts mainly led to: Jane G. Gravelle and Donald J. Marples, "The Economic Effects of the 2017 Tax Revision: Preliminary Observations," Congressional Research Service, May 22, 2019.

78 According to the Tax Policy Center: Tax Policy Center calculations cited by Zachary A. Goldfarb, "The Legacy of the Bush Tax Cuts, in Four Charts," *Washington Post*, Jan. 2, 2013.

79 "probably the largest peacetime tax increase": Katie Sanders, "Stephen Colbert Brings Up Ronald Reagan's Tax-Raising Record in Ted Cruz Interview," PolitiFact, Sept. 25, 2015.

80 the so-called sequestration budget deals: Dylan Matthews, "The Sequester: Absolutely Everything You Could Possibly Need to Know, in One FAQ," *Washington Post*, Feb. 20, 2013.

80 At a debate of GOP presidential contenders: All quoted in Steve Benen, "Ten-to-One Isn't Good Enough for the GOP," *Washington Monthly*, Aug. 12, 2011.

82 Of the fifteen leading candidates: All these minimum wage positions are from Joshua Ferrer, "Republican Candidates on Raising the Minimum Wage," OurFuture, July 24, 2015, ourfuture.org.

82   Exasperated at inaction on the federal level: All these states from "Minimum Wage Tracker," Economic Policy Institute, epi.org.

82   Numerous cities, from New York: All these cities from "Progress Report: Raise the Minimum Wage," reclaimtheamerican dream.org.

82   Even a number of companies: All these companies from Gabrielle Olya, "What Happened When These Places Raised the Minimum Wage to $15," *Yahoo! News*, Sept. 2, 2020.

83   this finding goes back: David Card and Alan B. Krueger, "Minimum Wages and Employment: A Case Study of the Fast-Food Industry in New Jersey and Pennsylvania" (National Bureau of Economic Research, NBER Working Paper 4509, Oct. 1993).

83   the researchers reversed field: See Noam Scheiber, "They Said Seattle's Higher Base Pay Would Hurt Workers. Why Did They Flip?," *New York Times*, Oct. 22, 2018. The lead author of the study was Jacob Vigdor, on faculty at the University of Washington but affiliated with the conservative Manhattan Institute. He had written a blog post in 2014 that he headlined "The Minimum Wage Is a Lousy Anti-poverty Program." Interestingly, he updated it in 2019 with a longish preface acknowledging that his experience studying the Seattle minimum wage had changed his thinking somewhat. Overall, his second study found that the higher minimum wage hurt people who weren't working but might seek entry-level work—in other words, that employers would take a chance on someone at $10 an hour, but maybe not at $13 an hour. However, for those already working at minimum wage, the second study found that they benefited substantially.

83   "no discernible effect on employment": Jason Bram, Faith Karahan, and Brendan Moore, "Minimum Wage Impacts Along the New York–Pennsylvania Border," Federal Reserve Bank of New York, Sept. 25, 2019.

84   "The minimum wage is a threat": Rubio was speaking at a forum at the Jack Kemp Foundation, Jan. 10, 2016, on YouTube.

84   too much economic inequality in America: See Oren Cass, "The Return of Conservative Economics," *National Review*, Feb. 18, 2020. This short essay announcing the formation of his group includes some fairly remarkable sentences coming from conservatives, like "Conservative economics will also accord equal respect to the concerns of capital and labor, rather than claiming that whatever is best for shareholders in the short run will eventually prove best for workers as well." I wish them Godspeed.

86   Trump never really pushed the issue: Alan Rappeport, "Trump

Promised to Kill Carried Interest. Lobbyists Kept It Alive," *New York Times*, Dec. 22, 2017.

86 Branko Milanovic offered an interesting take: Branko Milanovic, "Trump as the Ultimate Triumph of Neoliberalism," *Global Policy*, May 14, 2020.

CHAPTER FOUR: NEOLIBERALISM OF THE LEFT:
CONSIDERING CLINTON AND OBAMA

89 "The numbers almost certainly will cast": James Risen, "Bush's Budget Forecasts Rising Waves of Red Ink," *Los Angeles Times*, Jan. 7, 1993. Readers might know Risen today as a national-security reporter with *The New York Times* and more recently *The Intercept*. He's one of the best in the country.

90 "I was the one who ended up": Sperling, interview by author, Oct. 8, 2020.

90 "As we sat down to work": Bill Clinton, *My Life* (New York: Knopf, 2004), 459.

91 "You mean to tell me": Bob Woodward, *The Agenda: Inside the Clinton White House* (New York: Simon & Schuster, 1994), 84.

91 "thirty-year-old bond traders": Clinton, *My Life*, 459.

91 "if they didn't like what they saw": James Surowiecki, "Bonds and Domination," *New York*, March 1, 1999.

92 "I guess in some ways": Sperling, interview by author, Oct. 8, 2020.

94 between 2 and 3 percent most years: See Macrotrends, U.S. Inflation Rate 1960-2022, at https://www.macrotrends.net/countries/USA/united-states/inflation-rate-cpi.

94 More liberal critics have argued: See, for example, "The High Cost of Rubinomics," a really interesting exchange in *The American Prospect* between Jeff Faux and Brad DeLong from 2004. Faux was critic, and DeLong, who worked in Clinton's Treasury Department, defender. Faux acknowledges that "Rubin's plan worked," but argues the cost in terms of absent public investment was too high. DeLong retorted that for Clinton to have not addressed deficit concerns first was "politically infeasible."

95 vastly increased "extreme poverty": On extreme poverty, see H. Luke Shaefer and Kathryn Edin, "Extreme Poverty in the United States, 1996–2011," Policy Brief 28, National Poverty Center, Feb. 2012.

95 rose from 40.5 percent to 47.6 percent: Thomas Piketty, Emmanuel Saez, and Gabriel Zucman, "Distributional National Accounts:

Methods and Estimates for the United States," *Quarterly Journal of Economics* 133, no. 2 (2018).

96　In the House, Democrats voted for the bill: House Roll Call Vote 276, 106th Cong., July 1, 1999.

96　in the Senate only 8 Democrats were opposed: Senate Vote 354, 106th Cong., Nov. 4, 1999.

96　"This was an area": Sperling, interview by author, Oct. 8, 2020.

96　video of the signing ceremony: Remarks at the signing of the Gramm-Leach-Bliley Act, Nov. 12, 1999, courtesy William J. Clinton Presidential Library.

97　"What we are creating now": Rep. John Dingell on House floor, Nov. 4, 1999, C-SPAN, www.c-span.org/video/?c41620/user-clip -clip-house-session.

97　"many of the same people": David Leonhardt, "Washington's Invisible Hand," *New York Times Magazine*, Sept. 26, 2008.

98　"there's a virtual consensus": "The Right Minimum Wage: $0.00," *New York Times*, Jan. 14, 1987.

100　A 2014 audit by the department's Office: Audit of the Department of Justice's Efforts to Address Mortgage Fraud, Department of Justice, Office of the Inspector General, Audit Division, Audit Report 14-12, March 2014.

101　"I would just not understate": Furman, interview by author, July 22, 2020.

101　"That was the mentality": Sperling, interview by author, Oct. 8, 2020.

102　"Even if I drop to 5 percent": Clinton, *My Life*, 682.

102　"more than 50 percent bigger": Michael Grunwald, *The New New Deal* (New York: Simon & Schuster, 2012), 10.

104　"is conjured into existence": Stephanie Kelton, *The Deficit Myth: Modern Monetary Theory and the Birth of the People's Economy* (New York: PublicAffairs, 2020), 235.

CHAPTER FIVE: THE LEGACIES OF NEOLIBERALISM: INEQUALITY, MONOPOLY, AND PRIVATE EDUCATION

107　there were 161 billionaires: "Bloomberg Billionaires Index," Bloomberg News, Dec. 9, 2020, www.bloomberg.com.

107　Gini score, of 35: From a chart, "Income Gini Ratio of Families by Race of Householder, All Races," made by the St. Louis Federal Reserve, using Census Bureau figures, which can be found at economistsview.typepad.com/.a/6a00d83451b33869e201a51157 29b5970c-popup.

107   49 in 2020, for example: See Table 4 on the U.S. Census Bureau web page "Historical Income Tables: Income Inequality," www .census.gov.

108   "The Perils Awaiting Conservatives": Ryan Bourne, "The Perils Awaiting Conservatives Who Seek to Reduce Inequality," Cato Institute, Jan. 22, 2020.

108   "Capitalism is a competition": Binyamin Appelbaum, *The Economists' Hour: False Prophets, Free Markets, and the Fracture of Society* (New York: Little, Brown, 2019), 327.

108   according to two scholars: John E. Elliott and Barry S. Clark, "Keynes' *General Theory* and Social Justice," *Journal of Post-Keynesian Economics* 9, no. 3 (1987): 382–94.

109   "a belief in equality of income": Friedman, *Capitalism and Freedom*, 161.

109   "inequalities are arbitrary unless": John Rawls, "Justice as Fairness," *Philosophical Review* 67, no. 2 (April 1958): 165.

109   Because he argues for a lessening: Rawls's difference principle held that yes, inequalities of income will indeed exist, and they will be acceptable as long as the worst off benefit more (comparatively) than the best off. So, for example, imagine two societies, one in which everyone earned $40,000 and a second in which the worst off earned $50,000, the people in the middle earned $100,000, and the people at the top $200,000. Rawls's principle would prefer the second society over the first, because those at the bottom are doing better by $10,000.

110   "The impact of inequality on growth": Federico Cingano, "Trends in Income Inequality and Its Impact on Economic Growth" (OECD Social, Employment, and Migration Working Papers, No. 163, 2014), 17.

110   "redistributive policies achieving greater equality": Ibid., 28.

110   "Raising the income share of the poor": Era Dabla-Norris et al., "Causes and Consequences of Economic Inequality: A Global Perspective," International Monetary Fund, June 2015.

111   After the Great Society kicked in: U.S. Census Bureau, "Historical Poverty Tables: People and Families, 1959–2019," Table 3, www .census.gov.

112   "While there may be underlying economic forces": Joseph E. Stiglitz, *The Price of Inequality: How Today's Divided Society Endangers Our Future* (New York: Norton, 2012), L.

112   "Lack of opportunity": Joseph Stiglitz, "The Price of Inequality," *Guardian*, June 5, 2012.

113   Majorities of Americans tend to agree: Julianna Menasce Horo-

witz, Ruth Igielnik, and Rakesh Kochhar, "Most Americans Say There Is Too Much Inequality in the U.S., but Fewer Than Half Call It a Top Priority," Pew Research Center, Jan. 9, 2020.

114 "the world's first self-consciously libertarian": Quoted in Murray N. Rothbard, "Liberty and Property: The Levellers and Locke," Mises Institute, April 3, 2018, mises.org. That short essay is excerpted from Rothbard's book *Economic Thought Before Adam Smith: An Austrian Perspective on the History of Economic Thought*, vol. 1 (Aldershot: Edward Elgar, 1995).

114 "wretched spirit of monopoly": Phillipson, *Adam Smith*, 16.

114 "monopoly should be revoked": Ibid., 265–66.

114 Some scholars have argued: See, for example, Steven G. Calabresi and Larissa Price, "Monopolies and the Constitution: A History of Crony Capitalism" (Northwestern University School of Law Scholarly Commons, Faculty Working Papers, 2012), 27.

115 The leading voices here: Both Jefferson and Madison are quoted by Prateek Raj, "Antimonopoly Is as Old as the Republic," Pro-Market, May 22, 2017, promarket.org.

115 rights of equal protection to corporations: The story of corporate personhood is mind-blowing and wonderfully told by the UCLA law professor Adam Winkler in a 2018 *Atlantic* piece. A court reporter who wrote up the summary of the *Santa Clara* case—who had also been past president of a New York railroad company—wrote that the Court had ruled that "corporations are persons . . . within the Fourteenth Amendment." But the Court had ruled no such thing. On a subsequent case, a corrupt justice who was a confidant of Leland Stanford, the owner of the Southern Pacific Railroad, noted in an opinion that the Court had held that corporations were persons in *Santa Clara*. The Court had not, but somehow it stuck. It's been upheld many times since, but without that corrupt precedent who knows what might have happened? See Adam Winkler, "'Corporations Are People' Is Built on an Incredible 19th-Century Lie," *Atlantic*, March 5, 2018.

116 "the Democratic position": Louis Brandeis, "An Address to the Economic Club of New York," Nov. 1, 1912, Louis D. Brandeis School of Law Library, University of Louisville Brandeis School of Law.

116 "The elder J. P. Morgan died": Matt Stoller, *Goliath: The 100-Year War Between Monopoly Power and Populism* (New York: Simon & Schuster, 2019), 23.

116 "by Chicago-school economists": Robert E. Litan and Carl Shapiro, "Antitrust Policy in the Clinton Administration," UC Berkeley, Competition Policy Center, July 2001, 447.

117 "Classical liberals," wrote one scholar: Rob Van Horn, "Reinventing Monopoly and the Role of Corporations," in *The Road from Mont Pelerin: The Making of the Neoliberal Thought Collective*, ed. Philip Mirowski and Dieter Plehwe (Cambridge, Mass.: Harvard University Press, 2009), 204.

117 Antitrust Project headed by Aaron Director: Ibid., 205.

117 "retard the tendency (if it exists)": Ibid., 215.

117 "no longer regarded monopoly": Ibid., 229.

118 "over-estimation of the importance of monopoly": Friedman, *Capitalism and Freedom*, 123.

118 "are generally unstable and of brief duration": Ibid., 131.

118 "ended up having a far more": Barry C. Lynn, *Liberty from All Masters: The New American Autocracy vs. the Will of the People* (New York: St. Martin's Press, 2020), 192.

119 "You could not find a more": Lynn, interview by author, Nov. 23, 2020.

119 "as long as executives could make": Lynn, *Liberty from All Masters*, 206.

120 In that year's platform: The parties' platforms are most readily accessible through the American Presidency Project at the University of California at Santa Barbara. The 1988 platform reads, "We further believe in halting such irresponsible corporate conduct as unproductive takeovers, monopolistic mergers, insider trading, and golden parachutes for executives by reinvigorating our anti-trust and securities laws, reviewing large mergers, and discouraging short-term speculation taking place at the expense of long-term investment." The 1992 platform contains no such language.

121 Trump's old friend Rupert Murdoch: See, for example, Ben Chapman, "Google Must Be Broken Up to Save News Media, Says Rupert Murdoch's News Corp," *Independent*, March 12, 2019.

121 Chicken farmers, as Zephyr Teachout writes: Zephyr Teachout, *Break 'Em Up: Recovering Our Freedom from Big Ag, Big Tech, and Big Money* (New York: St. Martin's Press, 2020), 18–22.

121 "Even the cheerleading 'industry'": Sarah Miller, "End Monopoly Power," *Democracy: A Journal of Ideas*, no. 58 (Fall 2020): 38.

122 "an antitrust advocacy boutique": See the firm's website: kanterlawgroup.com.

123 It was 1918 before all: Deeptha Thattai, "A History of Public Education in the United States," Nov. 2017, researchgate.net.

123 One of the Black high schools: The student who attended that school and organized a strike to demand equal facilities, Barbara

Johns, has finally got her due: in early 2021, a statue of her replaced one of Robert E. Lee in the U.S. Capitol, as one of Virginia's two contributions to Statuary Hall.

124 "So long as the schools": Milton Friedman, "The Role of Government in Education," in *Economics and the Public Interest*, ed. Robert A. Solow (New Brunswick, N.J.: Rutgers University Press, 1955), 6.

124 "the actual administration of educational": Ibid., 3.

124 A number of southern counties: See, for example, Chris Ford, Stephenie Johnson, and Lisette Partelow, "The Racist Origin of Private School Vouchers," Center for American Progress, July 12, 2017, for a solid summary of this history. In the main, the white people of the South preferred not to educate their children at all to having to send them to integrated schools.

125 School choice was also interesting: See James Forman Jr., "The Secret History of School Choice: How Progressives Got There First," *Georgetown Law Journal* 93, no. 4 (April 2005).

125 By the end of Freedom Summer: Ibid., 1299.

126 "hadn't said a word about any of these things": James Harvey and David Berliner, "'A Nation at Risk' Demanded Education Reform 35 Years Ago. Here's How It's Been Bungled Ever Since," *Washington Post*, April 26, 2018.

126 Bradley Foundation helped finance: *Buying a Movement: Right-Wing Foundations and American Politics* (Washington, D.C.: People for the American Way, 1996), 24, files.pfaw.org.

126 "have performed about the same": Tawnell D. Hobbs, "Do School Vouchers Work? Milwaukee's Experiment Suggests an Answer," *Wall Street Journal*, Jan. 28, 2018.

127 One prominent study, from Stanford: "Multiple Choice: Charter School Performance in 16 States," Center for Research on Education Outcomes, Stanford University, June 2009, credo.stanford.edu.

127 This study has been oft cited: For a good summary of the debate over the CREDO study, see Matthew DiCarlo, "A New Look at the CREDO Charter School Study," *Washington Post*, Oct. 11, 2011.

128 using the cover of the pandemic: Samantha Sokol, "Betsy DeVos Is Using the Coronavirus Pandemic to Push School Vouchers," Americans United for Separation of Church and State, May 21, 2020, www.au.org.

128 The overall state of American public education: See the Nation's Report Card, published by the National Assessment of Educa-

tional Progress, www.nationsreportcard.gov. This site enables the user to look at a range of assessments in different subject matters from roughly 1990 to today. In most cases in the public schools, performance has increased. For example, in mathematics from 1990 to 2019, public school fourth graders improved by 28 percent, and eighth graders by 19 percent. Those increases were higher than increases in reading, history, and other subjects, but generally speaking, there were increases across the board.

129 "a series of structured choices": Kevin Carey, "No More School Districts!," *Democracy: A Journal of Ideas*, no. 55 (Winter 2020): 35.

129 "What much fewer people realize": Jason Blakely, "How School Choice Turns Education into a Commodity," *Atlantic*, April 17, 2017.

CHAPTER SIX: HOW ECONOMICS HAS CHANGED

135 "Why did nobody notice it?": "Sorry Ma'am—We Just Didn't See It Coming," Associated Press, July 26, 2009.

136 "an erosion of standards": Financial Crisis Inquiry Commission, Jan. 2011, xxii.

136 "In summary, Your Majesty": "Sorry, "Ma'am—We Just Didn't See It Coming."

136 Baker published a paper: Dean Baker, "Recession Looms for the U.S. Economy in 2007," Center for Economic and Policy Research, Nov. 2006.

137 "Lee Smolin begins *The Trouble with Physics*": Paul Romer, "The Trouble with Macroeconomics" (lecture delivered Jan. 5, 2016, published online Sept. 14, 2016).

137 "identification problem": Ibid., 8–14, and passim.

138 Paul Krugman did so at great length: Paul Krugman, "How Did Economists Get It So Wrong?," *New York Times Magazine*, Sept. 2, 2009.

139 "The authority of economics": Robert Skidelsky, *What's Wrong with Economics? A Primer for the Perplexed* (New Haven, Conn.: Yale University Press, 2020), xiv.

139 "I started to see": Romer, interview by author, May 10, 2021.

140 "they each point to contradictions": Justin Wolfers (@JustinWolfers), Twitter, Oct. 8, 2018, 5:57 a.m., twitter.com/JustinWolfers/status/1049237330647814144.

141 He also ruffled feathers: See, for example, Oliver Holmes, "World Bank Economist Sidelined After Demanding Shorter Emails and Reports," *Guardian*, May 26, 2017.

141   He celebrated the Nobel: Emily Badger, "A Nobel-Winning Economist Goes to Burning Man," *New York Times*, Sept. 5, 2019.

144   "allowed economists to estimate": Heather Boushey, "A New Economic Paradigm," *Democracy: A Journal of Ideas*, no. 53 (Summer 2019).

145   They found that since 1980: Piketty, Saez, and Zucman, "Distributional National Accounts," 557.

145   "Over the last fifteen years": Pamela Jakiela, "A Nobel Prize for the Randomistas," Center for Global Development, Oct. 14, 2019, www.cgdev.org.

147   "we need a real paradigm shift": Beinhocker, interview by author, April 20, 2020.

147   focus chiefly on "complexity economics": For a discussion of how "complexity economics" breaks from neoliberal orthodoxy, see Eric Beinhocker et al., "Forum Response: Inclusive Economics Is Complexity Economics," *Boston Review*, March 26, 2019, bostonreview.net.

148   "Where equilibrium economics emphasizes order": W. Brian Arthur, "Complexity Economics: A Different Framework for Economic Thought," Santa Fe Institute, March 12, 2013.

149   "Now it's changing": Shierholz, interview by author, Oct. 22, 2020.

149   Shierholz co-authored a 2018 paper: Josh Bivens and Heidi Shierholz, "What Labor Market Changes Have Generated Inequality and Wage Suppression?," Economic Policy Institute, Dec. 12, 2018.

150   "Those of us who have looked": Edmund L. Andrews, "Greenspan Concedes an Error on Regulation," *New York Times*, Oct. 23, 2008.

150   "empirical research is now the route": Boushey, "New Economic Paradigm."

152   "but it was very oriented toward": Folbre, interview by author, May 7, 2021.

152   Posts about men tended to use words: Alice H. Wu, "Gendered Language on the Economic Job Market Rumors Forum," *AEA Papers and Proceedings* 108 (2018): 175–79.

154   "If I am correct that altruism": Gary Becker, "Altruism in the Family and Selfishness in the Market Place," *Economica* 48, no. 189 (Feb. 1981): 12.

154   "the traditional family has never": Barbara Bergmann, "Becker's Theory of the Family: Preposterous Conclusions," *Feminist Economics* 1, no. 1 (1995): 141.

155   soft spot for polygamy: Becker wrote about polygamy and more

specifically polygyny (a man having several wives, as opposed to polyandry, a woman having several husbands) repeatedly over the years, sometimes trying to couch his arguments in quasi-feminist terms. See, for example, "Is There a Case for Legalizing Polygamy?," *The Becker-Posner Blog*, Oct. 22, 2006, www.becker-posner -blog.com, which concludes with his inquiring, "If modern women are at least as capable as men in deciding whom to marry, why does polygyny continue to be dubbed a 'barbarous' practice?" This is one of the most influential American economists of the twentieth century.

155 "Becker concentrates most attention": Bergmann, "Becker's Theory of the Family," 142.

155 "[Secretary of Labor] Robert Reich": Abraham, interview by author, June 3, 2021.

156 they'd earn $1.5 trillion: Gus Wezerek and Kristen R. Ghodsee, "Women's Unpaid Labor Is Worth $10,900,000,000,000," *New York Times*, March 5, 2020.

156 National Domestic Workers Alliance has passed: See the organization's website, at www.domesticworkers.org.

157 "As in our Robinson Crusoe stories": Julie A. Nelson, "Feminism and Economics," *Journal of Economic Perspectives* 9, no. 2 (Spring 1995): 135.

157 "What is needed is a conception": Ibid., 136.

158 "Americans are less eager": David Autor, "Good News: There's a Labor Shortage," *New York Times*, Sept. 4, 2021.

159 Sadie T. M. Alexander, the first Black woman: Lisa D. Cook and Ana Gifty Opoku-Agyeman, "'It Was a Mistake for Me to Choose This Field,'" *New York Times*, Sept. 30, 2019.

159 According to one 2017 study: Cory Kodel, "Examining Faculty Diversity at America's Top Public Universities," Brookings Institution, Oct. 5, 2017; based on Cory Kodel and Diyi Li, "Representation and Salary Gaps by Race-Ethnicity and Gender at Selective Public Universities," *Educational Researcher* 6, no. 7 (Oct. 2017).

159 "The officers and governance committees": Statement from the AEA Executive Committee, June 5, 2020, www.aeaweb.org.

160 "less likely to remain in business": Devah Pager, "Are Firms That Discriminate More Likely to Go out of Business?," *Sociological Science*, Sept. 19, 2016.

161 "unless you do research that says": Darity, interview by author, May 13, 2021.

162 *"the most robust indicator"*: William A. Darity and A. Kirsten Mullen, *From Here to Equality: Reparations for Black Americans in the*

Twenty-First Century (Chapel Hill: University of North Carolina Press, 2020), 263.

163   "Baby bonds offer you a chip": Hamilton, interview by author, May 25, 2021.

164   "most of these policies are now": Richard Rothstein, *The Color of Law: A Forgotten History of How Our Government Segregated America* (New York: Liveright, 2017), xvii.

164   female before the pandemic: Tara Law, "Women Are Now the Majority of the U.S. Workforce—but Working Women Still Face Serious Challenges," *Time*, Jan. 16, 2020.

165   The middle class is also racially diverse: See Christopher Pulliam, Richard V. Reeves, and Ariel Gelrud Shiro, "The Middle Class Is Already Racially Diverse," Brookings Institution, Oct. 30, 2020.

CHAPTER SEVEN: HOW POLITICS HAS CHANGED

169     $26.5 million of it supplied: This figure was given to me in an email by Gara LaMarche, who ran the Atlantic Philanthropies at the time.

170   nearly eight million jobs: Chris Isidore, "7.9 Million Jobs Lost—Many Forever," CNN.com, July 2, 2010.

171   "flood into lower Manhattan": Brian Greene, "How 'Occupy Wall Street' Started and Spread," *U.S. News & World Report*, Oct. 17, 2011.

172   "will be an asterisk": Andrew Ross Sorkin, "Occupy Wall Street: A Frenzy That Fizzled," *New York Times*, Sept. 17, 2012.

173   The National Employment Law Project estimates: Yannet Lathrop, T. William Lester, and Matthew Wilson, "Quantifying the Impact of the Fight for $15: $150 Billion in Raises for 26 Million Workers, with $76 Billion Going to Workers of Color," National Employment Law Project, Policy & Data Brief, July 27, 2021.

173   The Sunrise Movement: Ruairí Arrieta Kenna, "The Sunrise Movement Actually Changed the Democratic Conversation. So What Do You Do for a Sequel?," *Politico*, June 16, 2019.

174   "approached the research": Ryan Grim, *We've Got People: From Jesse Jackson to Alexandria Ocasio-Cortez, the End of Big Money and the Rise of a Movement* (Washington, D.C.: Strong Arm Press, 2019), 139.

176   "There is nobody in this country": The video clip can be viewed on YouTube at www.youtube.com/watch?v=htX2usfqMEs.

177   "a capitalist to my bones": First tweeted by Katie Lannan, a reporter with State House News Service, at Katie Lannan (@katielannan),

Twitter, July 16, 2018, 9:38 a.m., twitter.com/katielannan/status/1018852303212896257?lang=en.

177 "We had to struggle": Roosevelt Library, "Our Documents: Franklin Roosevelt's Address Announcing the Second New Deal," Oct. 31, 1936, docs.fdrlibrary.marist.edu.

178 "Biden carrying out maybe the same": Shakir, interview by author, Aug. 24, 2021.

181 "Enough is enough with Wall Street": Steven Mufson, "Treasury Nominee Antonio Weiss Withdraws from Consideration," *Washington Post*, Jan. 12, 2015.

181 "No. I'm not running for president": Colin Campbell, "Elizabeth Warren Just Actually Ruled Out Running for President in 2016," *Business Insider*, Jan. 13, 2021.

181 "It's obviously a real uphill battle": Donovan Slack, "Why Bernie Sanders Decided to Run for President," *USA Today*, Feb. 15, 2016.

181 "People should not underestimate me": Dan Merica, "Bernie Sanders Is Running for President," CNN.com, April 30, 2015.

183 The state has one Fortune 1,000 company: Evan Comen, "The Largest Company in Every State," 24/7 Wall St., July 3, 2019, 247wallst.com.

183 Not a single billionaire: Avery Koop, "Mapped: The Wealthiest Billionaires in Each U.S. State in 2021," Visual Capitalist, Feb. 3, 2021, visualcapitalist.com.

184 Sanders benefited heavily in several primaries: Nate Silver, "How Bernie's 2020 Map Might Change Without the #NeverHillary Vote," FiveThirtyEight, Feb. 19, 2021.

185 "converted itself . . . into a weapon": Grim, *We've Got People*, 230.

188 "seeking information and a photo": Tim Haddock, "Elections 2020: In Congressional District 44, Barragan Appears to Win Reelection over Joya," *Daily Breeze*, Nov. 4, 2020.

188 as documented most thoroughly: See, for example, Lara Putnam and Theda Skocpol, "Middle America Reboots Democracy," *Democracy: A Journal of Ideas*, Feb. 28, 2018. My *Democracy* colleagues (Jack Meserve and Sophia Crabbe-Field) edited this piece, which remains one of the highest-traffic pieces in the journal's sixteen-year history.

189 Consider these numbers from Pew: "Wide Gender Gap, Growing Educational Divide in Voters' Party Identification," Pew Research Center, March 20, 2018.

190 about 80 percent do: Wyatt Koma, Juliette Kubanski, and Tricia Neuman, "A Snapshot of Sources of Coverage Among Medicare

Beneficiaries in 2018," Kaiser Family Foundation, March 23, 2021, www.kff.org.

192   A Kaiser Family Foundation study: Lily Rubin-Miller et al., "COVID-19 Racial Disparities in Testing, Infection, Hospitalization, and Death: Analysis of Epic Patient Data," Kaiser Family Foundation, Sept. 16, 2020.

193   Some fast-food chains, struggling: See, for example, Mary Meisenzahl, "Fast Food Chains Are Offering Cash Bonuses, Raises, and Education Benefits in Order to Hire Enough Workers," *Business Insider*, April 24, 2021.

193   A study by the Federal Reserve Bank: These numbers are from an SCE Labor Market Survey, Federal Reserve Bank of New York, www.newyorkfed.org/microeconomics/sce/labor#/expectations -job-search18.

193   A 2021 report from the Conference Board: Frank Steemers et al., "The Reimagined Workplace a Year Later," Conference Board, June 10, 2021, conference-board.org.

194   "the core values of this nation": Alexander Burns, "Joe Biden's Campaign Video, Annotated," *New York Times*, April 25, 2019.

195   "I think it may not dwarf": Michael Tomasky, "Biden's Journey Left," *New York Review of Books*, July 2, 2020.

CHAPTER EIGHT: THE ROLE OF THE NONPROFIT WORLD

199   One day in 1967, an office phone: As recounted in John Markoff, "William Hewlett Dies at 87; a Pioneer of Silicon Valley," *New York Times*, Jan. 13, 2001.

211   "is sort of center-right-ish": Kramer, interview by author, Nov. 26, 2021.

212   believes the company should be broken up: See Chris Hughes, "It's Time to Break Up Facebook," *New York Times*, May 9, 2019.

212   "This is what movements do best": Warren, interview by author, Oct. 6, 2021.

213   Baker's Exhibit A here is patent: See Dean Baker, "Is Intellectual Property the Root of All Evil? Patents, Copyrights, and Inequality" (working paper, presented at the Great Polarization: Economics, Institutions, and Policies in the Age of Inequality conference, University of Utah, Department of Economics, Sept. 27–29, 2018).

216   "We were spending $4 million": Wong, interview by author, Sept. 30, 2021.

216   "The approach they were taking": Traister, "Biden's Big Left Gamble."

217 a call to raise his own taxes: See Chris Hughes, "Raise My Taxes!," *Democracy: A Journal of Ideas*, no. 53 (Summer 2019).

217 "organized around two fights": See Who We Are, Economic Security Project, www.economicsecurityproject.org.

218 "At some point, I got clarity": Hanauer, interview by author, June 2020.

218 "The problem isn't that we have *some* inequality": Nick Hanauer, "Beware, Fellow Plutocrats, the Pitchforks Are Coming," TED talk, Aug. 12, 2014.

218 "It isn't capital that creates economic growth": Nick Hanauer, "The Dirty Secret of Capitalism—and a New Way Forward," TED talk, Sept. 13, 2019.

219 "It's awfully telling": Michael Tomasky, "Score One for the Little Guys as W Hotel Drops Its Minimum Wage Surcharge in Seattle," *Daily Beast*, April 11, 2017.

220 "People came more or less consensually": LaMarche, interview by author, Sept. 28, 2021.

CHAPTER NINE: WHAT THE DEMOCRATS NEED TO DO

223 "I'm just not, so you know": Quoted in Jamelle Bouie, "Joe Manchin Should Stop Talking About 'Entitlement,'" *New York Times*, Oct. 8, 2021.

225 in October 2021, Gallup found: See Jeffrey M. Jones, "GOP Now Viewed as Better Party for Security, Prosperity," Gallup, Oct. 6. 2021, news.gallup.com.

228 Rosenberg's June 2020 PowerPoint: "With Dems Things Get Better," NDN PowerPoint presentation, June 2020, which Rosenberg shared with me (but which he presented publicly at the time). I wrote this up in a *Daily Beast* column, "Everyone Does Better When the President's a Democrat," June 17, 2020. In October 2021, Simon shared with me updated numbers to cover through the end of the Trump presidency. NDN's sources were official government data (Census Bureau, Bureau of Labor Statistics, and so on). I checked a combination of those sources and news accounts.

229 far better under Clinton: See, for example, William Watts, "Stock-Market Performance Under Trump Trails only Obama and Clinton," MarketWatch, Jan. 20, 2021.

229 But by all five of these measures: Now, conservatives will object to these numbers in three ways, so let me acknowledge them. First, these numbers just measure statistics from the month the person took office to the month the person left office. That is admittedly

imprecise, because no president's policies kick in his first month in office. But there's no real way to measure precisely when a president's policies do kick in. In addition, economic performance is a product of a host of factors, many outside a president's control. This is why I avoid the kinds of credit taking–blame assigning language that politicians favor. For example, "Bill Clinton created twenty-two million jobs." No; twenty-two million jobs were created during Clinton's presidency, but he didn't necessarily create them. His policies had something to do with it, obviously; maybe a lot to do with it (reminder: every Republican in Congress, every one, voted against his 1993 budget bill). But no president single-handedly creates or loses jobs or changes the Dow. Having said all that, these comparisons are reasonable to make; we have to have *some* way of measuring presidents' economic performance, and this method is fairer than any other I've seen. Rest assured that if the numbers tilted in the other direction, Republicans would be invoking them incessantly, and every person in America would know them.

Second, the conservative reader will notice that these numbers don't go back to Ronald Reagan, whose economic record is considerably better than either of the Bushes or Trump. That's a fair point. Including him changes things, but not that dramatically. The performance of the DJIA under Reagan was just under that of the Obama years, for example, by a percentage point, which means it was still well under the Clinton number. And while Reagan ranks second to Clinton in postwar job creation, the record of other GOP presidents is so bad that he doesn't help them make up much ground as a team. If one measures the number of jobs created month on month from 1961 through 2017—that's fifty-six years, during which this country had Democratic presidents for twenty-eight years and Republican presidents for twenty-eight years—the numbers are as follows: jobs created under Democrats, 51 million; Republicans, 24 million.

Finally, conservatives will object that the pandemic affected Trump's numbers, which were good before it hit. There's truth to this, and the pandemic was obviously not Trump's fault. His response to it, however, was entirely his fault, and his insane behavior—wishing it away, saying it would be gone by Easter (that was two Easters ago), suggesting that people inject Lysol, and of course knowing that it was worse than he was saying publicly—hindered economic recovery. A responsible president leading a rational government would have tailored emergency legislation with care to ensure that money got to the people who really needed it and would have set up a more stringent oversight structure on the $2 trillion or so Congress approved under the CARES Act. Trump did neither of those things. Certain provisions were smuggled into the CARES Act that benefited the rich, like a tax break for pass-through entities that went almost entirely to people earning $1 million or more a year. In addition, the act was badly monitored. So some of the economic fallout was his fault. And finally, even without the pandemic, Trump would have posted good numbers, but he was on track to finish roughly on par with Obama in most categories (except household income, which was up substantially in 2019 before falling in 2020), so a Trump tenure without the pandemic would not have altered the historical numbers very much. But the pandemic did happen, and Trump did botch it horribly. And the economic numbers tell only part of that story, of course. He all but committed negligent homicide. Hundreds of thousands of Americans died because of his sociopathic immaturity.

231 "Extra-rational motivations—those that transcend": Victor W. Hwang and Greg Horowitt, *The Rainforest: The Secret to Building the Next Silicon Valley* (Los Altos Hills, Calif.: Regenwald, 2012), 125.

233 "Sure. Yeah. Look, America": Nicole Belle, "Pete Buttigieg Reminds Chuck Todd That Capitalism Requires a Functioning Democracy," *Crooks and Liars*, April 7, 2019.

234 annual ranking of economic freedoms: Hong Kong's Economic Freedom score is 8.94, and Singapore's is 8.65. For comparison, the United States' score is 8.22. World Population Review, Freest Countries 2002, worldpopulationreview.com.

234 survey of political freedoms: Freedom House, Freedom in the World, 2022, Country Scores, freedomhouse.org.

235 incompatible with democracy: I wrote about this in *The New York Times*, "Is America Becoming an Oligarchy?," April 14, 2019.

236 "every member of society": Joseph Fishkin and William A. Forbath, *The Anti-Oligarchy Constitution: Reconstructing the Economic Foundations of American Democracy* (Cambridge, Mass.: Harvard University Press, 2022), 35.

237 Franklin Roosevelt's famous Four Freedoms: One can read or listen to the speech at the website American Rhetoric, www.americanrhetoric.com.

239 Most Productive Countries 2021: "Most Productive Countries 2021," World Population Review, worldpopulationreview.com.

The survey considers each country's gross domestic product, as well as workers' purchasing power parity, per hour worked.

239 The first, from 2017: Abhijit Banerjee et al., "Debunking the Stereotype of the Lazy Welfare Recipient: Evidence from Cash Transfer Programs," *World Bank Research Observer* 32, no. 2 (Aug. 2017), scholar.harvard.edu.

240 A second study from the World Bank: Sarah Baird, David McKenzie, and Berk Ozler, "The Effects of Cash Transfers on Adult Labor Market Outcomes," World Bank Group, Development Research Group, April 2018, documents1.worldbank.org.

242 She tells the story: See Elizabeth Warren (@ewarren), Twitter, Feb. 19, 2019, 4:02 p.m., twitter.com/ewarren/status/10979645805 82633476?lang=en.

INDEX

ABOUT THE AUTHOR

Michael Tomasky was appointed top editor of *The New Republic* in March 2021. He is also editor of *Democracy: A Journal of Ideas*, and a regular contributor to *The New York Review of Books*. He is the author of four books: *Left for Dead* (1996), *Hillary's Turn* (2001), *Bill Clinton* (2017), and *If We Can Keep It* (2019); also the e-book *Yeah! Yeah! Yeah!: The Beatles and America, Then and Now* (2014).